Anytime Korean

Intermediate 1

Sangbok Kim, Ph.D.
Sang-Seok Yoon, Ph.D.
Jieun Kim, Ph.D.

Anytime Korean Intermediate 1
애니타임 한국어 중급 1

Written by Sangbok Kim, Ph.D., Sang-Seok Yoon, Ph.D., and Jieun Kim, Ph.D.
Edited by Yejoo Lee
Designed by Eun Jeong Lim
Illustrations by Jae Young Lee

Published by KONG & PARK USA, INC.
1440 Renaissance Drive, Suite 430
Park Ridge, IL 60068 USA
Tel +1 (847) 241 4845
Fax +1 (312) 757 5553
usaoffice@kongnpark.com
www.kongnpark.com

1st published September 1, 2020
2nd printing, November 1, 2022

ISBN 978-1-63519-019-9

Library of Congress Control Number: 2020945003

DISTRIBUTORS

United States: KONG & PARK USA, INC.
1440 Renaissance Drive, Suite 430
Park Ridge, IL 60068
Tel +1 (847) 241 4845
Fax +1 (312) 757 5553
usaoffice@kongnpark.com

South America: KONG & PARK CHILE SPA.
Presidente Riesco 5435, Of. 1601, Las Condes
Santiago, 7561127 Chile
Tel: +56 22 833 9055
chileoffice@kongnpark.com

Other countries: KONG & PARK, INC.
85, Gwangnaru-ro 56-gil, Prime center 3411
Gwangjin-gu, Seoul, 05116 Korea
Tel +82 (0)2 565 1531
Fax +82 (0)2 6499 1801
info@kongnpark.com

Printed in Korea

Table of Contents

Preface

Anytime Korean is an interactive and engaging textbook series. It provides powerful practices for quickly acquiring listening, speaking, reading, and writing skills in Korean through carefully designed systematic learning steps grounded in pedagogic research that is proven most effective.

In our program, learners can practice Korean via various platforms, including print, website, and mobile app devices. The series and the accompanying audios, videos, and mobile application help learners build hands-on communication skills in Korean through an integrated practice of listening, speaking, reading, and writing.

Anytime Korean Intermediate 1 aims to build on the foundation of Korean gained in *Anytime Korean Beginning 1 and 2*. It includes high-frequency vocabulary, common sentence patterns, and speakers' daily communication skills. It emphasizes the ability to apply the target expressions and associated functions in various encounters in life.

Each lesson of the book consists of three major parts.

The first part includes model conversations, vocabulary, expressions, and culture. In the second part, students use that knowledge to write, engage in guided and spontaneous conversation, and give presentations, reflecting the theories of Scaffolding, Zone of Proximal Development, and Comprehensible Input. The third part provides students with a chance to prepare for the Test of Proficiency in Korean (TOPIK).

The content, procedures, and layout in this book are a result of the collaboration of the three authors, who have many years of Korean language teaching experience. The dialogues and examples are based on conversational analysis research and include authentic language and culture. The model conversations reflect contemporary Korean used by native speakers in their 20s and 30s and include contemporary and colloquial expressions, such as shortened forms of words, with explanations of formal and unabbreviated and formal expressions as needed.

Intended users

Anytime Korean Intermediate 1 is for learners who have already gained a solid foundation of Korean and are preparing for the Test of Proficiency in Korean (TOPIK). The book can be used for classroom instruction, online courses, or self-study. The book series comes with access to the accompanying Anytime Korean learning website, which provides interactive self-study material. (See AnytimeKorean.com for more information.)

Acknowledgements

The three authors contributed equally to this book. They would like to express their gratitude to the individuals who helped improve the manuscript of this book at different stages: Dr. Munsuk Lee, who reviewed the manuscript from teachers' perspectives; Alexander Daniel, who reviewed the manuscript closely from a learner's perspective and provided technical editing assistance; several Korean college students, who offered feedback and suggestions on the scripts of the model conversations.

How to use this book

Use the following chart to find the best sequence of study. The Listen & Discuss, Guided Conversation, and Spontaneous Conversation sections are included in the textbook. Pronunciation Practice, Interpretation Practice, and Performance Practice are available online at AnytimeKorean.com or with the mobile application.

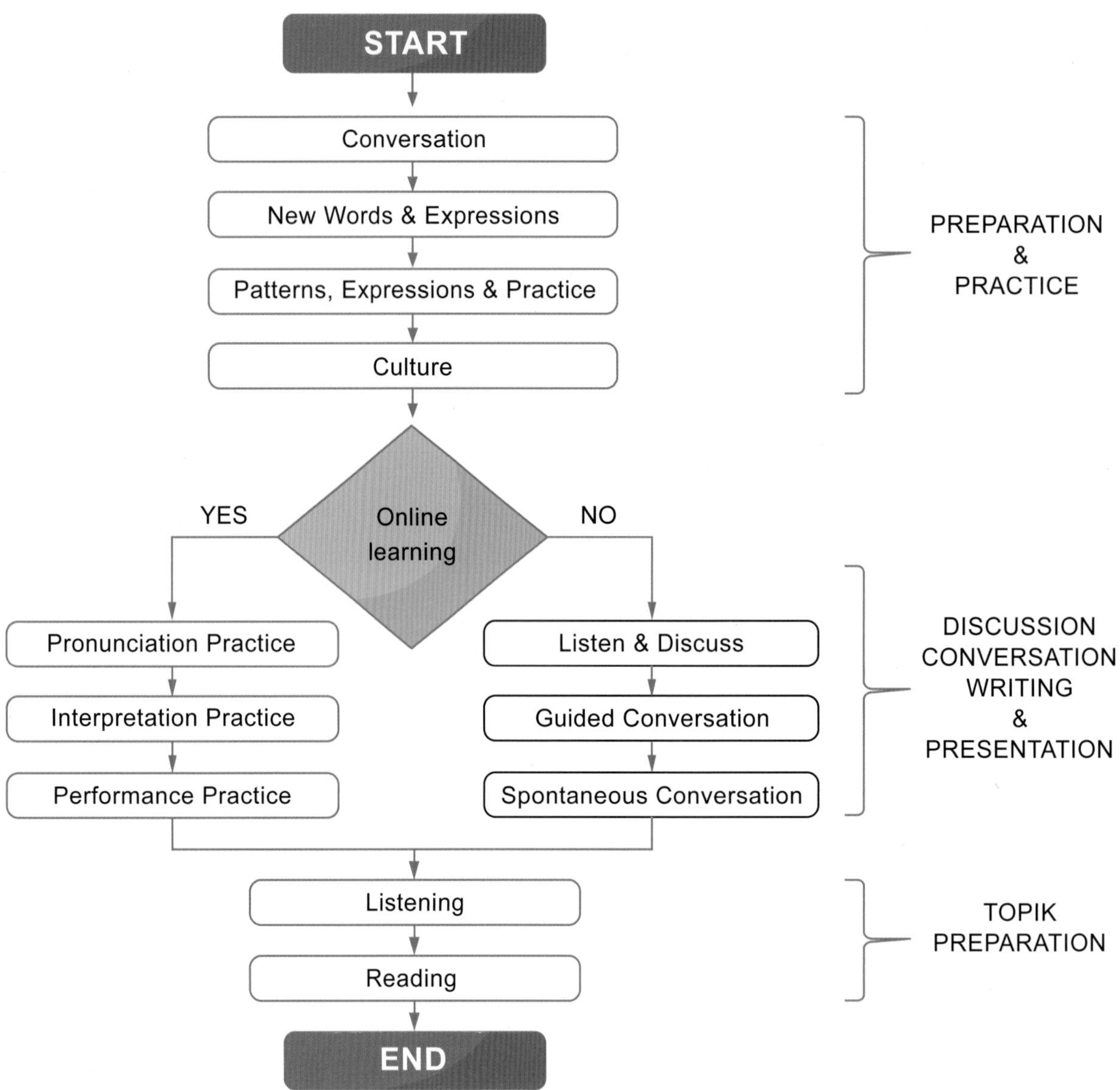

- **Title Page**

The title page of each lesson gives you an overview of the content, including the learning objectives, key expressions, culture notes, and conversation activities. It also features a comic that shows the context of the lesson's model conversation. A video dramatization of the model conversation is also available at AnytimeKorean.com.

- **New Words & Expressions**

This section includes vocabulary and expressions from the model conversation. Audio is available at AnytimeKorean.com to aid in your practice of the pronunciation of new words and expressions. The exercises that follow test your knowledge of not only the new words and expressions, but also the words and expressions you learned in previous lessons.

- **Patterns, Expressions & Practice**

Here you will find explanations of the key grammar patterns and expressions introduced in the model conversation and practice their usage through examples and exercises. This section will help you get ready for the following sections of Listen & Discuss, Guided Conversation, and Spontaneous Conversation. Audio is available at AnytimeKorean.com.

- **Culture**

The culture section offers insight into Korean culture. The information in this section provides additional vocabulary and expressions which will help you expand your Korean usage. They will be used in the next sections, Guided Conversation and Spontaneous Conversation.

• Listen & Discuss

This section checks your comprehension of the model conversation and provides space for discussion. While you discuss your understanding of the conversation with your classmates, you can practice writing in Korean simultaneously. Audio is available at AnytimeKorean.com.

• Guided Conversation

This section includes a script for you to complete and act out with a partner. Through this activity, you will learn and use additional expressions related to the topic, using the target grammar points actively in a different context to improve your fluency. You can also practice this guided conversation at AnytimeKorean.com.

• Spontaneous Conversation

In this section, the last of the conversation activities, you will interview your classmates and create your own script, based on the model conversation. Through this activity, you will gain fluency in all four areas of your Korean usage: listening, writing, reading, and speaking.

• Listening

Here you can practice your comprehension of Korean. The audio in this section ranges from informal conversations and announcements to news reports and formal interviews. Because the material closely relates to the topic of each lesson, you will practice and expand your vocabulary while improving your listening skills.

• Reading

The readings in this section span various genres of writing -- such as expository writing, public announcements, and emails -- and are similar to the types of readings that appear on the TOPIK test. As such, the questions in this section are useful when studying for the TOPIK test.

Main characters in this book

1. Hyunsoo Kim (김현수): A senior at a college in Korea

2. Jenny Smith (제니 스미스): An American exchange student studying as a sophomore at a college in Korea

3. Wei Wang (왕웨이): A Chinese male student who is a sophomore at a college in Korea

4. Minji Park (박민지): A senior at a college in Korea

5. Ted (테드): An American man who works at a company in the US and visits Korea to attend two international conferences

6. Miyoung (미영): A Korean woman who works at the Seoul branch of Ted's company

Hyunsoo Kim Jenny Smith Wei Wang Minji Park Ted Miyoung

Scope and sequence

Lesson	1	2	3
Topics	이번에 새로 온 유학생이죠? Are you the new international student?	다들 어디로 견학 갔다 왔어? Where did you all visit for the field trip?	명절 풍습도 조금씩 달라지는군요. Traditional holiday customs also gradually change.
Objectives	• Introducing yourself in an academic setting • Discussing Korean university culture	• Sharing your Korean travel experiences • Using casual speech	• Traditional Korean holidays and customs • Reporting the speech of others
Preparation & Practices	Conversation I. New Words & Expressions II. Patterns, Expressions & Practice 1. ~라고 하다 "to be called ~" 2. ~은/~ㄴ지 ... 이/가 되다 "It's been ... since ~" 3. NOUN밖에 "nothing/nobody/ no ~ but; only ~" 4. ~기 전에 "before ~ing" III. Culture 1. The Korean university academic calendar 2. Giving someone the option to speak in a non-honorific speech style	Conversation I. New Words & Expressions II. Patterns, Expressions & Practice 1. The ~는다 speech style 2. ~더라고 "I found out/realized that ~" 3. ~(는)구나 Expressing your realization of a new fact III. Culture 1. The KoreanDemilitarized Zone (DMZ) 2. Famous festivals in Korea	Conversation I. New Words & Expressions II. Patterns, Expressions & Practice 1. ~다고/~라고 하다 Reported statement 2. ~(으)라고 하다 Reported command 3. ~지 않 "not ~" 4. ~줄 알았다/몰랐다 "I mistakenly thought/ I did not know that~" III. Culture 1. Memorial service for ancestors 2. Traditional holidays in Korea
Discussion Conversation Writing & Presentation	IV. Listen & Discuss V. Guided Conversation VI. Spontaneous Conversation	IV. Listen & Discuss V. Guided Conversation VI. Spontaneous Conversation	IV. Listen & Discuss V. Guided Conversation VI. Spontaneous Conversation
TOPIK Preparation	VII. Listening • Conversation • Announcement VIII. Reading • Freshman welcome party • My reason for learning Korean	VII. Listening • Conversation • Annoucement VIII. Reading • Namsangol Hanok Village in Seoul • Museums in Seoul	VII. Listening • Conversation • News report VIII. Reading • 한가위 (Hangawi) • 세배 (Sebae)

4	5	6	7
교통편은 뭐가 좋을까요? What would be the best transportation?	한국시리즈 경기 봤어? Did you watch the Korean series game?	드라마 때문에 밤을 새웠다고? Did you say you stay up all night watching a drama?	인터넷으로 집 알아보고 있었어요. I was searching for a house on the internet.
• Local Korean specialties • Comparing modes of transportation in Korea	• Talking about popular sports in Korea • Reporting the questions and suggestions of others	• Talking about one's favorite dramas and movies • Places and events related to Korean dramas	• Talking about housing options for college students • Talking about pros and cons
Conversation I. New Words & Expressions II. Patterns, Expressions & Practice 1. ~을까/~ㄹ까 하다 "to be thinking of ~ing" 2. ~것 "the fact/thing that~" 3. ~(으)니까 "since ~ ; because ~; ~, so ..." 4. ~을/~ㄹ 줄 알다/모르다 "to know how to do ~" 을/~ㄹ 줄 모르다 "to not know how to do ~" III. Culture 1. Trains and express buses 2. Rest areas on expressways	Conversation I. New Words & Expressions II. Patterns, Expressions & Practice 1. ~거든 Indicating that you plan to continue talking 2. ~냐고 하다 Reported question 3. ~자고 하다 Reported proposal III. Culture 1. Baseball in Korea 2. Soccer in Korea	Conversation I. New Words & Expressions II. Patterns, Expressions & Practice 1. ~느라(고) "because of ~ ing" 2. ~아/~어 버리다 Declaring that an action has been completed 3. ~을/~ㄹ만큼 "to the extent that ~" III. Culture 1. Korean Dramas 2. Famous K-drama filming locations	Conversation I. New Words & Expressions II. Patterns, Expressions & Practice 1. ~은/~는 편이다 "to tend to ~; It is more the case of ~ than the other" 2. ~보다 (더/덜) "(more/less) ... than ~" 3. ~아야/~어야 할지 모르다 "to not know whether ... have to ~" III. Culture 1. Housing options for college students 2. Apartment in Korea
IV. Listen & Discuss V. Guided Conversation VI. Spontaneous Conversation	IV. Listen & Discuss V. Guided Conversation VI. Spontaneous Conversation	IV. Listen & Discuss V. Guided Conversation VI. Spontaneous Conversation	IV. Listen & Discuss V. Guided Conversation VI. Spontaneous Conversation
VII. Listening • Conversation • Annoucement VIII. Reading • Icheon Ceramics Festival • Cheonan Walnut Cookies	VII. Listening • Conversation • Interview VIII. Reading • Traffic announcement during the Korean Series final match • Popular sports in Korea	VII. Listening • Conversation • Interview VIII. Reading • Historical drama festival • Reasons for foreigners to learn Korean	VII. Listening • Conversation 1 • Conversation 2 VIII. Reading • Looking for a room • Housing options for college students

1 이번에 새로 온 유학생이죠?

Are you the new international student?

-Introducing yourself in an academic setting
-Discussing Korean university culture

I. New Words & Expressions

Study the words and expressions along with the audio. 01

NOUN

도움	help; assistance; support
반 년	half a year (= six months 육 개월)
사회학과	sociology department
선배	a classmate in a higher grade *선배님 (님 is honorific address term)
유학생	international student
후배	a classmate in a lower grade

PRONOUN

이쪽	this [this side; the person on this side]

VERB

도와주다	to give somone a hand; help
유학 오다	to come to study abroad
인사하다	to greet; introduce

ADVERB

새로	newly
서로	each other; one another
언제든지	anytime

EXPRESSION

·도움이 필요하면	when (you) need help [Literally, when help is necessary]
·연락(을) 주다	to give someone a call; to contact someone *(someone)한테/에게 연락(을) 주다

Listen to the audio and fill in the blanks. 

1. A: 안녕하세요? 저는 제니 스미스예요.

   B: 네, 반갑습니다. 저는 ________________ 4학년 김현수입니다.

2. A: 서로 인사하세요. ________________은 미국에서 온 제니 씨예요.

   B: 아, 안녕하세요? 만나서 반가워요.

3. A: 저는 1주일 전에 미국에서 와서 한국은 아직 잘 몰라요.

   B: 걱정하지 마세요. 웨이 씨가 많이 ____________________________.

4. A: 제 후배 웨이인데 서로 ________________________.

   B: 만나서 반갑습니다.

5. A: 넌 한국에 온 지 벌써 ____________쯤 됐지?

   B: 네. 벌써 6개월이 됐네요.

6. A: 이번에 새로 온 _______________이죠?

   B: 네, 미국에서 온 제니 스미스입니다.

7. A: _______________이 필요하면 저한테 연락 주세요.

   B: 네~. 많이 도와주시면 감사하겠습니다.

Exercise 2

Choose the best word to complete each sentence.

1. 요즘 저희 학교에 외국에서 온 ____2____이 많아졌습니다.

   ① 선배들 ② 유학생들 ③ 대학원생들 ④ 후배들

2. A: 한국은 처음이라서 ____4____이 많이 필요해요.

   B: 제가 많이 도와줄게요.

   ① 유학생 ② 반 년 ③ 후배들 ④ 도움

3. 오늘 동아리 모임에서 미국에서 온 유학생 제니 씨와 서로 ____4____.

   ① 도와줬습니다 ② 필요했습니다 ③ 연락을 줬습니다 ④ 인사했습니다

4. 4학년인 현수는 2학년인 웨이의 ____4____입니다.

   ① 후배 ② 유학생 ③ 대학원생 ④ 선배

5. 학기 시작하기 전에 제니는 도움이 ____2____해서 웨이한테 연락을 했습니다.

   ① 유학생 ② 필요 ③ 반 년 ④ 인사

II. Patterns, Expressions & Practice

1. NOUN + (이)라고 하다 "to be called + NOUN"

Usage

When you introduce your name, another's name, or the name of an object, use "NOUN 1은/는 NOUN 2(이)라고 하다," meaning "NOUN 1 am/are/is called NOUN2."

NOUN 1은/는 NOUN 2(이)라고 하다. (e.g., 저 사람은 김영철이라고 해요.)

"NOUN 1 am/are/is called NOUN 2." (e.g., That person is called 김영철.)

Form

Use the following rules to choose between ~이라고 하다 and ~라고 하다.

- ▶ NOUN 2 (ending in a consonant) + 이라고 하다 : 김영철이라고 합니다. [ㄹ + 이라고 합니다]
- ▶ NOUN 2 (ending in a vowel) + 라고 하다 : 박민지라고 합니다. [ㅣ + 라고 합니다]

Look at the following examples.

- A: 안녕하세요? 저는 제니 스미스라고 해요. (저 = NOUN1, 제니 스미스 = NOUN2) — Hi. I am Jenny Smith. [Literally, I am called Jenny Smith.]
  B: 저는 웨이 왕이라고 합니다. (저 = NOUN1, 웨이 왕 = NOUN2) — I am Wei Wang. [Literally, I am called Wei Wang.]
- A: 성함이 어떻게 되십니까? — May I have your name?
  B: (제 이름은) 김현수라고 합니다. (제 이름 = NOUN1, 김현수 = NOUN2) — I am Hyunsoo Kim. [Literally, (My name) is called Hyunsoo Kim.]
- A: "dining table" 은 한국말로 뭐예요? — What is "dining table" in Korean?
  B: ("dining table" 은) 식탁이라고 해요. ("dining table" = NOUN1, 식탁 = NOUN2) — It is 식탁. [Literally, It is called 식탁.]

Note

You may also use ~**(이)라고 하다** in a noun-modifying form: ~**(이)라고 하는** or its shortened form ~**(이)라는**.

1. 김치**라고 하는** (or 김치**라는**) 음식을 먹어 봤습니다.
   I have had food called *kimchi*.
2. 경복궁**이라고 하는** (or 경복궁**이라는**) 곳에 가 봤어요?
   Have you visited a place called Gyeongbokgung?
3. 혹시 사회학과 김현수**라고 하는** (or 김현수**라는**) 학생 아세요?
   Do you know a student called Hyunsoo Kim studying sociology?
4. 이것은 불고기**라고 하는** (or 불고기**라는**) 한국 음식입니다.
   This is a Korean food called *bulgogi*.

Complete each dialogue, using ~(이)라고 하다 or ~(이)라고 하는, or ~(이)라는.

1.

김지호

린다 존슨

지호: 안녕하세요? 저는 ______________________.

린다: 네, 안녕하세요? 저는 ______________________.

2.

제니: 이 스포츠는 뭐라고 하죠?

웨이: ______________________________________.

3. 

김세훈/컴퓨터 프로그래머

현수: 혹시 ______________________________ 알아?

웨이: 모르는데요? 왜요?

4. 

요리 1

요리 2

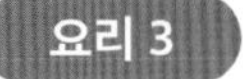

요리 3

요리 4

제니: 이 음식들 이름은 뭐예요?

웨이: (요리 1) 이건 ____________________ 음식이고,

(요리 2) 이건 ____________________ 음식이고,

(요리 3) 이건 ____________________ 음식이고,

(요리 4) 그리고 이건 ________________ 음식이야.

Respond to each question, using the appropriate noun from the box and the expression ~(이)라고 하다.

유학생	취미	이틀	요리사	소개팅	기자

1. A: 아는 사람의 소개로 남자와 여자가 만나는 것을 뭐라고 합니까?

   B: 소개팅이라고 합니다.

2. A: 음식을 만드는 일을 하는 사람을 뭐라고 합니까?

   B: ______________________________.

3. A: 시간이 있을 때 자주 하고 좋아하는 일을 뭐라고 합니까?

   B: ______________________________.

4. A: 신문이나 잡지에 글을 쓰는 사람을 뭐라고 합니까?

   B: ______________________________.

5. A: 2일을 다른 말로 뭐라고 합니까?

   B: ______________________________.

6. A: 외국에서 공부하는 사람을 뭐라고 부릅니까?

   B: ______________________________.

Exercise 3

Complete the dialogues, using ~(이)라고 하는 or ~(이)라는.

1. A: 한국에 와서 처음 먹어 본 음식은 뭐였어요?

   B: ______________ 음식이었어요.

2. A: 이번에 새로 온 유학생인데, 어디서 유학생을 도와줘요?

   B: ______________ 곳에서 외국 유학생을 도와줘요.

3. A: 이번에 한국에 가는데, 어디에 가 보면 좋을까?

   B: 서울에 ______________ 곳이 있는데, 볼 게 많아요.

4. A: 어느 교수님이 학점을 잘 줘요?

   B: ______________ 교수님 수업을 들어 보세요.

5. A: 혹시 이 학교 정문 근처에 서점 있어?

   B: 버스 정류장 앞에 ______________ 작은 서점이 있는데, 왜?

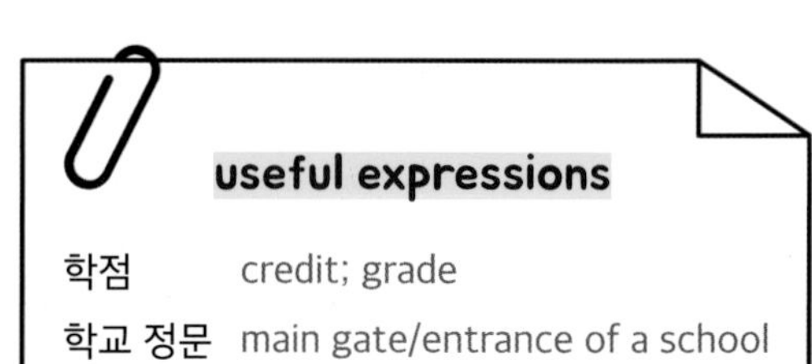

useful expressions

학점 credit; grade

학교 정문 main gate/entrance of a school

Listen to the phone conversation between two friends and mark each statements T(True) or F(False). 

1. ______ The man is at the student union building now.
2. ______ There is a freshman welcome party at the school auditorium.
3. ______ The school auditorium is behind the coffee shop called "friends."

useful expressions

대강당	auditorium
학생회관	student union building
신입생 환영회	freshman welcome party; freshman orientation

2. Verb base + 은/ㄴ 지 TIME SPAN이/가 되다 "It's been TIME SPAN since ~"

Usage When you express how much time has passed since you did something or something happened, use "**verb base + 은/ㄴ 지 TIME SPAN 이/가 되다**," meaning, "**It's been [time span] since...**"

verb base + **은/ㄴ 지 TIME SPAN 이/가 되다** (e.g., **한국에 온 지 반 년이 됐어요.**)

"**It's been TIME SPAN since** ~" (e.g., **It's been** half a year **since** I came to Korea.)

Form Use the following rules to choose between **~은 지** and **~ㄴ 지** (as in **verb base + 은/ㄴ 지 TIME SPAN 이/가 되다**).

Past noun-modifying form of a verb

▶ Verb base (ending in a consonant) + 은 지 TIME SPAN 이/가 되다: **먹은 지 3일이 돼요.**

▶ Verb base (ending in a vowel) + ㄴ 지 TIME SPAN 이/가 되다: **간 지 3일이 돼요.**

* Verb base (ending in ㄹ): 만들-다 → 만들 + ㄴ 지 → 만드 +ㄴ 지 → 만든 지

살-다 → 살 + ㄴ 지 → 사 +ㄴ 지 → 산 지

▷ TIME SPAN expressions

오래, 일 년/이 년 ... , 한 달/두 달 ... , 일 주일/이 주일 ... , 하루/이틀 ... ,
한 시간/두 시간 ... , 일 분/이 분 ...

Look at the following examples.

● A: 한국에 온 **지** 얼마나 **됐어요**? — How long has it been since you came to Korea?

B: (한국에 온 **지**) 이제 일주일**(이) 됐습니다**. — It has been a week now (since I came to Korea).

> ▷ Remember this set of Q-A.
>
> Q: ~ **은/ㄴ 지 얼마나 됐어요?** — How long has it been since ~ ?
>
> A: ~**은/ㄴ 지 TIME SPAN이/가 됐어요.** — It has been TIME SPAN since ~.

● A: 지금 대학교 3학년이죠?

B: 네, 고등학교를 졸업한 **지** 벌써 3년**(이) 지났네요**. *지나다 "to pass" can also be used instead of 되다.

> ▷ The subject-focus marker "-이/-가" often drops in conversation. You may use the topic/contract marker "-은/-는" instead of "-이/-가" depending on the context. (For the usage of the markers, see Lesson 7 in Beginning 1.)

● A: 대학교를 다닌 **지**가 벌써 4년**이** 다 **돼 가네요**. 저는 내년 2월이면 졸업해요.

B: 저는 졸업하려면, 아직 2년 더 공부해야 돼요.

Using ~은/~ㄴ 지 TIME SPAN 이/가 되다, describe the following pictures, as shown in the first example.

1. 
3 hours ago

아침 먹은 지 3 시간이 됐어요 .

2. 
1 year ago

한국어를 ______________________.

3. 
6 months ago

엄마한테 편지를 ______________________.

4. 
2 weeks ago

극장에서 영화를 ______________________________.

5. 
one month ago

새 차를 .

6. 
3 years

한국 음악을 ______________________________.

Respond to each question, using ~은/~ㄴ 지 TIME SPAN 이/가 되다, as shown in the first example.

1. A: 언제 한국에 유학을 왔어요?

   B: 유학 온 지 1년이 됐어요.

2. A: 언제 고등학교를 졸업했어요?

   B: ______________________________.

3. A: 한국에 가 본 지 얼마나 됐어요?

   B: ______________________________.

4. A: 얼마 동안 한국어 수업을 들었어요?

   B: ______________________________.

5. A: 언제부터 웨이 씨를 알았어요?

   B: ______________________________.

6. A: 한국에 얼마 동안 살았어요?

   B: ______________________________.

Listen to the conversation between two friends and mark each statement T(True) or F(False). 04

1. _____ The woman likes watching a movie.

2. _____ The man has not watched the movie yet.

3. NOUN + 밖에 "nothing/nobody/no~ but NOUN~ ; only NOUN"

Usage Use "NOUN + 밖에 ... negative verb/adjective." to express that the noun in question is fewer or lesser than you think.

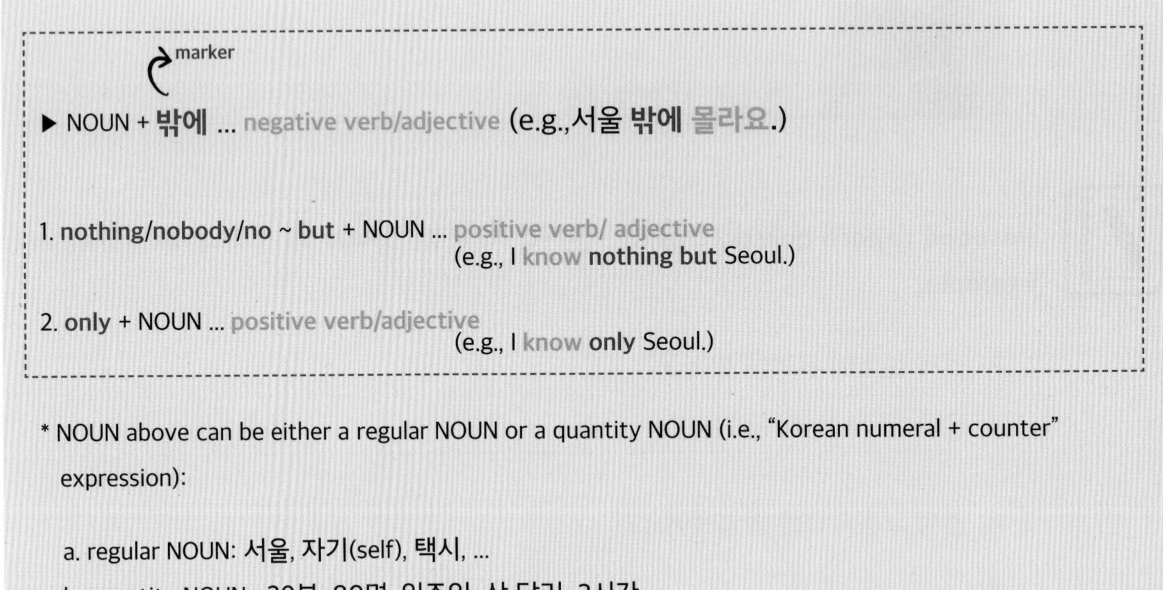

marker

▶ NOUN + **밖에** ... negative verb/adjective (e.g.,서울 **밖에** 몰라요.)

1. **nothing/nobody/no** ~ **but** + NOUN ... positive verb/ adjective (e.g., I know **nothing but** Seoul.)

2. **only** + NOUN ... positive verb/adjective (e.g., I know **only** Seoul.)

* NOUN above can be either a regular NOUN or a quantity NOUN (i.e., "Korean numeral + counter" expression):

a. regular NOUN: 서울, 자기(self), 택시, ...

b. quantity NOUN : 20분, 80명, 일주일, 삼 달러, 3시간, ...

Look at the following examples where "a regular NOUN + **밖에** ... negative verb/adjective" is used.

● A: 한국에 온 지 3년이 됐는데, 아직 서울**밖에** 몰라요.
(서울: NOUN)

B: 시간 있을 때, 부산에 한번 가 보세요.

A: It's been three years since I came to Korea, but I know nothing but Seoul (= I know only Seoul.).

B: When you have time, try to visit Busan.

- A: 왜 현수 씨를 싫어하죠?
  B: 현수 씨는 자기밖에 모르는 사람이에요.
  NOUN

  A: Why do you hate 현수?

  B: He knows only himself.

The following examples show cases where "a quantity NOUN + **밖에** ··· negative verb/adjective" is used.

- A: 신입생 환영회에 늦겠어요, 지금 20분**밖에** 안 남았어요.
  NOUN
  B: 그럼 우리 택시 타고 가요. 이 시간에는 택시**밖에** 없어요.
  NOUN

  A: We may be late for the freshman welcome party. We have only 20 minutes.

  B: Then let's go by taxi. There is no transportation other than a taxi at this time.
  (or There is only a taxi at this time.)

- A: 어제 신입생 환영회에 사람들이 많이 왔어요?
  B: 다음 주에 시험이 있어서 80명**밖에** 안 왔어요.
  NOUN

  A: Did many people come to the freshman welcome party?

  B: Only eighty people came since there is an exam next week.

Describe the situation in each picture, using "NOUN 밖에 ··· negative verb/adjective."

1.

가방 안에 책이 ______________________.

2.

A: 형 있으세요?

B: 아니요, 저는 ______________________.

3.

A: 커피 마시러 갈래요?

B: 지금 돈이 ______________________________.

4.

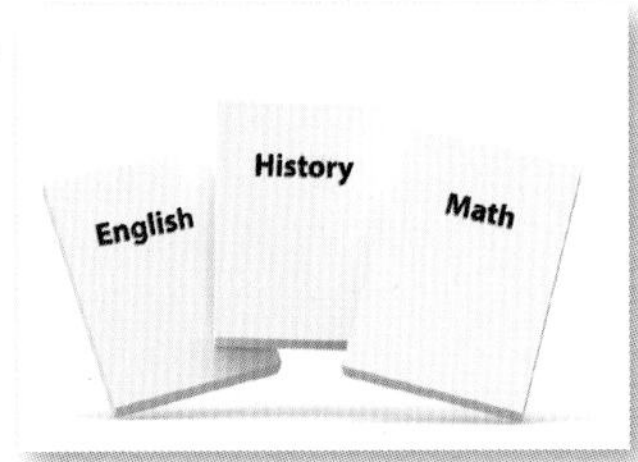

A: 이번 학기에도 수업 많이 들어요?

B: 아니요, 이번에는 ______________________________.

5.

A: 마이클하고 샌디 둘 다 잘 알죠?

B: 저는 마이클 ____________________. 샌디가 누구죠?

Listen to the conversation between two friends and mark each statements T(True) or F(False). 05

1. ______ The man bought his current cell phone one year ago.
2. ______ The man wants to buy a new cell phone because his current phone doesn't look good.

Exercise 10

Listen to the conversation between two friends and mark each statements T(True) or F(False). 06

1. ______ The woman studied Korean by herself for two years.
2. ______ It has been two years since the woman took a Korean class.

4. Verb base + 기 전에 "before ~ ing"

Usage

▶ Use "verb base + **기 전에**" to say "**before** ~ing."

▶ Verb base + **기 전에** (e.g., **오기 전에**)
: "**before** + verb base -ing" (e.g., **before** coming)

Look at the following examples.

● A: 한국에 유학 오**기 전에** 어디서 대학교 다녔어요? *유학을 오다 to come to study abroad
[오다: 오 + **기 전에**]
B: 미국에서 다녔어요.

A: Where did you go before coming to study abroad in Korea?

B: I attended in the U.S.

● A: 새 학기가 시작되**기** (일주일) **전에** 보통 뭐 해요? *새 학기 new school term
[시작되다: 시작되 + **기 전에**]
B: 기숙사에 들어 가서 새 학년을 준비해요.

A: What do you usually do during the week before a new semester begins?

B: I move into the dorm and prepare for the new school year.

Use "verb base + **은/ㄴ 후에**" or "verb base + **은/ㄴ 다음에**" to say "**after** ~ing."

은/ㄴ → past noun-modifying form of a verb

▶ Verb base + **은/ㄴ 후에** (e.g., 읽은 **후에**, 마친 **후에**)
은/ㄴ 다음에 (e.g., 읽은 **다음에**, 마친 **다음에**)

: "**after** + verb base -ing" (e.g., **after** reading/ finishing)

● A: 한국 역사 세미나는 언제 들으면 좋을까요?

B: 고급 한국어를 마친 **후에** (or 마친 **다음에**) 들으세요.
[마치다: 마치 + ㄴ **후에**/ㄴ **다음에**]

A: When would it be good to take the Korean history seminar course?

B: Take it after finishing advanced Korean courses.

Describe the sequence of events in the pictures using ~기 전에 or ~은/~ㄴ 후에, as shown in the first example.

1. 어제 저녁에 영화를 봤어요. 그리고 저녁을 먹었어요.

저녁을 먹기 전에 영화를 봤어요 ____________________.

영화를 본 후에 저녁을 먹었어요. ____________________.

2. 숙제를 했어요. 그리고 수업에 갔어요.

____.

____.

3. 식사를 했어요. 그리고 약을 먹었어요.

____.

____.

4. 준비 운동을 했어요. 그리고 수영을 했어요.

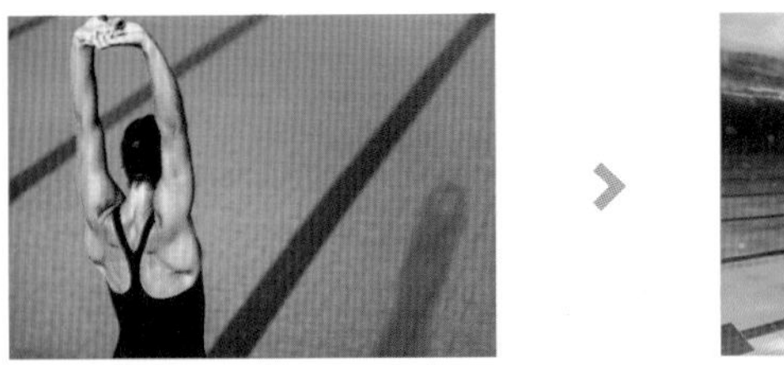

____.

____.

5. 취직을 했어요. 그리고 졸업을 했어요.

____.

____.

6. 양치질을 했어요. 그리고 잤어요.

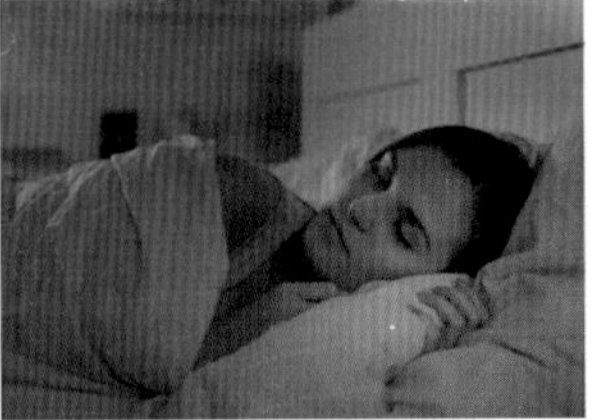

____.

____.

useful expressions

준비 운동을 하다	to do warm-up exercise
취직을 하다	to get a job
양치질을 하다	to brush one's teeth

Answer each question in your own words.

1. A: 50살이 되기 전에 꼭 하고 싶은 일 3가지는 뭐예요?

   B: ______________________________

   ____

   ______________________________.

2. A: 보통 잠자기 전에 뭐 하세요?

   B: ______________________________.

3. A: 10년 전과 지금은 뭐가 달라졌어요? *달라지다 to become different

   B: ______________________________.

4. A: 2시간 전에 뭐 하고 있었어요?

   B: ______________________________.

5. A: 내일 점심 먹기 전에 뭐 할 거예요?

   B: ______________________________.

Exercise 13

Listen to the phone conversation between two friends and mark each statement T(True) or F(False). 07

1. ______ The man is at a restaurant.
2. ______ The woman is going to the restaurant.
3. ______ It will take a long time for the woman to get to the restaurant.
4. ______ The woman will order after arriving at the restaurant.

useful expressions

~고 있다	be ~ ing (action in progress)
도착하다	to arrive

III. Culture

1. 한국 대학교들의 학사일정 The Korean university academic calendar

Unlike in America, the school year starts in spring for Korean universities. **1학기** (the first semester) runs from **3월 초** (early March) to **6월 중순** (mid-July). Each university has a student orientation for freshmen in **2월**, and **입학식** (entrance ceremony) in **3월 초** as they start the new school year. Academic departments and student associations run group activities, during which students get to know new people and adjust to college life. After **1학기**, **여름방학** (summer vacation) follows until **9월 초** (early September). Then, **2학기** begins in **9월 초** and lasts until **12월 중순** (mid-December). There are also various student activities in **2학기**. Senior students graduate in **2월 중순** (mid-February) and each school has **졸업식** (graduation commencement) by **2월 말** (end of February).

Culture

2. 다른 사람에게 반말 사용을 제안하기
Giving someone the option to speak in a non-honorific speech style

You should use honorific forms not just for those who are older than you, but also for people you are not yet close with, even if they are your same age or even younger than you are. When you get to know new people in college, it is generally safe to use **존대말** (honorific language) in the beginning. If you think you are close enough to someone who is your same age, you can ask that person, "Should we speak in **반말** with each other?" by saying "**우리 말 놓을까요?**" You can also give those older than you the option to address you in **반말** by saying "**말씀 편하게 하세요.**" or "**말 놓으세요.**" When speaking in **반말**, avoid using the endings ~**다** (for statements), ~**니**/~**냐** (for questions), and ~**아라**/~**어라** (for commands) because they have the connotation of lowering the listener. Instead, use ~**아**/**어** (for statements/commands/proposals).

IV. Listen & Discuss

제니 is an international student who recently came to Korea to attend university. In the following conversation, she meets 현수 and 웨이 during freshman orientation.

First, listen to the conversation. With your classmates, discuss the answers to the questions that follow. Finally, write each answer in a full Korean sentence in the space provided.

1. 현수와 웨이는 어떤 사이입니까?

2. 제니는 언제 한국에 왔습니까? (Include "~밖에 안 ..." in your answer.)

3. 웨이는 언제 한국에 왔습니까? (Include "~은/~ㄴ 지 ...이/가 되다" in your answer.)

4. 제니가 도움이 필요하면 누가 도와줍니까?

Script

☞ **제니 is an international student who recently came to Korea to attend university. In this conversation, she meets 현수 and 웨이 during freshman orientation.**

01 현수: 안녕하세요? 이번에 새로 온 유학생이죠?
02 제니: 네, 안녕하세요? 제니 스미스라고 해요.[II.1]
03 현수: 저는 사회학과 4학년 김현수라고 해요.
04 제니 씨, 이쪽은 제 후배 웨이인데 서로 인사하세요.
05 제니: 안녕하세요? 만나서 반갑습니다.
06 웨이: 네, 반갑습니다. 왕웨이라고 합니다.
07 현수: 제니 씨, 한국에 온 지 얼마나 됐어요?[II.2]
08 제니: 아직 일주일밖에[II.3] 안 됐어요.
09 현수: 웨이, 넌 한국에 온 지 벌써 일 년쯤 됐지?
10 학기 시작하기 전에[II.4] 제니 씨 좀 많이 도와줘.
11 웨이: 네~ 선배님!
제니 씨, 도움이 필요하면 언제든지 연락 주세요.
12 제니: 네~ 감사합니다.

01 현수: Hi! You are a new international student, right?
02 제니: Oh, hi! I'm Jenny Smith.
03 현수: I'm Kim Hyunsoo, and I'm a senior studying sociology.
04 Oh, Jenny, this is Wei, my junior in school. Please introduce yourselves.
05 제니: Hi. Nice to meet you.
06 웨이: Hi! Glad to meet you. I am Wei Wang.
07 현수: How long has it been since you came to Korea, Jenny?
08 제니: It's only been 1 week.
09 현수: Wei, it's already a year since you came to Korea, right?
10 Before the semester begins, please help Jenny.
11 웨이: Yes~ sir!
Jenny, please contact me whenever you need help.
12 제니: Yes, thank you!

V. Guided Conversation

Keeping in mind the organization of the model conversation in Listen & Discuss (Script), practice the modified conversation below with your partner.

At an information session for international students at a college in Korea, two students are talking to each other.

Practice the following conversation with your partners, using the prompts in (parenthesis) to fill in the blanks and make the conversation flow naturally.

01 A: 안녕하세요? 이번에 새로 온 유학생이죠?

02 B: 네, 안녕하세요? __________ (Introduce your name, using ~이라고/~라고 하다.). [II.1] 저는 __________ (your country name) 에서 왔어요.

03 A: 저는 __________ (Introduce your name, major, and school year, using ~이라고/~라고 하다.). 만나서 반갑습니다.

04 B: 저도 만나서 반가워요.

05 A: __________ (Ask B how long it has been since she/he came to Korea.)? [II.2]

06 B: __________ (Say, "It's been only 1 week, 2 weeks, or 3 weeks."). [II.3]

07 A: 그럼, 아직 시차 적응도 못 했겠네요.

08 B: 아뇨, 이제 거의 다 했어요.

Guided Conversation

09 A: 혹시 학기 시작하기 전에[11.4] 도움이 필요하면 언제든지 연락 주세요.

10 B: 네~ 감사합니다!

(Switch roles and continue to practice.)

useful expressions

L07 시차 적응도 못 했겠네요
I bet you haven't adjusted to the time difference, or You must be jet lagged.

Present the conversation above in front of the class. Try not to look at your paper!

VI. Spontaneous Conversation

This is your chance to have a realistic interaction with your classmates in Korean. You can practice writing, speaking with your classmates, and presenting in front of the class!

You are meeting another international student at a welcome party in a college in Seoul. Introduce yourself. Including the information (in the table below) into your conversation, create a meaningful conversation with your partner similar to the one that you practiced in the Guided Conversation!

- Show your interest in getting to know the other person by introducing yourself with your name, school year, etc.
- Ask the length of his/her stay in Korea.
- Exchange personal information (e.g., phone number) with him/her so you can contact each other to ask for or provide help in the future.
- Try to use ~(이)라고 하다, ~은/~ㄴ 지 TIME SPAN 이/가 되다, ~ 밖에, ~기 전에, ~은/~ㄴ 후에/다음에 in your conversation if possible.

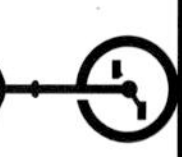

Write down the conversation you had with your partner in Step 1.

Step 3

While taking a summer intensive Korean class in Seoul, your teacher suggests that you create a blog site for your class. Write a paragraph introducing yourself. Include ~(이)라고 하다, ~은/~ㄴ TIME SPAN 이/가 되다, ~밖에/~이나, ~기 전에, ~은/ ~ㄴ 후에/다음에 in your writing.

Present what you wrote in Step 3 in front of the class. Try not to look at your paper!

VII. Listening

Listen to the following conversation between a man and a woman during a freshman welcome party at a college in Korea. Then, answer the questions. 09

1. 들은 내용과 같은 것을 고르십시오.
   ① 여자는 3년 전에 한국에 유학을 왔습니다.
   ② 남자는 한국에 온 지 3개월 됐습니다.
   ③ 남자는 학기 시작하기 전에 궁금한 게 많습니다.
   ④ 여자는 학기가 시작되기 전에 남자를 도와주고 싶어합니다.

Listen to the following announcement from a university broadcasting station and mark each statement is T(rue) or F(alse). 10

2. ______ This event is hosted by a student union.
3. ______ This is not an annual welcome party for the freshmen.
4. ______ The party is scheduled from 5~ 7pm next Friday.
5. ______ All faculty members will also attend the event.

Words & Expressions

01 **학생회** student union/association **도와주고 있다** to be helping [Literally, to be giving help for someone]
궁금한 게/것이 things to be curious about

02-05 **신입생** incoming students; freshman **총학생회** student body **학교 대강당** school auditorium
참석하다 to attend; participate in; join **(이야기를) 나누다** to have a talk [Lit., to share (stories)]
바라다 to wish; hope **학교 방송국** university broadcasting station
알려 드리다 to announce (*humble form of 알려 주다)
합격하다 to be admitted (to a college); pass **여러분(들)** all of you, literally several persons

VIII. Reading

신입생 환영회 (Freshman welcome party)

한국 대학교에 합격하신 여러분들을 진심으로 환영합니다.
신입생 환영회에 많이 참석해 주시기 바랍니다.

■ 일시: 2020년 2월 20일, 오전 9시~11시
■ 장소: 대강당
■ 대상: 신입생
■ 프로그램
9:00-9:30 인사말, 교수 소개
9:30-10:00 신입생 소개
10:00-11:00 대학 생활 안내, 도서관 이용 안내

1. 위의 내용과 같은 것을 고르십시오.
① 신입생 환영회는 저녁에 합니다.
② 2월 20일에 신입생들이 첫 번째 수업을 합니다.
③ 신입생 환영회는 도서관에서 합니다.
④ 신입생들은 신입생 환영회에서 교수님들을 만날 수 있습니다.

Words & Expressions

01 합격하다 to be admitted (to a college); pass 여러분(들) all of you [Literally, several persons]
진심으로 sincerely 환영하다 from the bottom of one's heart to welcome
(참석해) 주기 바라다 to wish (to participate in; join)
일시 date and time 대상 target guest 인사말 greeting [Lit., greeting words]
교수 소개 introduction to professors 대학 생활 안내 guide to school life
도서관 이용 안내 guide to using the library verb base + 을/ㄹ 수 있다 can ~

한국어를 배우는 이유 (My reason for learning Korean)

제가 한국에 오기 전에는 한국어를 취미로 배웠습니다. 그 때는 한국의 유명한 가수들과 배우들을 만나는 것이 제 꿈이었습니다. 그런데 제가 한국에 온 지 벌써 3년이 됐습니다. 지금은 한국의 역사와 문화에 관심이 많아졌습니다. 그리고 한국에서 일을 하고 싶습니다. ___㉠___ 지금 저의 계획은 대학원에 다니면서 더 공부를 하는 것입니다.

2. ㉠에 들어갈 알맞은 말을 고르십시오.
① 그런데 ② 하지만 ③ 그래서 ④ 왜냐하면

3. 이 글의 내용과 같은 것을 고르십시오.
① 저는 한국에 오기 전에 한국 가수를 만났습니다.
② 저는 한국에서 대학원에 다니고 싶습니다.
③ 저는 한국어를 취미로 배우고 있습니다.
④ 저는 앞으로 한국에서 3년동안 살 것입니다.

02-03 꿈 dream 많아지다 to increase; grow (대학원)에 다니면서 while attending (a graduate school)

2 다들 어디로 견학 갔다 왔어?

Where did you all visit for the field trip?

-Sharing your Korean travel experiences
-Using casual speech

01 지난 주말에 다들 어디로 견학 갔다 왔어?
02 전 DMZ에 갔다 왔어요.

03 DMZ? 거기서는 북한이 정말 가깝게 보이니?

04 어, 망원경으로 보니까 사람들이 걸어 다니는 것도 다 보이더라고.
05 와아~! 되게 가깝구나!
06 민지 누나는 어디 갔었어요?
07 난 보령에 갔다 왔어!
08 거기 머드 축제에 가 봤어요?
09 당연하지! K-pop 공연도 봤는데, 정말 재밌더라~.

10 전 전주 한옥 마을에 갔다 왔어요. 이거 거기서 찍은 사진이에요.
11 와~ 너 한복이 참 잘 어울리는구나! 꼭 한국 사람 같아!
12 그리고 한옥에서 묵었는데, 온돌방이 생각보다 편하더라구요.
13 와~! 모두 좋은 경험을 했구나!

Preparation & Practice	I. New Words & Expressions II. Patterns, Expressions & Practice 1. ~는다 speech style Used in casual conversations 2. ~더라고 "I found out/realized that ~" 3. ~(는)구나 Expressing your realization of a new fact	**Conversation Activities**	III. Culture 1. The Korean Demilitarized Zone (DMZ) 2. Famous festivals in Korea
			IV. Listen & Discuss V. Guided Conversation VI. Spontaneous Conversation
		TOPIK Preparation	VII. Listening • Conversation • Announcement
			VIII. Reading • Namsangol Hanok Village in Seoul • Museums in Seoul

I. New Words & Expressions

 **Study the words and expressions along with the audio.** 

NOUN

견학	field trip
공연	performance
망원경	telescope; binocular
보령	Boryeong (a city in South Korea)
보령 머드 축제	Boryeong Mud Festival
북한	North Korea
온돌방	*ondolbang*, a room with the Korean floor heating system
전주	Jeonju (a city in South Korea)
전주 한옥 마을	Jeonju Hanok Village
축제	festival
한옥	*hanok* (a traditional Korean house)
DMZ	demilitarized zone

VERB

걸어 다니다	to walk around
묵다	to stay (at a hotel) *(a hotel)에/에서 묵다
보이다	(for a person/thing) to be seen
어울리다	to look good on (a person) *(a person)한테/에게 어울리다
찍다	to take (photos)

ADJECTIVE

편하다	to be comfortable; convenient

ADVERB

가깝게	near; not far away

EXPRESSION

·당연하지!	Of course!
·(망원경으로 보)니까	(I looked at it with a telescope), so... , and...
·생각보다	more than (I) thought; unlike what (I) thought
·(한국 사람) 같아!	(You) look like (a Korean)!

Listen to the audio and fill in the blanks. 

1. A: 지난 주말에 어디로 ______________ 갔다 왔어?

   B: ____________________ 에 갔다 왔어.

2. A: 이거 어디서 찍은 사진이야?

   B: ____________________ 에서 찍은 거야.

3. A: 그럼, ____________________ 에 묵었어?

   B: 응, ___________ 편했어!

4. A: 난 거기서 K-pop ____________________을 봤는데, 너는 뭐 했어?

   B: 나는 머드 축제에 갔어.

5. A: 한복이 너한테 정말 잘 ____________________!

   B: 그래? 너도 다음에 한번 입어 봐.

Exercise 2

Choose the best word to complete the sentences.

1. 제니는 전주에 있는 ____________에 갔다 왔고, 웨이는 북한이 가깝게 보이는 DMZ에 갔다 왔습니다.

   ① 도움 ② 한옥 마을 ③ 연락 ④ 견학

2. 제니는 한옥 마을에 묵었는데, ____________ 편했습니다.

   ① 언제든지 ② 서로 ③ 생각보다 ④ 새로

3. 제니는 한옥 마을에서 한복을 입고 사진을 ____________________.

   ① 잤습니다 ② 보였습니다 ③ 찍었습니다 ④ 어울렸습니다

4. 한옥 마을의 온돌방은 생각보다 ______________.

   ① 어울렸습니다 ② 보였습니다 ③ 걸어 다녔습니다 ④ 편했습니다

5. ________으로/로 보니까 북한 사람들이 걸어 다니는 것도 다 보였습니다.

   ① 온돌방 ② 경험 ③ 사진 ④ 망원경

II. Patterns, Expressions & Practice

1. The ~는다 speech style

Usage

Use the ~는다 speech style in a situation where the honorific style is not required. When used in casual conversation, there is no difference in formality between the ~는다 and ~아 speech style. However, the ~는다 style can be used in writing, formal announcements, or military commands, while the ~아 style is mostly used in casual conversations.

Form

The form of the ~는다 speech style varies according to the sentence types, as shown in the table below.

Sentence types			
Statement	**Question**	**Proposal**	**Command**
~는다/~ㄴ다/~다	~니? or ~냐?	~자	~아라/~어라
친구를 만난다. 책을 읽는다. 책이 많다.	친구를 만나니/냐? 책을 읽니/냐? 책이 많니/냐?	친구를 만나자. 책을 읽자. --	친구를 만나라. 책을 읽어라. --

(For the whole table of the speech styles in Korean, see Appendix IV.)

In statement

Use ~는다, ~ㄴ다, or ~다 in statement sentences. Use the rules below to choose among the three forms.

▶ Verb base (ending in a consonant) + 는다 : 먹 + 는다 → 먹는다

Verb base (ending in a vowel) + ㄴ다 : 가 + ㄴ다 →간 다

하 + ㄴ다 →한 다

▶ Adjective base + 다 : 좋 + 다 → 좋다

Look at the following examples.

- 나는 아침 7시쯤에 일어나서 버스를 타고 학교에 간다. [가+ㄴ다]
- 나는 점심은 보통 학교 식당에서 먹는다. [먹+는다]
- 어제는 흐렸는데, 오늘은 날씨가 좋다. [좋+다]
- 이 백화점에 있는 한복들은 모두 싸고 예쁘다. [예쁘+다]

Note 1

The 이다 verb takes the form of "the base + 다."

- (verb) 이 + 다 → 이다
  아니 + 다 → 아니다

Note 2

The past tense form of any verb or adjective is "the base + 았다/었다."

- (verb) 먹 + 었다 → 먹었다
  가 + 았다 → 갔다
- (adjective) 좋 + 았다 → 좋았다
- (verb) 이었다/였다
  아니었다

Note 3

Conjugate "ㄹ-ending" irregular verbs (but not adjective) as follows.

- 놀다 (to hang out) → 놀 + ㄴ다 → 노 + ㄴ다 → 논다
- 만들다 (to make) → 만들 + ㄴ다 → 만드 + ㄴ다 → 만든다

For the conjugation rule of "ㄹ-irregular" verbs, see Appendix Ⅴ.

Note 4

You can also use the ~는다 speech style in writing that does not have any specific recipient (for example, newspaper articles or scholarly papers), or writing to oneself (for example, a personal diary). In these cases, the ~는다 speech style does not carry any honorific meaning.

In question Use ~니? or ~냐? in question sentences.

Look at the following examples.

- A: 너, 지금 어디 가니?/가냐?
  B: 동아리 모임이 있어서 학교 앞에 있는 커피숍에 가.

- A: 민수 방금 여기 있었는데, 어디 갔니?/갔냐?
  B: 다른 건물에서 수업이 있어서, 오 분 전에 나갔어.

In proposal Use ~자 when you make a proposal.

Look at the following examples.

- A: 오늘 모임 여섯 시 반에 시작하니?
  B: 그래. 우리 모임에 늦겠다. 빨리 가자.

- (식당에서)
  A: 이 식당은 뭐가 맛있지?
  B: 순두부찌개가 맛있으니까 순두부찌개 먹자!

In command Use ~아라/~어라 in command sentences according to the rules below.

▶ Verb base (ending in 아 or 오) + 아라 : 가 + ~~아~~라 → 가라
Verb base (ending in other vowels) + 어라 : 먹 + 어라 → 먹어라

▶ Verb base (ending in ~하) + 여라 : 공부하 + 여라 → 공부해라

Patterns, Expressions & Practice

Look at the following examples.

- 어머니: 벌써 12시인데, 아직 안 자고 뭐하니? 빨리 **자라**!
  아들 : 네. 안녕히 주무세요! *주무시다 to sleep [honorific equivalent of 자다]
- 어머니: 밖에 나갔다 오면 꼭 손을 **씻어라**. *씻다 to wash; clean
  딸 : 네, 알았어요.
- A: 요즘 날씨도 좋은데, 밖에 나가서 운동 좀 **해라**.
  B: 귀찮아. 그냥 집에 있을래.

In each blank, switch the ~아 speech style to the ~는다 speech style.

1. A: 지난 번에 소개팅에서 만난 친구 (1)____________? (어땠어)
   B: 좋았어! 근데 어떻게 (2)____________? (알았어)

2. A: 오늘 모임에 몇 명쯤 (1)____________? (와)
   B: 150명쯤 와. 여기 쇼핑 리스트가 있어. 한 번 (2)____________. (봐)
   A: 우리 음료수는 다섯 상자만 (3)____________. (사)
   B: 어. 그런데, 지금까지 (4)____________? (얼마야)
   A: 음... 23만 원 나왔어.
   B: 그럼, (우리) 이제 야채 코너로 (5)____________. (가)

The following is a personal diary entry. In each blank, change the ~아 speech style to the ~는다 speech style.

나는 지난 금요일 민준 씨의 소개로 민준 씨 친구와 소개팅을 (1) ______________________ (했어요). 그런데, 그 친구가 안 와서 혼자서 한 시간 동안 기다리다가 그냥 집에 (2) ______________________ (갔어요).

나는 학교 앞 별카페에서 기다렸는데 그 친구는 학교 뒤 별카페에서 기다렸다는 것을 나중에서야 알았다. 금요일에 우리는 다시 (3) ______________________ (만날 거예요).

이번 주 금요일이 너무 (4) ______________________ (기다려져요).

useful expressions

기다렸다는 것을 알았다	(I) know that (he) waited ~
나중에서야	only later
기다려지다	to look forward to ~

Two close friends are talking about their field trip. Using your knowledge of honorifics and speech styles, find and correct the unnatural words and expressions in the dialogue.

01 웨이: 전주 한옥 마을에서 재미있었어?

02 제니: 네, 한옥들도 예쁘고 맛집도 많이 있어서 너무 좋았어.

____.

03 웨이: 잠은 어디서 잤어? 한옥 마을에 호텔도 있었습니까?

____.

04 제니: 아뇨. 그런데 호텔처럼 돈을 내고 묵을 수 있는 한옥들이 있어서 한옥에서 묵었어.

____.

05 웨이: 아~ 그랬어요? 어땠어?

____.

06 제니: 첫째 날은 좀 불편했는데, 둘째 날부터는 괜찮았어. 그리고 아침 식사도 나왔는데, 정말 맛있었습니다.

____.

07 웨이: 저도 한번 가 보고 싶다.

____.

08 제니: 서울에도 한옥 마을이 있는데, 같이 가요!

____.

09 웨이: 그럼 그럽시다.

____.

useful expressions

맛집	a restaurant which is famous for serving delicious food.
돈을 내다	to pay for ~ [Literally, to put out money]

2. ~더라고: I found out/realized that ~

Usage

Use ~**더라고** when reporting what you notice, learn, or realize from your past experience. ~**더라고** is used to describe firsthand experience obtained personally or directly.

Form

Dictionary form (Word base + 다)	Present tense (Verb/Adjective base + 더라고)	Past tense (Verb base + 았/었 + 더라고)
Verb 참가하다	참가하더라고	참가했더라고
Adjective 불편하다	불편하더라고	--

Use ~**았**/~**었더라고** to report an action that was completed at or before the time of observation, as in the following examples.

- (마이클이 말하는 걸 들었는데) 마이클이 한국 사람처럼 한국말을 잘 하**더라고요**.

  (I heard Michael speaking and) I noticed that he spoke Korean like a native Korean.

- 아침에 샌디 집에 가니까, 벌써 학교에 **갔더라고**.

  I went to Sandy's house in the morning and found out that she had already gone to school.

- (오늘 시험을 봤는데) 이번 시험이 생각보다 어렵**더라고**.

  (I took the exam today and) I realized that the exam was harder than I thought.

- 새 컴퓨터를 사려고 했는데, 너무 비싸**더라고요**.

  I was going to buy a new computer but I realized that it was too expensive.

Note 1

In colloquial speech, ~**더라고** is often used as ~**더라구**.

A: 오늘도 또 서울식당에 가?

B: 응, 그 식당 아주머니가 진짜 친절하시더라고/ 친절하시더라구.

Yeah, I noticed that the lady of the restaurant was really kind.

Note 2

고 in ~더라고 can be omitted in the ~아 speech style.

오늘 아침 날씨 진짜 춥**더라**.
I noticed that it was really cold this morning.

Note 3

~(으)니까 "~, I found out that …" is used to express that the event/situation (in the first clause) brings about your realization or discovery of the following event/situation (in the second clause). In this case, ~**(으)니까** is often used with ~**더라구/더라고** ending, as shown in 아침에 샌디 집에 가**니까**, 벌써 학교에 갔**더라고**. This will be discussed in detail in Lesson 4, II.3.

- Verb / Adjective base (ending in a consonant) + **으니까**: 먹**으니까**
- Verb / Adjective base (ending in a vowel) + **니까**: 사**니까**

아침에 일어나**니까** 눈이 오고 있더라구요.
I woke up in the morning and found out that it was snowing.

Column A is what you experienced in the past, and Column B is what you learned or realized from that experience. Match the most suitable clause in Column A with the most suitable clause in Column B. Then, combine the clauses into a complete sentence using 더라고, as in the first example.

A	B
1. 어제 집에 갔는데	a. 엄청 맵다
2. 디즈니랜드에서 롤러코스터를 타봤는데	b. 뉴욕에 눈이 많이 왔다
3. 저번에 에이미 남자 친구를 만났는데	c. 벌써 12시다
4. 뉴스를 봤는데	d. 메뉴에 한국 음식이 있다
5. 파티에서 떡볶이를 먹어 봤는데	e. 되게 무섭다
6. 학교 앞 식당에 가 봤는데	f. 진짜 잘생겼다

1. 어제 집에 갔는데 벌써 12시더라고 .

2. ______________________________.

3. ______________________________.

4. ______________________________.

5. ______________________________.

6. ______________________________.

Report the experiences in each question to a friend, using ~더라고 or ~았/었더라고, as in the first example.

1. 
지난 학기에 다섯 과목을 들었는데 너무 힘들더라고.
(five classes; to have a hard time)

2. 
______________________________.
(to go to New York; heavy traffic)

3. 

______________________________.
(to go shopping; cheap TV)

4. 

______________________________.
(to take a Korean class; to be easy)

5. 
______________________________.
(to meet an actor; to be handsome)

Report what you found out or realized through your own experiences by completing the following sentences.

1. ________________________________, 너무 맛있더라고요.
2. ________________________________, 사람들이 정말 많더라구요.
3. ________________________________, 불편하더라고요.
4. ________________________________, 어려보이더라고.
5. ________________________________, 시험이 어렵더라고.

Listen to the conversation between two friends and mark each statement T(rue) or F(alse).

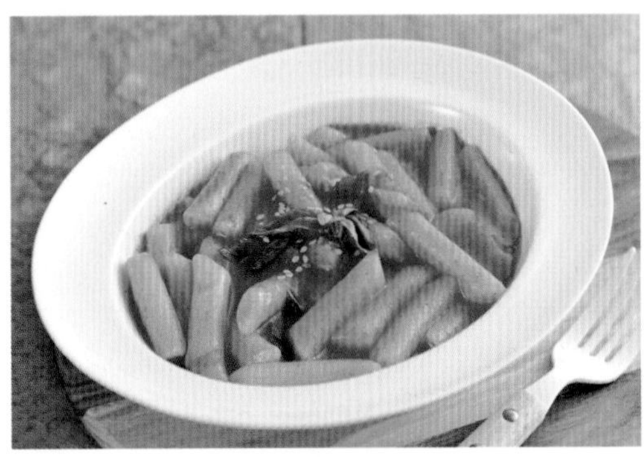

1. _____ The man heard that 떡볶이 is tasty.
2. _____ The woman thinks that 떡볶이 is spicy.

Listen to the conversation between two classmates and mark each statement T(rue) or F(alse).

1. _____ The man thinks Economics class was too hard for him.
2. _____ The woman heard that Economics class is not fun.

Listen to the conversation between two classmates and mark each statement T(rue) or F(alse). 15

1. _____ The woman didn't go to the library because she thought there might be too many people.
2. _____ The man thought the woman was not at home because no one answered the phone.

Listen to the conversation between classmates and mark each statement T(rue) or F(alse).

1. _____ The man heard that a pretty T-shirt will be given as a gift.
2. _____ The man heard that the marathon is not that hard.

Patterns, Expressions & Practice

3. ~(는)구나 Expressing your realization of a new fact

Usage

Use ~는구나/~구나 (or the reduced form ~는군/~군) to talk about something you not only realized, but which may also be a little surprising to you.

Form

Dictionary form	Present tense	Past tense
(Verb base + 다) 찍다	(Verb base + 는구나) 찍는구나	(Verb base + 았/었구나) 찍었구나
(Adjective base + 다) 좋다	(Adjective base + 구나) 좋구나	(Adjective base + 았/었구나) 좋았구나
(Noun이다) 이다	(Consonant-ending Noun + 이구나) 사진이구나	(Consonant-ending Noun + 이었구나) 사진이었구나
	(Vowel-ending Noun + 구나) 축제구나	(Vowel-ending Noun + 였구나) 축제였구나

Look at the following examples.

1. 와아~! 북한이 되게 가깝구나!
   Wow! North Korea is really close!

2. 저 사람이 진짜 범인이었구나! *범인 culprit
   That person was the real culprit!

3. 너 한국어 많이 늘었구나! *늘다 to improve
   Your Korean has improved a lot!

Note 1

~는군요/~군요 (coming from the combination of **~는군/~군** and the **~아요** speech style) is the only honorific form.

1. A: 서울이 더울 때는 39도까지 올라가요.
   B: 와~ 정말 덥군요!
   A: When it gets really hot in Seoul, the temperature reaches up to 39°C.
   B: Wow! It is really hot.

2. 한국 음식을 좋아하는 미국 사람들이 많군요.
   There are many Americans who like Korean food!

3. 저 사람이 진짜 범인이었구나! *범인 culprit
   That person was the real culprit!

Note 2

~구나/~군요 is often used with **겠**, which expresses the speaker's conjecture or guess, as in **~겠구나/~겠군요**. Use **~겠구나/~겠군요** to talk about your guess or conjecture, based on the information you just received or realized.

1. 내일은 비가 오겠구나. (Considering the current weather condition)
   It will be raining tomorrow.

2. 선생님도 요즘 바쁘시겠군요. (After hearing the teacher's current situation)
   You must also be busy recently.

Using ~(는)구나 or ~(는)군, write what you would say in the situations described below.

1. You noticed that your friend bought a new cell phone.

   ______________________________.

2. You realized that there is a test tomorrow, which you had forgotten about.

   ______________________________.

3. You went to 전주한옥마을 from Seoul and found out that it is very close and it only takes 2 hours.

   ______________________________.

4. When your friend cooks for you, you realize what a good cook he is.

______________________________.

5. You just found out that Jenny and Sophia are roommates.

______________________________.

Complete each dialogue, using ~겠구나/~겠군요.

1. 가: 어제 친구들하고 제일 좋아하는 가수 콘서트에 갔어.

   나: ______________________________.

2. 가: 다음 주에 시험이 세 개 있어요.

   나: ______________________________.

3. 가: 제 고양이가 아파서 지난 주에 죽었어요.

   나: ______________________________.

4. 가: 저 다음 달에 결혼해요.

   나: ______________________________.

5. 가: 다음 학기에는 한국에서 공부할 거야.

   나: ______________________________.

Listen to the conversation between two friends and mark each statement T(rue) or F(alse). 17

1. ______ 여자는 가방을 사고 싶어해요.
2. ______ 남자는 인터넷으로 가방을 샀어요.
3. ______ 여자는 세일하는 것을 몰랐어요.
4. ______ 이 쇼핑몰은 다음 주에 또 세일을 해요.

useful expressions

쇼핑몰 shopping mall

III. Culture

1. 비무장지대 (The Korean Demilitarized Zone, DMZ)

비무장지대 (The Korean Demilitarized Zone), often simply called the the DMZ, is an area spanning two kilometers (km) north and south of **휴전선** (the armistice line) which was set at the end of **한국 전쟁** (the Korean War, 1950-1953). DMZ is about 250 kilometers (160 miles) long, dividing North and South Korea. There is a small place where **남한** (South Korean) and **북한** (North Korean) forces meet, called **공동경비구역** (Joint Security Area: JSA). There used to be armed military guards from the South and North Korea that confronted each other at the borderline of the JSA. However, following an agreement between South and North Korean officials in 2018, JSA is now cleared of all landmines, weapons, guard posts and personnel, and now the JSA just contains 35 unarmed security guards.

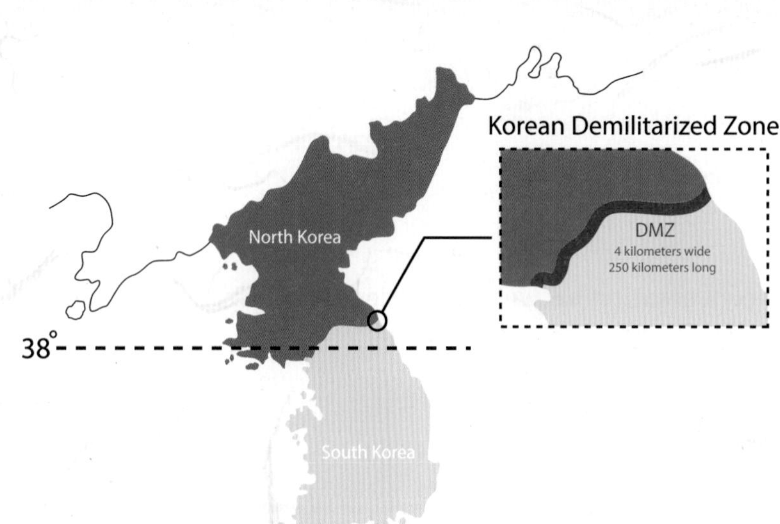

2. 한국의 유명한 축제 (Famous festivals in Korea)

2월: 보성차밭빛축제 (Boseong Tea Plantation Light Festival)

보성(Boseong) is a city located in **전라남도**(South Jeolla Province), famous for its green tea leaves. At **보성차밭빛축제**, you can enjoy the view of the famous **차밭** (tea plantation), which is beautifully lit up at night, as well as fun activities such as **차 잎따기** (picking tea leaves), **차 끓이기** (making tea), and **녹차 과자 먹어보기** (sampling green tea snacks).

4월: 진해군항제 (Jinhae Gunhangje Festival)

진해 (Jinhae) is a city located in **경상남도** (South Gyeongsang province). It is known for its large Korean and American naval base and beautiful **벚꽃** (cherry blossoms). During **진해군항제**, you can enjoy the beautiful view of **벚꽃**, shop at **전통시장** (traditional market), and take in a variety of **문화공연** (cultural performances).

7월: 보령 머드축제 (Boryeong Mud Festival)

보령 (also known as 대천) is a city located on the coast of 황해 (Yellow Sea) in 충청남도 (South Chungcheong Province). The mud in 보령 is considered rich in minerals and is used to manufacture cosmetics. In 보령머드축제, visitors enjoy 머드 레슬링 (mud wrestling), 머드 슬라이드 (mudslide), 머드런 (mud run), and even swimming in 머드 목욕탕 (giant mud bath) on 바닷가 (the beach). You can also visit 머드박물관 (the mud museum) and learn about 머드 (mud).

10월: 부산국제영화제 (Busan International Film Festival)

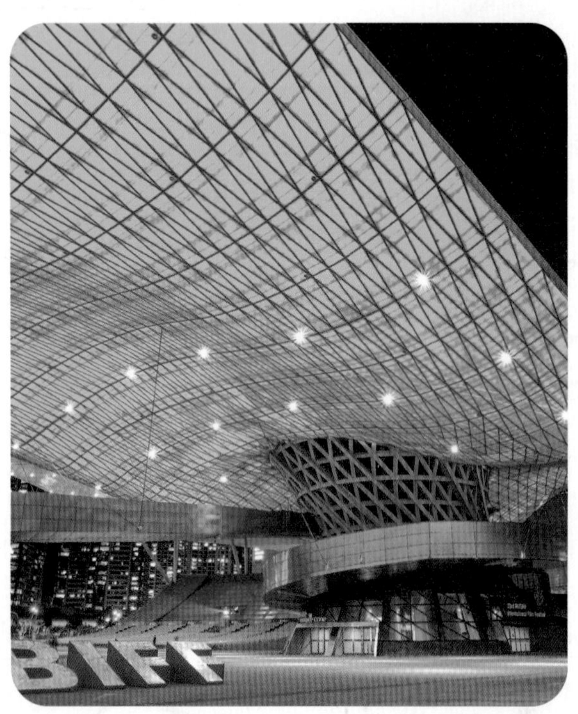

부산 국제 영화제 (The Busan International Film Festival) is one of the most significant film festivals in Asia. It is held annually early in October at 해운대, a district in Busan, which is famous for its beautiful beach. At the festival, you can watch various new films and learn about Asian movies. If you are lucky, you will see 유명한 영화 배우 (famous movie stars) or 영화 감독 (movie directors) on the streets.

IV. Listen & Discuss

민지, 웨이, and 제니 are chatting in the school cafeteria.

First, listen to the conversation. With your classmates, discuss the answers to the questions that follow. Finally, write each answer in a full Korean sentence in the space provided.

1. 민지, 웨이, 제니는 어디로 견학을 갔다 왔습니까?

2. DMZ에서 망원경으로 북한을 보면 무엇이 다 보입니까?

3. 민지는 보령에 가서 무엇을 했습니까?

4. 제니는 전주한옥마을에서 무엇을 했습니까?

5. 온돌방은 제니한테 어땠습니까?

Script

민지, 웨이, and 제니 are chatting in the school cafeteria.

01 민지: 지난 주말에 다들 어디로 견학 갔다 왔어?

02 웨이: 전 DMZ에 갔다 왔어요.

03 제니: DMZ? 거기서는 북한이 정말 가깝게 보이니?[II.1]

04 웨이: 어, 망원경으로 보니까 사람들이 걸어 다니는 것도 다 보이더라고.[II.2]

05 제니: 와아~! 되게 가깝구나!

06 웨이: 민지 누나는 어디 갔었어요?

07 민지: 난 보령에 갔다 왔어!

08 웨이: 거기 머드 축제에 가 봤어요?

09 민지: 당연하지! K-pop 공연도 봤는데, 정말 재밌더라~.

10 제니: 전 전주 한옥 마을에 갔다 왔어요. 이거 거기서 찍은 사진이에요.[II.2]
(Showing a photo)

11 민지: 와~ 너 한복이 참 잘 어울리는구나![II.3] 꼭 한국 사람 같아!

12 제니: 그리고 한옥에서 묵었는데, 온돌방이 생각보다 편하더라구요.[II.2]

13 민지: 와~! 모두 좋은 경험을 했구나!

01 민지: Where did you all visit for the field trip last weekend?

02 웨이: I visited the DMZ.

03 제니: DMZ? Can you see North Korea up close from there? (Literally, is North Korea seen really close from there?)

04 웨이: Yeah, I looked at it with a telescope, so I could see people walking.

05 제니: Wow! It is really close!

06 웨이: Minji, where did you go?

07 민지: I visited Boryeong!

08 웨이: Did you go to the mud festival there?

09 민지: Of course! I also watched K-pop performances. That was very fun!

10 제니: I visited Jeonju *Hanok* Village. I took this photo there.
(제니 shows 민지 a photo.)

11 민지: Wow~ This *hanbok* looks good on you! You look just like a Korean!

12 제니: And I stayed at *Hanok*. I found out that *Ondolbang* is more comfortable than I thought.

13 민지: Wow~! You both had good experiences.

V. Guided Conversation

 **Keeping in mind the organization of the model conversation in Watch & Discuss (Script), practice the modified conversation below with your partner.**

Step 1

Two classmates are talking to each other.

Practice the following conversation with your partner, using the prompts in (parenthesis) to fill in the blanks and make the conversation flow naturally.

01 A: ________ 동안 어디 갔다 왔니?[II.1]
(봄 방학; 여름 방학; 겨울 방학; 연휴)

02 B: 응, ________ 에 갔었어.
(name of a famous place in Korea or US: 보령머드축제; …)

03 A: ________? ________ 어땠어?
(Clarify yourself by repeating the place name: 보령머드축제; …) (세계인의 축제라고 하던데; 유명하다고 하던데; 좋다고 하던데; …)

04 B: ________!
(사람도 엄청 많고 되게 재미있었어; 볼거리/할거리가 정말 많았어; 경치가 정말 아름다웠어; …)

05 A: ________?
(Respond to B's experience, asking how it was: ㅎㅎ 뭐가 그렇게 재미있었어; 무슨 볼거리/할거리가 그렇게 많았어; 뭐가 그렇게 아름다웠어; …)

06 B: ________.
(List experiences you had: 낮에는 머드 슬라이드, 머드 레슬링, 머드 런, … 그리고 밤에는 K-pop공연도 있었어; 아름다운 호수도 보고 오래된 건물도 구경하고 ….; 보트도 타고 수영도 하고...; 바위들이 정말 아름다웠어; …)

07 A: ________!
(스트레스 다 풀렸겠네; 재미있었겠네; 와~좋았겠네; …)

08 B: 응. ________! 근데 넌 뭐 했니?
(너무 ~ 좋았어; 엄청 재미있었어; …)

09 A: 난 ________ 에 갔다 왔어. 이거 거기서 찍은 사진이야.
(name of a famous place in Korea or US: 전주한옥마을; …)

(Showing a photo)

10 B: 와~ ________![II.3]
(Make a positive surprising comment on the photo: 한복이 너한테 진짜 잘 어울리는구나; 경치가 진짜 예쁘구나;…)

11 A: 그리고 ______________________________ 는데,
(List experiences you had: 한옥에서 잤; 하이킹했; 놀이 기구 탔; ..)

생각보다 ______________________________.
(Report what you newly learned from them: 편하더라구; 재미있더라구; 무섭더라구;...)

(Switch roles and continue to practice.)

useful expressions

L03 (세계인의 축제라)고 하던데 I heard that (it is a worldwide festival).

L04 엄청 very much; 볼거리 things to see, attractions; 할거리 things to do; 경치 scenery

L06 머드 런 mud run; 머드 레슬링 mud wrestling; 머드 슬라이드 mudslide; 호수 lake; 바위(들) rock(s)

L07 스트레스가 다 풀렸겠네! It must have been completely relieved!

L11 놀이 기구 the rides at an amusement park; 무섭다 to be scary

Present the conversation above in front of the class. Try not to look at your paper!

VI. Spontaneous Conversation

This is your chance to have a realistic interaction with your classmates in Korean. You can practice writing, speaking with your classmates, and presenting in front of the class!

You and your classmate are talking about famous places in Korea or any country. (Refer to "Section III: Culture" for famous places.) Include the information (in the table below) in your conversation. Create a meaningful conversation with your partner similar to the one that you practiced in the Guided Conversation!

- Where you visited (Choose a place from Section III. Culture.)
- Why you chose that place
- What activities you did there
- What you learned/realized after visiting there (Use ~더라고.)
- Show your reaction to your partner's experience. (Use ~겠구나, ~는구나/~구나.)

Write down the conversation you had with your partner in Step 1.

Based on the conversation in Step 2, write a journal about the places you and your friend visited in Korea or any country. Use the ~는다 speech style.

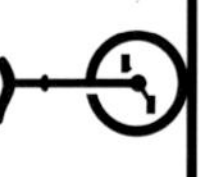

Present what you wrote in Step 3 in front of the class. Try not to look at your paper!

VII. Listening

Listen to the following conversation between a man and a woman and mark each statement T(rue) or F(alse). 19

1. ______ They didn't go to 전주한옥마을 last week.
2. ______ They're going to take a subway to 남산골한옥마을.
3. ______ They're preparing their lunch box in order not to eat at a restaurant.
4. ______ There is an admission fee for using facilities in 남산골한옥마을.

Listen to the following announcement at a museum and mark each statement T(rue) or F(alse). 20

5. ______ This museum has a program for children.
6. ______ You can learn about Korean traditional clothes, but cannot wear them.
7. ______ You can eat food on the third floor of the museum.
8. ______ This museum is open five days a week.

Words & Expressions

01-04 대중교통 public transportation 남산골한옥마을 Namsangol Hanok Village 도시락 lunch box
싸가지고 가다 to pack (thing) and go 입장료 admission fees

05-08 박물관 museum 어린이 박물관 children's museum 행사가 진행되다 an event is going on
전시실 exhibition hall 전시를 하다 to exhibit 체험 행사 hands-on experience event
참여를 부탁하다 to ask for participation (humble expression: 참여를 부탁드립니다)
편의 시설 amenities, accommodation 방문하다 to visit

VIII. Reading

남산골한옥마을 (Namsangol Hanok Village)

- **입장료** 무료
- **시간** 4월-10월 (09:00-21:00)
  11월-3월 (09:00-20:00)
- **오시는 길**
  지하철: 충무로역 4번 출구
  버스: 140번, 604번 버스, 퇴계로 3가 한옥 마을 정류장 하차
- **편의시설**
  한식당 "남산각", 전통 찻집 "국향방" 있음.
  공원 잔디밭에서 도시락을 드실 수 있음.
  공원에서 음식을 만들어 먹을 수 없음.
- **체험 프로그램**
  한복 입기, 한글 쓰기, 한국 차 마시기

자세한 내용은 웹사이트를 참고하세요.
https://www.hanokmaeul.or.kr/

1. 윗 글의 내용과 같은 것을 고르십시오.

① 남산골한옥마을은 입장료가 필요 없다.

② 남산골한옥마을에서는 식당에서만 음식을 먹을 수 있다.

③ 남산골한옥마을의 한옥에서 잘 수 있다.

④ 남산골한옥마을은 꼭 버스를 타고 가야 한다.

Words & Expressions

01 오시는 길 directions 출구 exit 하차 getting off from a transportation 한식당 Korean restaurant 전통 찻집 traditional teahouse (-을/-를) 참고하다 to refer (to ~)

서울의 박물관 (Museums in Seoul)

서울에는 많은 박물관이 있지만, 그 중에서 국립중앙박물관과 전쟁기념관은 특히 외국인들에게 인기가 많다. 국립중앙박물관은 한국에서 제일 큰 박물관이다. 이곳에서는 한국의 유명한 문화재들을 볼 수 있고, 한국의 역사와 문화에 대해 배울 수 있다. 전쟁기념관에서는 한국에서 일어났던 전쟁의 역사에 대해 배울 수 있고, 전쟁에서 사용되었던 여러 가지 무기들을 직접 볼 수 있다. 국립중앙박물관과 전쟁기념관은 서울 중심에 위치해 있고, 지하철 역에서 가까워 방문하기 편리하다. 그리고 입장료는 무료이다. ______㉠______ 항상 관람객들로 복잡하기 때문에 일찍 가는 것이 좋다. 그리고 전시품들이 아주 많기 때문에 오랫동안 둘러볼 수 있도록 계획을 하는 것이 좋다.

2. ㉠ 에 들어갈 알맞은 말을 고르십시오.

① 그리고 ② 그래서 ③ 또한 ④ 그래도

3. 이 글의 내용과 일치하는 것을 고르십시오.

① 한국에서 제일 큰 박물관은 서울에 있다.
② 국립중앙박물관은 외국인들이 잘 모르는 박물관이다.
③ 전쟁기념관은 서울에서 가까워서 방문하기 편리하다.
④ 이 박물관들은 입장료가 싸서 인기가 많다.

02-03 그 중에서 among them 국립중앙박물관 the National Museum of Korea
전쟁기념관 War Memorial of Korea 특히 especially 문화재 cultural assets 일어나다 to break out
사용되다 to be used 무기 weapon 중심에 위치하다 to be located at the center
전시품 exhibition (방문하)기 편리하다 It is convenient to (visit)
둘러보다 to look around

3 명절 풍습도 조금씩 달라지는군요.

Traditional holiday customs also gradually change.

-Traditional Korean holidays and customs
-Reporting the speech of others

Preparation & Practice	I. New Words & Expressions II. Patterns, Expressions & Practice 1. ~다고/라고 하다 Reported statement 2. ~(으)라고 하다 Reported command 3. ~지 않 "not ~" 4. ~줄 알았어요/몰랐어요 "I (mistakenly) thought/I did not know that ~"		III. Culture 1. Memorial service for ancestors 2. Traditional holidays in Korea
		Conversation Activities	IV. Listen & Discuss V. Guided Conversation VI. Spontaneous Conversation
		TOPIK Preparation	VII. Listening • Conversation • News report VIII. Reading • 한가위 (Hangawi) • 세배 (Sebae)

I. New Words & Expressions

 **Study the words and expressions along with the audio.** 

NOUN

기차표	train ticket
명절	traditional holidays
송편	half-moon-shaped rice cake
연휴	holidays (in a row); consecutive holidays
추석	Chuseok, the Korean (version of) Thanksgiving Day (celebrated on August 15 on the lunar calendar)
추석 연휴	Chuseok holiday
친척	relatives
풍습	customs
표	ticket

VERB

달라지다	to change
보내다	to spend one's time
초대하다	to invite

EXPRESSION

·(표 사)기가 쉽지 않다.
It is not easy to (buy a ticket).
*verb base + 기가 쉽다/어렵다:
it is easy/difficult to ~

Listen to the audio and fill in the blanks. 

1. A: 다음 주가 ____________인데, 넌 무슨 요일에 ______________에 내려가니?
   B: 화요일 저녁에 가. 너는?

2. A: 너 고향 가는 ______________는 샀니? ______________사기가 쉽지 않을 건데.
   B: 벌써 샀어.

3. A: 나는 일찍 ______________를 사서 이번 주말에 고향에 내려갈 거야.
   B: 이번 추석은 ______________가 길어서 난 추석 하루 전에 갈 거야.

4. A: ____________에도 서울에서 부산으로 내려가는 길은 엄청 복잡할 거야. 힘들겠다.
   B: 걱정해 줘서 고마워. 근데, 이번 ______________에는 부모님께서 서울로 올라오셔!

5. A: 이번 추석 어떻게 보냈니?
   B: 친구 집에 가서 ______________도 먹고 추석 게임들도 하고 재미있게 보냈어.

Choose the best word to complete the sentences.

1. 이번 추석은 ____________이/가 길어서 일찍 고향으로 간 사람들이 많았다.
   그래서 고속도로(highway)에는 생각보다 차가 없었다.
   ① 여행 ② 연휴 ③ 공연 ④ 견학

2. 이번 추석은 친구 부모님이 초대해 주셔서 한국에 와서 즐거운 ____________을 보냈다.
   ① 축제 ② 맛집 ③ 명절 ④ 고향

3. 이번 추석 연휴는 이틀밖에 안 되어서 고향에 안 가고 그냥 집에서 ___________ 사람들이 많다.
   ① 끝내주는 ② 어울리는 ③ 기다려지는 ④ 보내는

4. 나는 한국에 가족이 없어서 이번 추석 때 친구 부모님께서 댁에 ________________.
   ① 보냈다 ② 기다려졌다 ③ 묵었다 ④ 초대해 주셨다

5. A: 이번 추석에는 기차표 사기가 쉽지 않을 거야. 내 차로 고향에 같이 가자.
   B: ________________? 정말 고마워!
   ① 언제 내려가 ② 어떻게 보낼 거니 ③ 연락 줄래 ④ 그래도 돼

II. Patterns, Expressions & Practice

1. Reported statement: ~다고/~라고 하다

Usage

Use ~다고/~라고 하다, when you report a person's statement (e.g., what was stated in the past).

▶You (Reporter): person -이/가 [what was stated + 다/라]고 하다.
WHO (subject) WHAT (object) SAY(verb)

"A person **says/said that** ~."

* The expression in [ ] is called "reported statement." Let's use [ ] to mark the boundary of reported statement.

* The verb/adjective used in "reported statement" is called "reported verb/adjective."

* 하다 in ~고 하다 is called "reporting verb" or "saying verb."

Form

Use the ~는다 speech style for the reported verb/adjective in a reported statement, as shown below.
The ~는다 speech style in a reported statement is ~는다, ~ㄴ다, ~다, or ~(이)라. (For more, see Appendix. IV.)

Present tense

▶ [... Verb base + 는다/ㄴ다]고 하다 (e.g., .. 읽는다고 해요, 어울린다고 해요)

▶ [... Adjective base + 다]고 하다 (e.g., .. 예쁘다고 해요)

▶ [... Noun (이)라]고 하다 (e.g., .. 학생이라고 해요, 가수라고 해요)

Past tense

▶ [... Verb/Adjective base + 았다/었다]고 하다 (e.g., .. 맑았다고 해요, 읽었다고 해요)

▶ [... Noun + 이었다/였다]고 하다 (e.g., .. 학생이었다고 해요, 가수였다고 해요)

You can use the reduced form "~대요/~래요" instead of the full form "~다고 해요/~라고 해요" in reporting hearsay (in other words, things you have heard from unspecified speakers) or in more casual conversation, as shown in the table below.

Dictionary form	Present / Past	Reported statement	
		Full form	Reduced form
(Verb) 읽다 가다	읽는다 읽었다 간다 갔다	읽는다고 해요 읽었다고 해요 간다고 해요 갔다고 해요	읽는대요 읽었대요 간대요 갔대요
(Adjective) 예쁘다	예쁘다 예뻤다	예쁘다고 해요 예뻤다고 해요	예쁘대요 예뻤대요
(Consonant-ending Noun + 이다) 학생이다	학생이다 학생이었다	학생이라고 해요 학생이었다고 해요	학생이래요 학생이었대요
(Vowel-ending Noun + 다) 가수다	가수다 가수였다	가수라고 해요 가수였다고 해요	가수래요 가수였대요

Look at the following examples.

- 사람들이 나한테 [한복이 잘 어울린다]고 해요.
  사람들이 나한테 [한복이 잘 어울린]대요. *다고 해요 becomes 대요.
  (People) say that *Hanbok* looks good on me.

- 사람들이 나한테 [한복이 잘 어울린다]고 해.
  사람들이 나한테 [한복이 잘 어울린 어울린]대. *다고 해 becomes 대.
  (People) say that *Hanbok* looks good on me.

- 현수: 제니야, 너 한복이 진짜 잘 어울리는구나!
  제니: 그렇죠? 사람들이 [한복이 저한테 잘 어울린다]고 해요.
  그렇죠? 사람들이 [한복이 저한테 잘 어울린]대요.
  It does, right? People say that it looks good on me.

- 제니: 현수 오빠는 지난 주말에 어디로 견학 갔다 왔대요?

  민지: [DMZ에 갔다 왔다]**고 했어**.

  DMZ에 갔다 왔대.

  (He) said that he visited DMZ.

- (Looking at 제니's photo)

  민지: 와~ 제니가 한복을 입고 있네! 너무 잘 어울린다!

  현수: 이거 전주한옥마을에서 찍은 사진**이래**.

  It is said that this is the photo Jenny took at 전주한옥마을.

- 에이미: 샤오밍 씨는 [온라인 게임이 취미라]**고 해요**.

  샤오밍 씨는 온라인 게임이 취미**래요**.

  민준 : 그래요? 몰랐어요.

Note

The reporting verb **하다** in ~다고 하다 means "to say" and can be replaced with such verbs as **말하다** (to talk) or **얘기하다** (to tell).

민지: 현수는 이번 추석 때 부산에 안 내려가니?

웨이: 다음 주에 중요한 시험이 있어서 안 내려간다고 얘기했어요.

(He) told (me) that he would not go to his hometown because he has an important exam next week.

Tell your classmate what someone else said to you. The 👂 icon in each question indicates what you were told in the past.

1. 👂 브라이언: 저는 한국어를 잘 못해요.

   Classmate: 브라이언 씨는 한국어를 잘 해요?

   You: ______________________________.

2. 👂 마크: 어제 우리 집에서 친구들하고 같이 한국 드라마 봤어.

   Classmate: 마크는 어제 뭐 했대?

   You: ______________________________.

3. 👂 민서: 나 지금 열심히 공부하는 중이야.

   Classmate: 민서는 지금 뭐 해?

   You: ______________________________.

4. 👂 샤오밍: 사실 마크 씨가 파워블로거예요.

   Classmate: 샤오밍이 너한테 뭐래?

   You: ______________________________.

5. 👂 에이미: 저는 일 주일에 한 번 정도 블로그에 글을 쓸 거예요.

   Classmate: 에이미는 뭐 할 거래?

   You: ______________________________.

Imagine you heard the following conversation in the past. Report to your classmate what 제니퍼 mentioned about her trip to Korea.

데이빗: 이번 겨울 방학에 한국으로 여행 가려고 해요. 제니퍼 씨는 한국에 가 본 적이 있어요?

제니퍼: 네, 고등학교 졸업하고 나서 가족들하고 같이 일주일 동안 여행했어요.

데이빗: 어땠어요?

제니퍼: 정말 재미있었어요. 그런데 날씨가 생각보다 덥더라구요.

데이빗: 어떻게 다녔어요? 차를 렌트했어요?

제니퍼: 서울은 지하철하고 버스가 아주 편리해서 차가 필요 없었어요.

데이빗: 참, 한국에서는 공원에서 음식도 주문할 수 있다던데, 진짜예요?

제니퍼: 네, 그래서 우리 가족도 한강에서 치킨을 배달시켰어요.

useful expressions

배달시키다	to have things delivered
(차를) 렌트하다	to rent (a car)
한강	the Hangang River in Seoul

1. (제니퍼는) 한국에 가 본 적이 있다고 해요. (or 있대요.)

2. ______________________________.

3. ______________________________.

4. ______________________________.

5. ______________________________.

Listen to each conversation and then answer the following questions using a reported statement. 23

1. What does the woman say to the man?

____.

2. What does the man say to the woman?

____.

3. What does the woman say to the man?

____.

4. What does the man say to the woman?

____.

5. What does the man say to the woman?

____.

6. What does the woman say to the man?

____.

7. What does the man say to the woman?

____.

2. Reported command: ~(으)라고 하다

Usage

Use **~(으)라고 하다** when you report a person's command (e.g., what was commanded in the past).

▶You (Reporter): Person-이/가 [what was commanded ~(으)라]고 하다.
WHO (subject) WHAT (object) SAY(verb)

"A person **tells/told** another to do ~."

* The expression in [ ] is called "reported command." " Let's use [ ] to mark the boundary of reported statement.

Form

Use the ~(으)라 form of the verb in the reported command, as shown below.

▶ [... Verb base (ending in a consonant) + 으라]고 하다 (e.g., .. 읽으라고 해요)

▶ [... Verb base (ending in a vowel) + 라]고 하다 (e.g., .. 가라고 해요)

You can use the reduced form **~으래요/~래요** instead of the full form **~으라고 해요/~라고 해요** in more casual conversations, as shown in the table below.

Dictionary form (word base + 다)	Command	Reported command	
	Present	Full form	Reduced form
Consonant-ending verb base + 다 (읽다)	읽어라	읽으라고 해요	읽으래요
Vowel-ending verb base + 다 (오다)	와라 (오+아라)	오라고 해요	오래요

Patterns, Expressions & Practice

Look at the following examples.

- (Looking at a photo)

  웨이: 어! 너 한복 입었구나!

  제니: 응, 사람들이 [한번 입어 보라]**고 해서**, 입고 사진도 찍은 거야.

  응, 사람들이 한번 입어 보**래서**, 입고 사진도 찍은 거야.

  Because people told (me) to try wearing 한복, (I) did and took a photo as well.

- 현수: 너 오늘 영화 보러 안 갈 거야?

  민지: 부모님께서 [집에 있으라]**고 하**셔서, 오늘은 힘들겠어.

  Because my parents told (me) to stay home, it's hard (to go to the movies) today.

Note

In reported commands, **하다** in ~다고 하다 means "to say" and can be replaced with such verbs as **명령하다**(to command), **충고하다**(to advise), and **초대하다**(to invite).

민지: 웨이야, 넌 추석 어떻게 보낼 거니?

웨이: 친구가 [송편 먹으러 오라]고 **초대해 줘서**, 친구 집에 갈 거예요.

Since a friend of mine invited me to eat 송편, I'll go to his home.

Tell your classmate what someone else said to you. The icon in each question indicates what you were told in the past.

1. 마크: 지금 빨리 가려면 버스 말고 지하철을 타세요.

   Classmate: 마크 씨가 뭐라고 했어요?

   You: ______________________________.

2. 민준: 제 친구 되게 잘 생겼는데, 한번 만나보세요!

Classmate: 민준 씨가 뭐라고 했어요?

You: ____.

3. 제시카: 이 근처에 새로 생긴 한국 식당이 있는데, 거기 한번 가 봐.

Classmate: 제시카 씨가 뭐라고 했어요?

You: ____.

4. 제니: 전주한옥마을에 가면 한복도 입어 보고 온돌방에서도 한번 자 봐.

Classmate: 제니 씨가 뭐라고 했어요?

You: ____.

5. 샤오밍: 온라인 게임 해 보세요. 스트레스도 풀고 친구도 사귈 수 있는 좋은 기회예요.

Classmate: 샤오밍 씨가 뭐라고 했어요?

You: ____.

Imagine you heard the following conversation in the past. Now report what 제니퍼 told David to do when he visits Korea.

데이빗: 이번 겨울 방학에 한국으로 여행 가려고 하는데, 제니퍼 씨는 한국에 가 본 적이 있지요? 어땠어요?

제니퍼: 정말 재미있었어요. 그런데, 서울 겨울 날씨가 생각보다 춥더라구요. 옷을 따뜻하게 입고 모자하고 장갑도 꼭 가지고 가세요.

데이빗: 한국은 대중 교통이 편리하다던데, 어떻게 다녔어요?

제니퍼: 대중 교통이 아주 편리하니까 차를 빌리지 말고, 지하철이나 버스를 타세요.

데이빗: 네, 알겠어요.

제니퍼: 참, 시간 있으면 제주도에 꼭 가 보세요. 제주도가 정말 아름답다던데, 우리는 시간이 없어서 못 가 봤거든요.

제니퍼는 데이빗한테

1. ____ 했어요.

2. ____ 했어요.

3. ____ 했어요.

Listen to each conversation and then answer the question using a reported command.

1. What does the woman tell the man to do?

   여자는 남자한테 ______________________________.

2. What does the man tell the woman to do?

   남자는 여자한테 ______________________________.

3. What does the woman tell the man to do?

   여자는 남자한테 ______________________________.

4. What does the woman tell the man to do?

   여자는 남자한테 ______________________________.

5. What does the man tell the woman to do?

   남자는 여자한테 ______________________________.

3. ~지 않 "not ~"

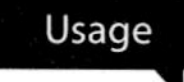

There are two ways of making a negative sentence in Korean. One way is to place **안** before a verb/adjective, which you studied in Lesson 4 (Beginning 1). Another way is to attach **지 않** after a verb/adjective base.

Dictionary form (Verb/Adjective base + **다**)	Negative forms	
	Verb/Adjective base + **지 않** + **아요**	**안** + Verb/Adjective + **아요/어요**
쉬다 (to take rest)	쉬**지 않**아요 (do **not** rest)	**안** 쉬어요 (do **not** rest)
편하다 (to be comfortable)	편하**지 않**아요 (is **not** comfortable)	**안** 편해요 (is **not** comfortable)

Look at the following examples. Generally speaking, **안** and **지 않** can be used interchangeably.

- A: 이번 추석에 고향에 안 내려갔니?
  B: 매년 내려갔는데, 올해는 좀 쉬고 싶어서 내려가**지 않**았어/**안** 내려갔어.
  I used to go down to my hometown every year, but I didn't go down this year because I wanted to rest a bit.

- A: 한국어 수업에 학생이 많아요?
  B: 보통 15명이 **안** 넘어요./보통 15명이 넘**지 않**아요.
  Usually it doesn't exceed 15.

- A: 한옥에서 자는 거 괜찮았어?
  B: 어, 하나도 불편하**지 않**더라구/**안** 불편하더라구.
  Yes, I realized that it wasn't uncomfortable at all.

Both **안** and **지 않** mean "**not**." In order to mean "**cannot**," use either **못** or **지 못하**.

Dictionary form (Verb base + 다)	Negative forms	
	Verb base + ~지 못하 + 아요/어요	못 + Verb + 아요/어요
쉬다 (to take rest)	쉬**지 못**해요 (**cannot** rest)	**못** 쉬어요 (**cannot** rest)
먹다 (to eat)	먹**지 못**해요 (**cannot** eat)	**못** 먹어요 (**cannot** eat)

Look at the following examples.

- 집이 좁아서 생일 파티에 친구들을 많이 초대하**지 못**했다/초대 **못** 했어요.
  I couldn't invite many friends to my birthday party because my house is too small.

- A: 여행하는 동안 카메라가 고장났어.
  B: 아~ 그래서 사진을 많이 찍**지 못**했구나/**못** 찍었구나.
  A: My camera was broken while traveling.
  B: Oh~ I see that's why you couldn't take many photos.

- 한복을 빌려주는 데가 많았는데, 돈이 없어서 빌리**지 못**했어요/**못** 빌렸어요.
  There were many places that lend out hanbok, but I couldn't try one on because I didn't have money.

useful expressions

고장나다	to be broken	
빌려주다	to lend (thing) to (person)	*(thing)을/를 (person)한테/에게 빌려주다
빌리다	to borrow (thing) from (person)	*(thing)을/를 (person)한테서 빌리다

Note

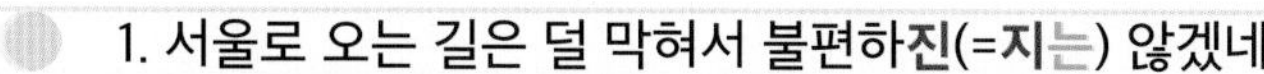

Additional markers can be attached after ~**지** in 지 않 in order to add some nuance or place emphasis on the negative meaning.

1. 서울로 오는 길은 덜 막혀서 불편하**진**(=**지는**) 않겠네.
   The traffic to Seoul would be less crowded, so I guess it would be less troublesome.

2. A: 고속도로에 차가 많이 막혀서 피곤했겠다.
   B: 응. 그리고 이번 추석은 짧아서 고향에서 쉬**지도** 못했어. 지금 엄청 피곤하네.
   Right. Because this 추석 was short, I couldn't even rest in my hometown. I'm really tired now.

Exercise 7

Complete each dialogue, using either ~지 않 or ~지 못하.

1. A: 이번 추석에 고향에 내려갈 거예요?
   B: 아뇨, 부모님이 올라오시기 때문에 저는 내려가지 않을 거예요.

2. A: 학교에 올 때 차가 많이 막혔어요?
   B: 아니요, ______________________.

3. A: 피곤해 보여요. 어제 잘 못 잤어요?
   B: 네, 오늘까지 내는 숙제가 있어서 ______________________.

Patterns, Expressions & Practice

4. A: 너는 왜 항상 바지만 입어?

   B: 나한테 치마가 잘 ______________________ 것 같아서.

5. A: 왜 가을을 좋아하세요?

   B: 여름은 너무 덥고, 겨울은 너무 추워요.

   그런데, 가을은 날씨가 ____________ 고, ____________ 잖아요.

6. A: 오늘 점심에 김밥 먹으러 갈래요?

   B: 죄송해요. 제가 오이 알레르기가 있어서 김밥을 ______________________.

   A: 그래요? 오이 없는 김밥도 있어요.

useful expressions

알레르기	allergy
알레르기가 있다	to have an allergy
내다	to submit (thing) *(thing)을/를 내다
치마	skirt

Exercise 8

Convert the following 안/못 negative sentences into the 지 않/지 못하 form, or vice versa.

1. 나는 룸메이트랑 같이 방을 쓰는 게 하나도 안 불편하다.

   나는 룸메이트랑 같이 방을 쓰는 게 하나도 불편하지 않다.

2. 아르바이트 때문에 겨울 방학에 집에 못 갔다 왔다.

   ____.

3. 참가비가 비싸서 그 행사에 참가하지 못했다.

   ____.

4. 아버지께서 바쁘셔서 가족들과 시간을 많이 못 보내신다.

   ____.

5. 서울타워에서는 북한이 안 보인다.

____.

6. 지난 주에 DMZ에 견학을 갔다 온 학생은 10명을 넘지 않았다.

____.

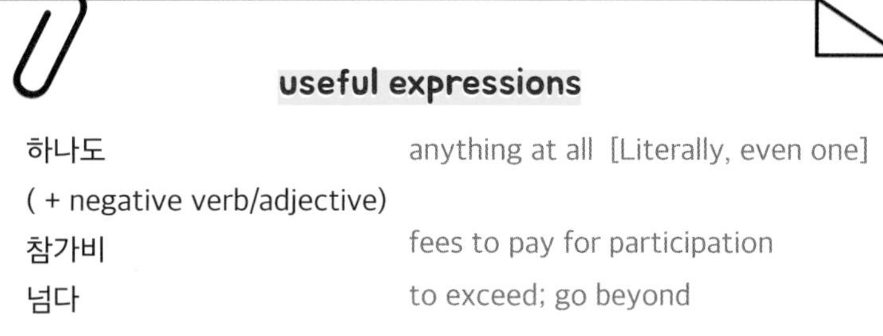

useful expressions

하나도 (+ negative verb/adjective)	anything at all [Literally, even one]
참가비	fees to pay for participation
넘다	to exceed; go beyond

민지 called 현수 but he didn't answer, so she left a message. Listen to her message and answer the following questions in Korean. 25

1. Why is 민지's home not available for the party?

____.

2. Why did 민지 suggest gathering at 웨이's house?

____.

*모이다 to gather; to meet

In this audio, two friends talk about a restaurant that recently opened. Listen to their conversation and mark each statement T(rue) or F(alse). 26

1. ______ The man knows that the food of the restaurant is tasty.

2. ______ The woman heard about the restaurant.

useful expressions

식당이 생긴 줄 모르다	to not know if a restaurant opened
(a place)에 들어가다	to enter (a place)

4. ~줄 알았다/몰랐다 "I mistakenly thought/I did not know that ~"

Usage

Use **~줄 알았다** to express your realization that something is not true, even though you originally thought that it was. It means "**I mistakenly thought that ~**" or "**I thought that ~ (but it was not true).**" On the contrary, use **~줄 몰랐다** to express your realization that something is true, even though you originally thought that it was not. "**I did not know that ~**" or "**(I just realized that) I did not know that something was true.**"

Form

~줄 알았다/몰랐다 is preceded by various noun-modifying forms. (For noun-modifying forms, see Appendix VI.)

Dictionary form	Noun-modifying forms + 줄 알았다		
	Past tense	Present tense	Future tense
(Verb base + 다) 먹다 자다	(Verb base + 은/ㄴ줄 알았어요) 먹은 줄 알았어요 잔 줄 알았어요	(Verb base + 는 줄 알았어요) 먹는 줄 알았어요 자는 줄 알았어요	(Verb base + 을/ㄹ 줄 알았어요) 먹을 줄 알았어요 잘 줄 알았어요
(Adjective base + 다) 좋다 크다	---	(Adjective base + 은/ㄴ 줄 알았어요) 좋은 줄 알았어요 큰 줄 알았어요	(Adjective base + 을/ㄹ 줄 알았어요) 좋을 줄 알았어요 클 줄 알았어요
(Consonant-ending Noun +이다) 한국사람이다	---	(Consonant-ending Noun + 인 줄 알았어요) 한국사람인 줄 알았어요	(Consonant-ending Noun + 일 줄 알았어요) 한국사람일 줄 알았어요
(Vowel-ending Noun+다) 가수다	---	(Vowel-ending Noun + ㄴ 줄 알았어요) 가수인 줄 알았어요 (Colloquial: 가순 줄 알았어요)	(Vowel-ending Noun + ㄹ 줄 알았어요) 가수일 줄 알았어요 (Colloquial: 가술 줄 알았어요)

Look at the following examples.

- A: 나는 민지가 집에 있는 **줄 알았어**.
  B: 지난 주에 한국에 갔는데, 몰랐구나.
  I thought that Minji was at home, (but I just found out that she is not.)

- A: 제니퍼가 영국 사람**인 줄 몰랐어요**.
  B: 어떻게 그걸 몰랐어요? 제니퍼는 영국식 영어를 쓰잖아요.
  I did not know that Jennifer was British, (but I just found out that she is.)

- A: 남자 친구와 일 년 전에 헤어졌어요.
  B: 그래요? 그렇게 일찍 헤어**진 줄 몰랐어요**!
  A: 사실, 저도 그렇게 빨리 헤어**질 줄 몰랐어요**.
  Really? I didn't know that you had broken up with him that early.
  In fact, I didn't even know that I would break up with him that quickly.

Describe the situation in (parenthesis), using ~줄 알았어요 or ~줄 몰랐어요.

1. (You didn't know it was raining outside, but it is.)

____.

2. (You didn't know Seoul's winters would be this cold, but it is.)

____.

3. (You didn't know college life would be this hard, but it is.)

____.

4. (You thought your roommate was sleeping, but she's not.)

____.

5. (You didn't know it was going to rain today, so you didn't bring your umbrella.)

____.

Exercise 12

Fill in the blanks, using ~줄 알았어요 or ~줄 몰랐어요.

1. A: 제니는 도서관에 있어요?

   B: 아니요. 집에 갔어요.

   A: 그래요? 저는 제니가 ____________________.

2. A: 마이클, 너 술 마셔도 돼?

   B: 그럼. 내가 지난 달에 20살이 됐잖아.

   A: 아, 그래? 나는 네가 아직 ____________________.

3. A: 날씨가 이렇게 추운데 왜 반팔을 입고 왔어? 안 추워?

   B: 나는 날씨가 이렇게 ____________________.

4. A: 이 해물 파전 정말 제니퍼 씨가 만들었어요?

   B: 네, 어때요?

   A: 정말 맛있어요. 제니퍼 씨가 요리를 이렇게 __________

   ____________________.

5. A: 여보세요? 거기 제니 씨 있어요?

   B: 잠깐만 기다리세요. (after a while) 죄송합니다.

   저는 제니가 자리에 ______________는데

   지금 보니까 없네요. 메시지를 남겨 드릴까요?

useful expressions

술 alcohol
반팔 short-sleeved shirt, half-sleeved shirt
자리 one's seat
메시지를 남기다 to leave a message

In this audio, two friends are talking about where 제니 is. Listen to their conversation and mark each statement T(rue) or F(alse). 27

1. ______ 여자는 제니를 찾고 있어요.
2. ______ 제니는 방에 있어요.
3. ______ 남자는 제니하고 같이 있어요.
4. ______ 남자는 제니가 방에 있는 줄 알았어요.

*나가다 to go out
*찾다 to look for

In this audio, two friends are talking about the weather. Listen to their conversation and mark each statement T(rue) or F(alse). 28

1. ______ 여자는 일기 예보를 봤어요.
2. ______ 남자는 짧은 옷을 입었어요.
3. ______ 여자는 오늘 날씨가 추울 거라고 알고 있었어요.
4. ______ 남자는 오늘 날씨가 추울 거라고 들었어요.

*일기 예보 weather forecast

In this recording, two classmates talk about taking a Chinese class. Listen to their conversation and mark each statement T(rue) or F(alse). 29

1. ______ The woman did not know that the man did not take the Chinese class.
2. ______ The man thought that the woman is interested in Chinese culture.

*전공 수업 major class/course

III. Culture

1. 차례 (Memorial service for ancestors)

On the morning of 설날 and 추석, Koreans hold a memorial service called 차례 in honor of their ancestors. They set out a table of dishes, including 고기 (meat), 생선 (fish), 과일 (fruit), 나물 (seasoned vegetables), 떡 (rice cake), and more. The dishes used in this ritual vary from region to region. During the service, family members take deep bows (절) and offer 술 (wines) to their ancestors.

To commemorate/honor the day of their ancestors' death, Koreans hold a similar service called 제사.

Traditionally, ancestral rites, such as 제사 and 차례, were considered an important obligation of "the" offspring, but in more recent times, the ancestral rites have been simplified. In addition, many people, including Protestants, do not hold memorial services. As you can see, 설날 and 추석 traditions (gradually) change over time.

2. 한국의 명절 (Traditional holidays in Korea)

양력설 (New Year's Day), 설날 (Lunar New Year's Day)

Koreans celebrate the New Year twice--once on January 1, as westerners do, and once on the first day of the lunar calendar. January 1 is known as **양력설**, and it is a public holiday, so many people take the day off. On the lunar calendar, New Year's Day is called **설날**, and it generally occurs in late January or early February. It is one of the most important Korean holidays, lasting three days, and most people don't have to work during this time. During **설날**, people travel to their hometowns to visit their families, which leads to congested roads across the country.

세배

떡국

On **설날 아침**, people wear **한복** (Korean traditional clothes), perform **차례** and eat **떡국** (rice cake soup). Children give **세배** (formal bows) to their elders while greeting them with phrases such as "**새해 복 많이 받으세요!**" (May you receive many blessings this new year!) or "**새해에도 건강하세요!**" (May you have good health this year as well!). In turn, the parents and elders give children **덕담** (well-wishing remarks) along with **세뱃돈** (bow money).

부처님 오신 날

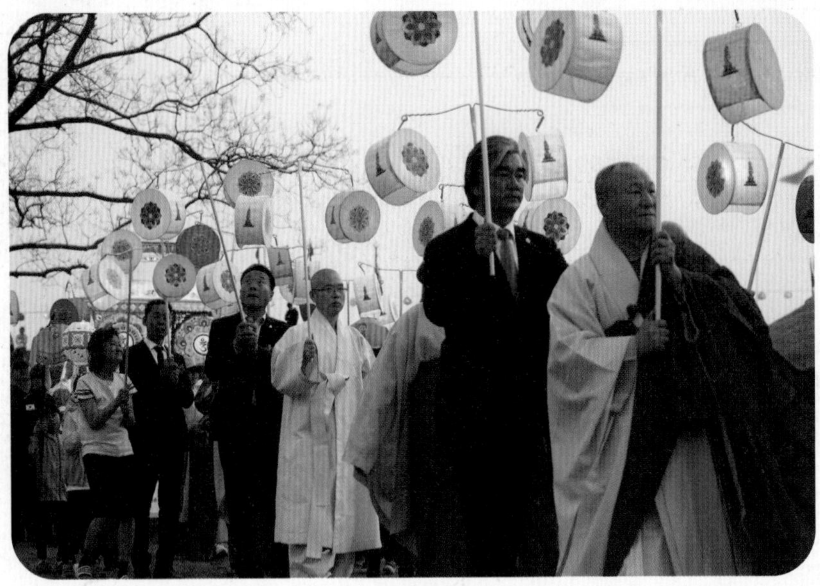

Both Buddha's birthday and Jesus's birthday are official Korean holidays. For most of Korean history. Buddhism has been the country's most popular religion. **부처님 오신 날** (the day when Buddha came) is the 8th day of the 4th month of the lunar calendar. On this day, people visit **절** (Buddhist temples) and enjoy the view of **연등** (lotus lanterns), which hang all around **절** or on the streets.

성탄절

Christianity is one of the most popular religions in contemporary Korea. Christmas is called **성탄절** or **크리스마스** in Korean. Rather than a day spent exchanging presents with family, it is a time when young people go out and have fun. Many places are decorated with Christmas lights and everyone enjoys the Christmas spirit regardless of their faith.

IV. Listen & Discuss

웨이, 현수, and 민지 are talking to one another.

First, listen to the conversation. With your classmates, discuss the answers to the questions that follow. Finally, write each answer in a full Korean sentence in the space provided.

1. 세 사람은 무엇에 대해서 이야기하고 있습니까?

2. 웨이는 이번 추석에 대해서 무엇을 들었습니까?

3. 현수는 고향에 언제 어떻게 갑니까?

4. 민지는 이번 추석에 무엇을 합니까?

5. 추석 명절에 대해서 웨이가 몰랐던 사실은 무엇입니까?

6. 웨이의 이번 추석 계획은 무엇입니까?

Script

While moving to another building on campus, 웨이 is asking questions for 현수 and 민지 about a Korean national holiday.

01 웨이: 이번 추석에는 표 사기가 쉽지 않다고 들었어요.[II.1]
형하고 누나도 고향에 가세요?

02 현수: 어, 나는 올해 기차표를 일찍 사서 이번 주말에 고향에 내려갈 거야.

03 민지: 고향에 가면 친척들도 만나고 재미있겠네.

04 현수: 민지 너는 언제 갈 거야?

05 민지: 난 이번 추석에는 고향에 내려가지 않고,[II.3] 친구들이랑 여행가기로 했어.

06 웨이: 한국 사람들은 명절에 다 고향에 가는 줄 알았는데….[II.4]

07 현수: 요즘은 명절에 여행을 하는 사람도 많아졌어.

08 웨이: 그렇구나. 명절 풍습도 조금씩 달라지는군요.

09 민지: 웨이야, 너는 추석 어떻게 보낼 거니?

10 웨이: 교수님께서 송편 먹으러 오라고 초대해 주셔서,[II.2] 교수님 댁에 갈 거예요.

11 현수: 잘 됐네. 그럼, 다들 추석 연휴 즐겁게 보내고, 다음 주에 봐.

01 웨이: I heard that it's not easy to buy a ticket this Chuseok, too.
Are you both also going to your hometown?

02 현수: Yes. I bought a train ticket early this year. I'll head to my hometown this weekend.

03 민지: If you go back home, you'll get to see your relatives. I bet you'll have fun.

04 현수: When do you go, Minji?

05 민지: I won't go home this time. I decided to go on a trip with friends.

06 웨이: I thought most Koreans go home on national holidays.

07 현수: These days many people travel during national holidays.

08 웨이: I see. Traditional holiday customs also gradually change.

09 민지: Wei, what are you going to do over Chuseok?

10 웨이: My professor invited me to come and eat 송편, so I'll go to his house.

11 현수: That sounds great. Have a great 추석 holiday, and I'll see you next week.

V. Guided Conversation

Keeping in mind the organization of the model conversation in Watch & Discuss (Script), practice the modified conversation below with your partner.

Two close friends are talking about their plan for 추석.

Practice the following conversation with your classmate, using the prompts in (parenthesis) to fill in the blanks. Use non-honorific speech styles, and try to make the conversation flow naturally.

01 A: 이번 추석에는 ______________ 다고 들었어.[II.1]
(표 사기가 쉽지 않다; 많은 사람들이 서울에서 지방으로 내려가다; 많은 사람들이 집에 가다; …)

너는 언제 고향에 가니?

02 B: 난 올해 ______________ 를 일찍 사서 ______________.
(기차표; 버스표;비행기표) (State when you plan to go to your hometown)

03 A: ______________ 좋겠다.
(가족들/친척들도 만나고;고향 친구들도 만나고;맛있는 음식도 많이 먹고;....)

04 B: 너는 언제 가?

Option (1)

05 A: 이번 추석에는 고향에 가지 않기로 했어.[II.3]

06 B: 그래? 난 너도 집에 가는 줄 알았는데….[II.4] 그럼 추석은 어떻게 보낼 거니?

07 A: ______________[II.2] 에 가려고.
(친구가 송편/저녁 먹으러 오라고 초대해 줘서 친구 집; 친구가 놀러 오라고 해서 친구 집; …)

08 B: 잘 됐네! 그럼 추석 연휴 즐겁게 보내고, 다음 주에 보자.

Option (2)

05 A: 난 이번 추석에는 고향에 가지 않고,[II.3]

____.

(Tell B your different plan, using ~기로 하다: 친구들이랑 여행 가기로 하다; …)

06 B: 난 너도 당연히 집에 가는 줄 알았는데….[II.4]

07 A: 우리 부모님께서 괜찮다고 하셨어.[II.1] 요즘은 명절에 여행하는 사람들이 많으니까 이해해 주시더라구.

08 B: 넌 좋겠다~. 우리 부모님께서는 집에 꼭 오라고 하셨어.[II.2]

(Switch roles and continue to practice.)

useful expressions

L01 서울에서 지방으로 내려가다 to go to the provinces from Seoul

L02 버스표 bus ticket

L03 즐겁게 pleasantly; joyfully

Present the conversation above in front of the class. Try not to look at your paper!

VI. Spontaneous Conversation

This is your chance to have a realistic interaction with your classmates in Korean. You can practice writing, speaking with your classmates, and presenting in front of the class!

You and your classmate are talking about national holidays in your home county. (Refer to Section "IV. Culture" for national holidays in Korea.) Include the information (in the table below) in your conversation. Create a meaningful conversation with your partner similar to the one that you practiced in the Guided Conversation!

- Choose one national holiday from Section IV. Culture and ask about your partner's plan. (Use ~기로 했어, ~을 거야.)
- Talk about traditional customs you've heard or read about the holiday. (Use ~다고 해, ~대.)
- Talk about anything new you've learned about the holiday. (Use ~는 줄 알다/모르다, ~는구나/구나.)
- Wrap up the conversation by wishing each other a great holiday.

Write down the conversation you had with your partner in Step 1.

Step 3

Based on the conversation in Step 2, write a short paragraph about one of the national holidays in Korea. Include what Korean people traditionally do on that day and also what you would do if you were celebrating the holiday in Korea. Use the ~는다 speech style. (Note: You may choose one of the holidays in your own country.)

Present what you wrote in Step 2 in front of the class. Try not to look at your paper!

VII. Listening

In this audio, two friends discuss New Year's Day in Korea. Listen to their phone conversation and mark each statement T(rue) or F(alse). 31

1. ______ It is going to be January 1st next Wednesday.
2. ______ Koreans celebrate a New Year twice.
3. ______ On 설날, people go to their hometown.
4. ______ 세배 is a traditional Korean food that you eat on 설날.

Listen to the following news report and answer the questions in English. 32

5. How long is the 추석 holiday?

______________________________.

6. Why are bus terminals and train stations busy now?

______________________________.

7. What do people buy at traditional markets?

______________________________.

8. Which place is the busiest at markets?

______________________________.

9. During the holiday, what would be the weather like?

______________________________.

Words & Expressions

01-09 기차역 train station 버스터미널 bus terminal 나와 있다 to come out 그중에서도 above all 떡집 rice cake shop

VIII. Reading

한가위 (Hangawi)

"더도 말고 덜도 말고 한가위만 같아라 (No more or no less, may it always be like 한가위)" 라는 말이 있다. 한가위는 추석과 같은 말인데 추석 때가 한국에서 일 년 중에 제일 좋은 시기이다. 먼저 추석 때는 더운 여름이 지나고 날씨가 시원해지기 때문에 지내기가 좋다. 그리고 옛날부터 추석 때면 맛있는 과일과 곡식이 풍성해서 가난한 사람들도 음식 걱정이 없었다. ( ) 옛날 사람들은 일년 내내 추석 때처럼 좋은 날이길 바라며 서로 이 말을 했다고 한다.

1. ( )에 들어갈 알맞은 것을 고르십시오.
   ① 그리고 ② 그렇지만 ③ 그래서 ④ 그래도

2. 이 글의 내용과 같은 것을 고르십시오.
   ① 추석 때는 음식이 많다.
   ② 추석보다 한가위 때가 날씨가 더 좋다.
   ③ 추석 때는 날씨가 덥다.
   ④ 옛날에는 추석이 자주 있었다.

Words & Expressions

01-02 같은 말 same word 시기 (period of) time 곡식 grains 풍성하다 to be plentiful, abundant 걱정 worries

세배 (Sebae)

설날 아침 어른들께 절을 하는 것을 세배라고 한다. (1) 1년을 시작하면서 집안 어른들께 인사를 하는 것이다. (2) 어른들께 세배를 할 때에는 절을 한 후에 "새해에는 더 건강하세요." "새해 복 많이 받으시고 오래 사세요."라고 새해 인사말을 한다. (3) 세뱃돈을 주면서 "새해에는 좋은 직장에 들어가라", "새해에 꼭 좋은 사람 만나서 결혼해라"등의 좋은 말을 하는데 이것을 덕담이라고 한다. (4)

3. 다음 문장이 들어갈 곳을 고르십시오.

어른들은 세배를 한 사람들에게 돈을 주는데 이것을 세뱃돈이라고 한다.

① (1) ② (2) ③ (3) ④ (4)

4. 이 글의 내용과 같은 것을 고르십시오.
① 세배는 집안 어른들이 하는 것이다.
② 세배를 할 때 어른들께 돈을 드린다.
③ 세배를 하면서 어른들께 하는 인사말을 덕담이라고 한다.
④ 세배는 새해 첫날 아침에 한다.

03-04 절을 하다 to give a big, Korean style bow 집안 어른 seniors (elders) in one's family
~(으)면서 while ~ing 직장 job, workplace

4 교통편은 뭐가 좋을까요?

What would be the best transportation?

-Local Korean specialties
-Comparing modes of transportation in Korea

Preparation & Practice	I. New Words & Expressions II. Patterns, Expressions & Practice 1. ~을까/~ㄹ까 하다 "to be thinking of ~ing" 2. ~ 것 "the fact/thing that ~" 3. ~(으)니까 "since ~ ; because ~; ~, so …." 4. ~을/~ㄹ 줄 알다 "to know how to do ~" ~을/~ㄹ 줄 모르다 "to not know how to do ~"		III. Culture 1. Trains and express buses 2. Rest areas on expressways
		Conversation Activities	IV. Listen & Discuss V. Guided Conversation VI. Spontaneous Conversation
		TOPIK Preparation	VII. Listening • Conversation • Announcement VIII. Reading • Icheon Ceramics Festival • Cheonan Walnut Cookies

I. New Words & Expressions

☞ **Study the words and expressions along with the audio.** 

NOUN

고속버스	express bus
교통편	means of transportation
관광 안내	sightseeing guidance
사흘	three days *사흘 후에: in four days
일정	daily schedule
제주도	Jeju-do (island of South Korea)
지역	area
컨퍼런스	conference
택시기사	taxi driver
휴게소	rest area
KTX	Korea Train Express

VERB

렌트하다	to rent (a car)
운전하다	to drive
추천하다	to recommend

ADJECTIVE

다양하다	to be various; diverse

ADVERB

오래	for a long time
즐겁게	pleasantly; joyfully

EXPRESSION

·(먹어 볼) 수 있다	to be able to (eat) *~을/~ㄹ 수 있다: to be able to~
·관광 안내를 잘 해주다	to give good tour information
·즐겁게 여행하세요!	Have a nice trip!

Listen to the audio and fill in the blanks. 

1. A: 테드 씨, 다음 ______________은 어떻게 되세요?

   B: ______________ 후에 제주도에서 컨퍼런스가 있어요.

2. A: KTX를 타면, 빠르고 편해요. 두 세 시간밖에 안 걸려요.

   B: 맞아요. 근데 저는 ______________를 타는 것도 좋아해요.

3. A: 고속버스를 타고 휴게소에 들르면, 그 ______________의 유명한 음식들을 먹어 볼 수 있어요.

   B: 그럼 고속버스를 타야겠네요!

4. A: 부산에서 제주도까지 가는 ______________은 뭐가 좋을까요?

   B: 보통 비행기를 많이 타요.

5. A: 제주도에 가서는 어떻게 다니실 거예요?

   B: 택시를 타고 다니려구요. ______________이 관광 안내도 해 준다고 들었어요.

Exercise 2

Choose the best word to complete the sentences.

1. 제주도에 가서는 차를 ____________게 다니기 편할 것이다.

   ① 추천할　② 도착할　③ 렌트하는　④ 초대하는

2. 나는 빠른 KTX를 좋아하지만, 시간이 많은 테드 씨한테는 고속버스를 ____________.

   ① 경험했다　② 즐겼다　③ 운전했다　④ 추천했다

3. 휴게소에서 ______________ 음식을 먹어 보고 싶어서 나는 고속버스를 타기로 했다.

   ① 무서운　② 편한　③ 필요한　④ 다양한

4. 제주도에서 택시를 탔는데, 택시 기사님이 ____________을/를 잘 해 주셨다.

   ① 일정　② 연휴　③ 관광 안내　④ 풍습

5. 택시 기사 아저씨들이 친절해서, 나는 제주도에서 ________여행을 할 수 있었다.

   ① 가깝게　② 즐겁게　③ 생각보다　④ 엄청

II. Patterns, Expressions & Practice

1. ~을/ㄹ까 하다 "to be thinking of ~ing"

Usage

Use **~을/~ㄹ까 하다** when you express your tentative plan for the near future.

▶ Verb base (ending in a consonant) + **을까** : 먹 + **을까 하다** → **먹을까 하다**

▶ Verb base (ending in a vowel) + **ㄹ까** : 가 + **ㄹ까 하다** → **갈까 하다**

*Verb base (ending in ㄹ) + **까** : 만들 + **까 하다** → **만들까 하다**

Note 1

"ㄷ-ending" irregular verbs conjugate as follows:

걷다 → 걷 + **을까 하다** → 걸 + **을까 하다**

듣다 → 듣 + **을까 하다** → 들 + **을까 하다**

(For "ㄷ- irregular" verb conjugation, see Appendix Ⅴ,1.)

Look at the following examples.

● A: 내일은 밖에 나가지 않고 집에서 책이나 읽**을까 해요**.
B: 가끔은 집에서 그냥 쉬는 것도 좋죠.

A: I'm thinking of reading books and not going out.
B: It's good to take a rest at home sometimes.

● A: 시험도 끝났는데 오늘 저녁에 뭐 할 거예요?
B: 친구하고 같이 놀**까 해요**.

A: Since the exam is over, what are you going to do tonight?
B: I'm thinking of hanging out with my friends.

● A: 컨퍼런스 끝나면 바로 돌아오실 거예요?
B: 아니요. 이번에는 여행도 좀 하고 싶어서 한 달 정도 머무**를까 해요**. *머무르다 to stay

A: Are you going to come back immediately when the conference is over?
B: No, I want to travel this time, so I'm thinking of staying for about one month.

Note 2

하다 can be replaced by **생각하다** "to think."

• 졸업하고 나서, 한국에서 영어를 가르칠까 생각하고 있어요.
I'm thinking of teaching English in Korea after graduation.

Express your tentative plan based on the pictures, using ~을/~ㄹ까 하다, as in the first example.

1. A: 오후에 뭐 할 거예요?

   B: 친구하고 커피를 마실까 해요.

2. A: 이번 주말에 뭐 할 거예요?

   B: 오래간만에 ______________________.

3. A: 내일 아침에 뭐 먹을 거예요?

   B: 새해라서 ______________________.

4. A: 지금 차가 막히니까 지하철을 ______________________.

   B: 저는 그냥 버스를 탈까 해요. 나중에 봐요.

5. A: 이번 추석에는 한복을 ______________________.

   B: 민지 씨한테 한복이 잘 어울릴 것 같아요.

Complete each dialogue, expressing your tentative plan, as in the first example.

1. A: 시험도 끝났는데, 주말에 뭐 할 거야?

   B: 이번 주말에는 오래간만에 영화를 볼까 해.
   (to be thinking of watching movies)

2. A: 어머니 생신 선물 준비했니?

   B: 이번 생신에는 어머니께 ______________________.
   (to be thinking of giving a birthday card and flowers)

3. A: 한국 음식이 먹고 싶어서 오늘 저녁에 ______________________.
   (to be thinking of making 잡채)

   B: 정말요? 잡채도 만들 수 있어요?

4. A: 다음 학기에 무슨 수업 들을 거니?

B: ________________________________ 생각하고 있어.
(to be thinking of taking Korean history)

5. A: 수영복은 왜 찾고 있어?

B: 오래간만에 ________________________________ 해서.
(to be thinking of going to the swimming pool)

6. A: 파티에 박 선생님도 ________________________ 는데, 어때?
(to be thinking of inviting)
B: 좋지. 그런데, 선생님께서는 바빠서 아마 못 오실 거야.

7. A: 내일도 도서관에 갈 거야?

B: 아니, 시험도 끝나서 오래간만에 친구랑 ________________________.
(to be thinking of hanging out)

Listen to the conversation between two friends and mark each statement T(rue) or F(alse). 35

1. ______ The woman bought a movie ticket.
2. ______ The woman watched a movie.

Exercise 4

Listen to the conversation between two friends and answer the following questions. 36

1. ______ The woman went to the department store to buy a present for Steve.
2. ______ The man bought a cell phone for Steve.

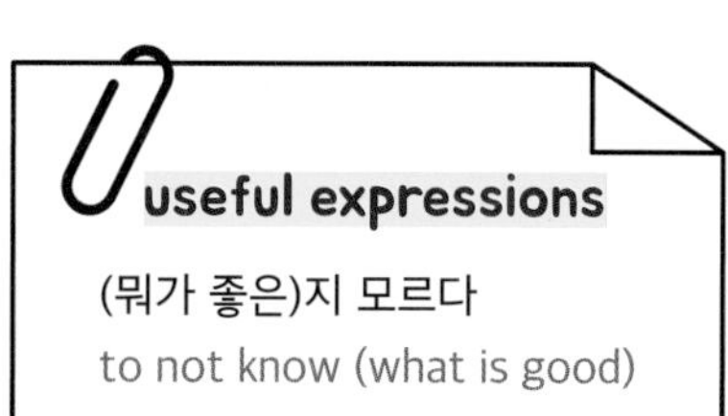

useful expressions
(뭐가 좋은)지 모르다
to not know (what is good)

2. noun-modifying form + 것 "the fact/thing that ~"

Usage Use "verb/adjective base + **noun-modifying form + 것**" to say "the fact that ~."

past/present/future noun-modifying form

Noun meaning "fact/thing"

▶ Verb base + 은/ㄴ/는/을/ㄴ 것 : 먹는 것 "the fact that one eats"

▶ Adjective base + 던/은/ㄴ/을/ㄹ 것 : 좋은 것 "thing that is good"

(For noun-modifying forms, see Appendix IV.)

Because "것" above is a noun, it can be followed by the topic/contrast marker (은), the subject-focus marker (이), the object marker (을), and other similar markers, as shown in the table below.

Noun-modifying form verbs/adjectives (e.g., 먹다, 좋다)			Dependent nouns (e.g., 것)	Subject-focus marker	Topic/contrast marker	Object marker
				이	은	을
Past tense form	Verb base + 은/ㄴ	먹은	것	먹은 것이 (먹은 게)	먹은 것은 (먹은 건)	먹은 것을 (먹은 걸)
Present tense form	Verb base + 는	먹는	것	먹는 것이 (먹는 게)	먹는 것은 (먹는 건)	먹는 것을 (먹는 걸)
	Adjective base + 은/ㄴ	좋은	것	좋은 것이 (좋은 게)	좋은 것은 (좋은 건)	좋은 것을 (좋은 걸)
Future tense form	Verb base + 을/ㄹ	먹을	것	먹을 것이 (먹을 게)	먹을 것은 (먹을 건)	먹을 것을 (먹을 걸)
	Adjective base + 을/ㄹ	좋을	것	좋을 것이 (좋을 게)	좋을 것은 (좋을 건)	좋을 것을 (좋을 걸)

Look at the following examples.

- A: 요즘 공부하는 **게** 힘들어서 졸업하고 대학원에는 안 가기로 했어.
  (것이)

  B: 나도 그냥 취직하는 **게** 더 나을 거 같아.
  (것이)

  A: Because I find studying difficult these days, I decided not to go to graduate school after graduation.

  B: I also think getting a job is better.

- A: 서울에서 부산까지는 어떤 교통편으로 가는 **게** 좋을까?
  (것이)

  B: 연휴라서 고속버스 타는 **건** 별로고 기차 타는 **걸** 생각해 봐.
  (것은) (것을)

  A: Which mode of transportation would be good for going from Seoul to Busan?

  B: Because it is a long holiday, taking an express bus is not good. Think of taking a train.

- A: 이 식당 뭐가 맛있을까?

  B: 비싼 **게** 맛있겠지!
  (것이)

The underlined parts below are reduced forms of "것 + marker" in "verb base + noun-modifying form + 것 + marker." Write the full forms, as shown in Line 01.

01 A: 주말에 뭐 하는 걸 좋아하세요?
(것을)

02 B: 저는 친구들 만나서 얘기하는 걸 제일 좋아해요.
(   )

03 A: 공원에서 산책하는 건 어때요?
(   )

04 B: 그것도 좋아요.

05 A: 그럼 이번 주말에 같이 산책하는 게 어때요?
(   )

06 B: 네, 좋아요.

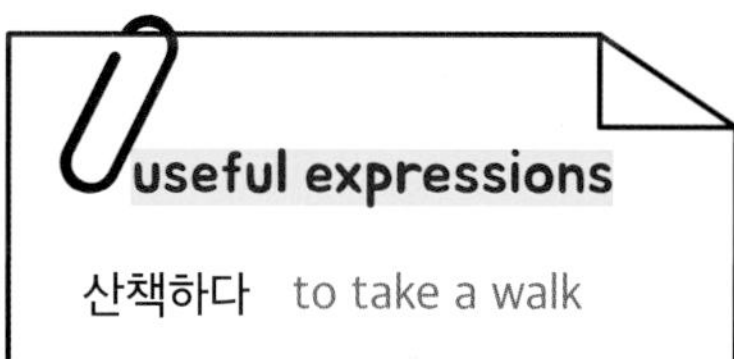

Exercise 6

Complete each dialogue, using "verb base + noun-modifying form + 것 + marker," as in the first example.

1. 민지: DMZ? 거기선 북한이 정말 가깝게 보이니?

   웨이: 어, 망원경으로 보니까 사람들이 (걸어 다니다) <u>걸어 다니는 게</u> 다 보일 정도야.

2. 웨이: 그럼... 한옥에서 묵었어?

   제니: 응. 온돌방에서 (자다) ____________________ 생각보다 편하더라고.

3. 샤오밍: 이 운동화 300불에 샀는데, 어때?

   에이미: 예쁘네! 근데 왜 그렇게 (비싸다) ____________________ 샀어?

4. 민준: 시간이 참 빨리 (가다) ____________________ 아쉬워요!

   샤나: 그러게요. 벌써 12월이 다 갔어요!

5. 에이미: 샤오밍한테 민준 씨 생일이 오늘이라고 들었어요. 이거 (비싸다) ________________ 아니지만... 제 선물이에요.

Exercise 7

Complete the following conversation by filling in the blanks, using "verb base + noun-modifying form + 것 + marker."

01 현수: 다음 주가 마크 생일이래. 우리 생일 파티 해 줄까?

02 민지: 그러자. 근데 어디서 모이지? 너네 집에서 해도 돼?

03 현수: 글쎄... 내 룸메이트가 ________________________ (having a party at home) 싫어해서 어려울 거 같아.

04 그냥, ________________ 어때?
(meeting at a restaurant)

05 민지: 연말이라서 ________________ 쉽지 않을 거야. 내가 한번 알아볼게.
(reserving a restaurant)

06 현수: 그래. 근데, 선물은 뭐가 좋을까?

07 마크가 ________________ 좋아하니까 ________________ 어때?
(listening to music) (buying earphones)

08 민지: 이어폰은 크리스마스 세일 때 벌써 샀대.

useful expressions

연말	the end of a year
이어폰	earphones
세일 때	on sale

Exercise 8

Listen to the conversation between two friends and answer the questions in English. 37

1. What does the man suggest the woman does?

a. ________________.

b. ________________.

2. Why does the woman not want to go to the Korean students' club?

________________.

3. ~(으)니까 (1) since ~; because ~; ~, so ... (2) ~, I found out that ...

Form

- ▶ Verb/Adjective base (ending in a consonant) + **으니까** : 먹**으니까**
- ▶ Verb/Adjective base (ending in vowel) + **니까** : 사**니까**
- * Past tense: ~았/~었 + **으니까** : 먹었**으니까**, 샀**으니까**
- * Future tense: ~을/~ㄹ 거 + **니까** : 먹을 거**니까**, 살 거**니까**

Usage 1

Use the ~**(으)니까** to indicate that the action or state in the preceding clause is the reason for that of the following clause.

Look at the following examples.

● 오늘은 눈이 오**니까** 집에 있을 거예요.

Since it's snowing today, I will be staying home.

● 이 영화는 재미있**으니까** 많은 사람들이 볼 거예요.

Because this movie is very entertaining, many people will watch it.

● 점심을 네가 샀**으니까** 커피는 내가 살게.

Because you bought lunch, I will buy coffee.

● 오늘 오후에 비가 올 것 같**으니까** 우산을 가지고 가세요.

It will rain this afternoon, so please take an umbrella with you.

Usage 2

Use ~**(으)니까** to express that the event/situation (in the first clause) brings about your realization or discovery of the following event/situation (in the second clause). In this case, ~**(으)니까** is often used with ~더라구/더라고 ending, as we discussed in Lesson 2.

● 아침에 일어나**니까** 눈이 오고 있었어요.

I woke up in the morning and found out that it was snowing.

● 샌디 집에 가**니까**, 벌써 학교에 갔더라고.

I went to Sandy's house and found out that she already went to school.

Note 1

Use ~**(으)니까** when you explain the reason why you are suggesting or asking someone to do, as in the following situations.

- 약속 시간에 늦었**으니까** 택시를 타고 갈까요?
- 오늘은 추우**니까** 내일 만나는 게 어때요?

Patterns, Expressions & Practice

Note 2

You should not use ~**(으)니까** when you apologize or express gratitude. For explaining the reason why you are apologizing or expressing gratitude, it's more common to use ~**아서**/~**어서**.

- 선생님, 수업에 늦**어서** 죄송합니다.
- 추천서를 써 주**셔서** 감사합니다.

Exercise 9

Complete each dialogue, using ~(으)니까, as in the first example.

1. A: 우리 오늘 수업 끝나고 만날까요?

   B: <u>오늘은 너무 늦었으니까</u>, 내일 만나요.

2. A: 오늘 무슨 옷을 입을지 잘 모르겠어요.

   B: ______________________, 따뜻하게 입으세요.

3. A: 어디서 저녁을 먹지요?

   B: ______________________, 저기로 갈까요?

4. A: 버스 타고 갈까요?

   B: ______________________, 지하철을 타는 게 좋겠어요.

5. A: 저녁 먹으러 갈래요? 제가 살게요.

   B: ______________________, 이번에는 제가 살게요.

useful expressions

(무슨 옷을 입)을지 모르다
not to know
(what clothes I will wear)

Complete each dialogue, using ~(으)니까, as in the first example.

1. A: 오늘 날씨가 어떨 것 같아요?

   B: 일기 예보를 보니까, 오후에 눈이 온대요.
   (to watch weather forecast)

2. A: 한국 여행 어땠어요?

   B: ________________________, 구경할 데가 정말 많더라구요.
   (to visit Jeju Island)

3. A: 스티브가 오늘 수업에 안 왔어요.?

   B: ________________________, 감기에 걸렸대요.
   (to call)

4. A: ________________________, 한국 역사가 재미있더라구요.
   (to take Korean history class)

   B: 한국 역사 수업은 언제 들었어요?

5. A: 떡볶이 좋아하세요?

   B: 음··· ________________, 저는 너무 맵던데요.
   (to eat)

Choose the appropriate form from the options presented in the brackets.

1. A: 10분만 있다가 출발하면 안 될까요?

   B: 지금 벌써 늦었어요. 시간이 [없으니까, 없어서] 빨리 준비하세요.

2. A: 집에 가야 하는데 버스 정류장이 어디에 있어요?

   B: 버스는 너무 [복잡하니까, 복잡해서] 택시를 타고 가는게 어때요?

3. A: 어제 파티에 못 [가서, 갔으니까] 정말 미안해.

   B: 할 수 없지 뭐. 다음에는 꼭 와.

4. A: 그동안 너무 바빠서 잠을 잘 못 잤어요.

   B: 수고 많으셨어요. 내일은 [일요일이니까, 일요일이라서] 집에서 푹 쉬세요.

5. A: 여러 가지로 [도와주셨으니까, 도와주셔서] 정말 감사합니다.

B: 아니에요. 제가 감사하지요.

6. A: 샌디가 일하는 커피숍에 가 [보니까, 봤으니까] 샌디가 없던데?

B: 걔 지난 주에 아르바이트 그만뒀어. *그만두다 to quit (a job)

Exercise 12

Listen to the conversation between two friends and mark each statement T(rue) or F(alse). 38

1. ______ The woman saw 민기 yesterday.

2. ______ The woman thinks that 민기 is tired.

Exercise 13

Listen to the conversation between 현수 and 민지 and answer the questions <u>in Korean</u>.

1. What is 민지 thinking of doing over the winter vacation?

____.

2. What does 현수 suggest for 민지 to do?

a. 현수는 민지한테 ______________________________.

b. 현수는 민지한테 ______________________________.

3. Why does민지 not like 현수's first suggestion?

____.

4. ~을/~ㄹ 줄 알다 "to know how to ~"
~을/~ㄹ 줄 모르다 "to not know how to ~"

Use the present tense form of~을/~ㄹ 줄 알다/모르다 to say one has the ability/inability to do something. Only the present tense form of the expression (e.g., ~을/~ㄹ 줄 알아요/몰라요) can mean "ability / inablilty."

- ▶ Verb base (ending in a consnant) + 을 줄 알다/모르다 : 읽을 줄 알다 / 모르다
- ▶ Verb base (ending in a vowel) + ㄹ 줄 알다/모르다 : 할 줄 알다 / 모르다
- *Verb base (ending in ㄹ) + 줄 알다/모르다 : 만들 줄 알다 / 모르다

Note 1

* ㄷ in the verb base changes to ㄹ when followed by a vowel: 걷 + 을 줄 알다 → 걸을 줄 알다.

(For irregular verbs and adjectives, see Appendix V.)

Look at the following examples.

- A: 미영 씨 남자 친구는 매운 음식을 먹을 줄 알아요?
  B: 네, 아주 잘 먹어요.

- A: 피아노 칠 줄 알아요?
  B: 어렸을 때 배워서 칠 줄은 아는데 잘 못 쳐요.

- A: 우리 바닷가에 가서 수영해요.
  B: 미안해요. 제가 수영을 할 줄 몰라요.

- A: 찬영이는 걸을 줄 알지?
  B: 아니, 걸을 줄 몰라. 아직 한 살이잖아.

Note 2

"Noun-modifying form + 줄 알아요/몰라요 (present tense)" has a different meaning from "Noun-modifying form + 줄 알았어요/몰랐어요 (past tense)." The former means "One knows how to do ~/ One does not know how to do~)." The latter means "I mistakenly thought that ~/ I did not know that ~."

- 저는 스키 탈 줄 몰라요.

  I don't know how to ski.

- 오늘 비가 올 줄 몰랐어요.

  I didn't know it would rain today.

Note 3

While ~을/~ㄹ 수 있다 and ~을/~ㄹ 수 없다 can be used to talk about both the possibility of doing something and the ability to do something, ~을/~ㄹ 줄 알다/모르다 is used to talk about ability only.

- A: 운전할 줄 아세요? (ability)

  B: 네. 하지만 지금은 술을 마셔서 운전할 수 없어요. (possibility)

  A: Do you know how to drive?

  B: Yes, I do, but I cannot now because I drank alcohol.

Note 4

~을/~ㄹ 줄 알다 does not imply that someone is good at doing something, only that they have the ability. It is unnatural to say ~을/~ㄹ 잘 할 줄 알다. Instead, to say someone is good at doing something, simply add 잘 before the verb.

마크는 한국어를 잘 할 줄 알아요. (unnatural)

마크는 한국어를 잘 해요. (natural)

Exercise 14

Complete the following dialogues. Use ~을/~ㄹ 줄 알다 or ~을/~ㄹ 줄 모르다 in your answers.

1. A: 어떤 외국어를 할 줄 아세요? *외국어 foreign language

   B: ______________________________.

2. A: 스키 탈 줄 아세요? *스키(를) 타다 to ski

   B: ______________________________.

3. A: 기타 칠 줄 아세요? 어떤 악기(instrument)를 할 줄 아세요? *기타(를) 치다 to play guitar

   B: ______________________________.

4. A: 한국 음식 만들 줄 아세요?

   B: ______________________________.

5. A: 포토샵 할 줄 아세요?

   B: ______________________________.

Exercise 15

Write 5 sentences describing your ability to do something, using ~을/~ㄹ 줄 알다.

1. ______________________________.
2. ______________________________.
3. ______________________________.
4. ______________________________.
5. ______________________________.

Write 5 sentences describing your inability to do something that you wish you could do, using ~을/~ㄹ 줄 모르다.

1. ______________________________.
2. ______________________________.
3. ______________________________.
4. ______________________________.
5. ______________________________.

Listen to the conversation between 남자 and 여자 and mark each statement T(rue) or F(alse). 40

1. ______ 여자는 독일어를 할 줄 몰라요.
2. ______ 남자는 외국어를 공부하고 있어요.

Listen to the conversation between 남자 and 여자 and mark each statement T(rue) or F(alse). 41

1. ______ 민지 남자 친구는 한국말을 할 줄 알아요.
2. ______ 민지 남자 친구는 송편을 만들 수 있어요.

Patterns, Expressions & Practice

III. Culture

1. 기차와 고속버스 (Trains and express buses)

It is convenient to travel by 기차 in Korea. Korean 기차 can be classified based on speed and amenities. Among the different types of 기차, KTX (Korea Train Express) trains are the fastest, designed to run at 330 km/h with the top operational speed being 305 km/hr., but they only stop at major cities, such as 서울, 대구, 부산, 광주.

ITX (Intercity Train eXpress)-새마을 trains are the next class of trains, which also stop at major cities. 무궁화 trains and their planned successor 누리로 are regional train services. 무궁화 trains are slower than KTX or ITX-새마을, but they stop at more cities and have cafe cars where you can get snacks, coffee, and even beer during your trip. There are also cinema-trains where you can watch movies while traveling.

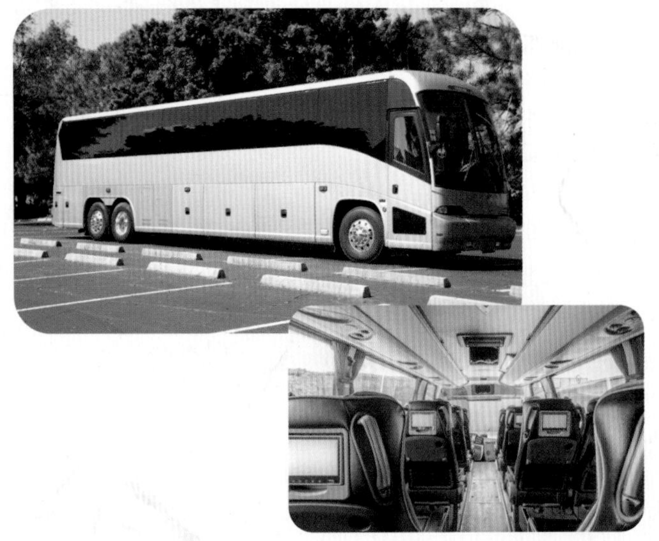

고속버스 is another popular option for traveling from region to region. 고속버스터미널 (express bus terminals) are located at the center of most cities in Korea. 고속버스 run on 고속도로 (expressways), and can be classified into 일반(regular), 우등(luxury) and 프리미엄 (premium) buses. 우등 버스 offer additional comfort with wider seats and 프리미엄 offers even better amenities. 고속버스 generally make a stop at a 휴게소 (rest area) where you can taste local specialty dishes. 고속버스 are slower but more affordable than 기차. If you are not in a hurry and want to enjoy your travels, 고속버스 is a good option.

2. 고속도로 휴게소 (Rest areas on expressways)

휴게소 is a place on the **고속도로** where you can use the **화장실** or **주유소** (gas station), and have some **간식** (snacks). In Korea, many **휴게소** offer more services than necessary and become tourist attractions in their own right. While driving, you can visit a **휴게소** to take a quick rest, enjoy local foods, buy local specialties, or even enjoy leisure activities. Some **휴게소** are situated in places that command a fine view.

금산인삼랜드 휴게소 is famous for its **인삼 갈비탕** (ginseng beef-rib soup), because they use **금산**'s high-quality **인삼** (ginseng).

여주 휴게소 is located along **영동고속도로**. It has a ceramic museum and offers a cultural program for making ceramics.

금강 휴게소 is famous for its beautiful view of **금강**(Geum river).

마장 프리미엄 휴게소 is the biggest rest area in Korea. You can have **간식** (snacks), **식사** (meals), and **디저트**(desserts). Also, there are **편의점** (convenient stores), **도넛 가게**, **커피숍** and outlet stores.

Culture

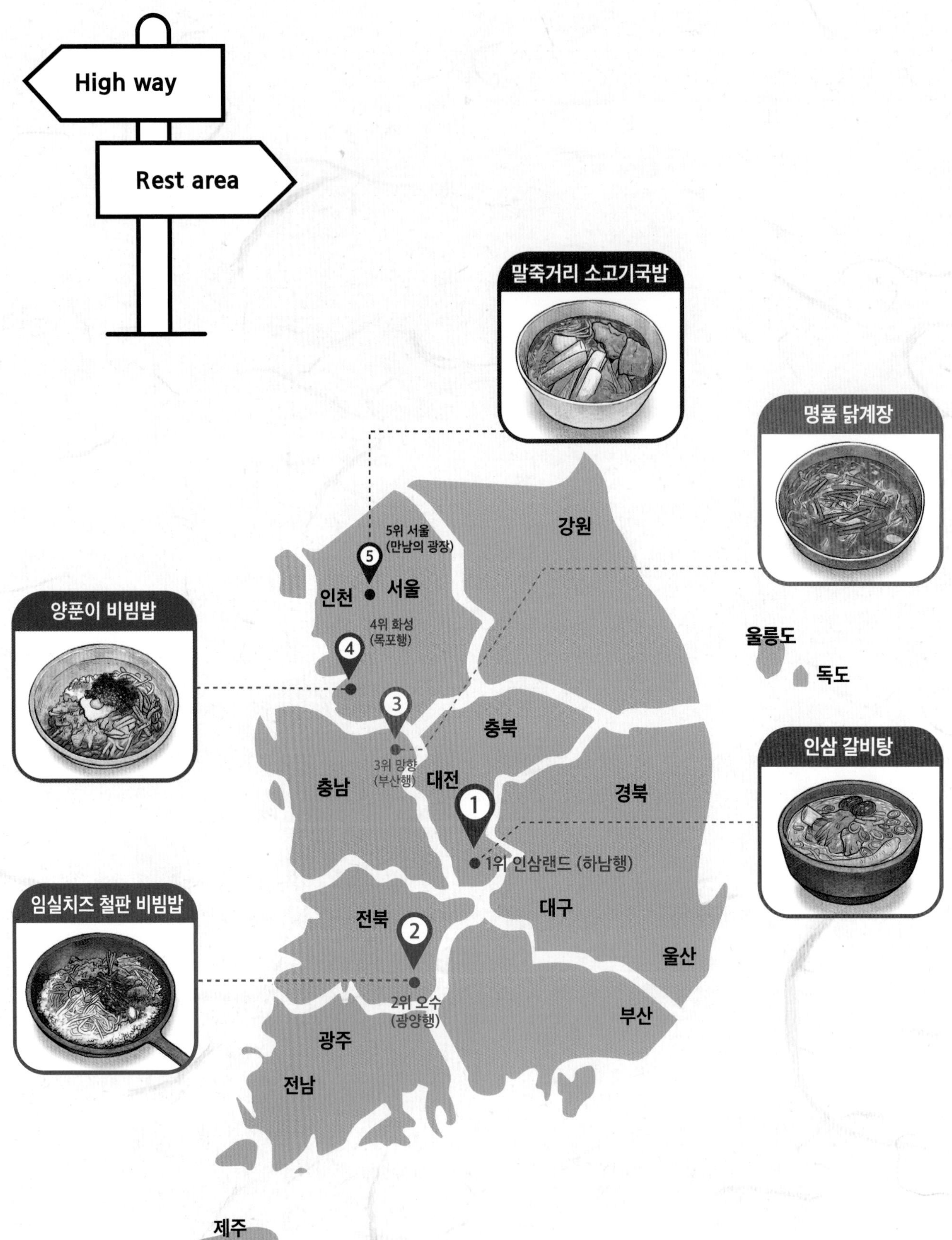

High way
Rest area
말죽거리 소고기국밥
명품 닭계장
양푼이 비빔밥
인삼 갈비탕
임실치즈 철판 비빔밥
강원
5위 서울
(만남의 광장)
인천
서울
4위 화성
(목포행)
울릉도
독도
충북
3위 망향
(부산행)
충남
대전
경북
1위 인삼랜드 (하남행)
대구
전북
울산
2위 오수
(광양행)
부산
광주
전남
제주

IV. Listen & Discuss

An American business man (테드) visits Korea to attend two international conferences. After finishing the first, he is talking with his colleague (미영) who works at a branch of his company in Seoul.

First, listen to the conversation. With your classmates, discuss the answers to the questions that follow. Finally, write each answer in a full Korean sentence in the space provided.

1. 미영은 KTX에 대해서 어떻게 말했습니까?

2. 고속버스는 오래 걸리지만 무엇이 좋다고 했습니까?

3. 테드는 부산에서 제주도까지 어떻게 가려고 합니까?

4. 미영은 제주도에서 택시를 타면 무엇이 좋다고 합니까?

Script

An American businessman (테드) visits Korea to attend two international conferences. After finishing the first conference in Seoul, he is talking with his colleague (미영) who works at the Seoul branch of his company.

01 미영: 테드 씨, 다음 일정은 어떻게 되세요?

02 테드: 제주도 컨퍼런스 전에 부산에 한번 가 볼까 하는데,[II.1] 교통편은 뭐가 좋을까요?

03 미영: KTX를 타면 편하고 빠르지만, 고속버스 타는 걸[II.2] 추천해요.

04 테드: 고속버스는 오래 걸리지 않나요?

05 미영: 그렇긴 하지만, 휴게소에서 그 지역의 유명한 음식들도 먹어 볼 수 있거든요.

06 테드: 다양한 음식을 먹어 보고 싶었는데, 그럼 고속버스를 타야겠네요.

07 미영: 부산에서 제주도는 어떻게 가실 거예요?

08 테드: 비행기를 탈까 해요.

09 미영: 아~ 네. 그럼 제주도에 가서는 어떻게 다니실 거예요? 차를 렌트하실 거예요?

10 테드: 제가 운전할 줄 몰라서[II.4] 택시를 타고 다니려구요.

11 미영: 그것도 괜찮아요. 택시 기사님들이 관광 안내도 잘 해 주시니까요.[II.3]

12 그럼 즐겁게 여행하세요!

01 미영: 테드, May I ask what's next on your schedule?

02 테드: I'm thinking of visiting Busan before the Jeju conference. What would be the best means of transportation?

03 미영: The KTX is the fastest and most convenient, but I recommend you to take an express bus.

04 테드: Wouldn't it take long to take an express bus?

05 미영: Yes, but you can eat famous local foods at rest areas.

06 테드: I wanted to eat various foods (during my stay in Korea). Then, I would have to take an express bus.

07 미영: How will you get from Busan to Jeju-do?

08 테드: I am thinking of taking an airplane.

09 미영: Oh~ I see. Then when you arrive in Jeju-do, how will you get around? Will you rent a car?

10 테드: I don't know how to drive, so I plan to take a taxi to get around.

11 미영: That's also good. Taxi drivers will give you good sightseeing tips/information on the area.

12 Have a great trip!

V. Guided Conversation

Keeping in mind the organization of the model conversation in Listen & Discuss (Script), practice the modified conversation below with your partner.

Two students at a college in Seoul are talking about their weekend trip.

Practice the following conversation with your partner, using the prompts in (parenthesis) to fill in the blanks and make the conversation flow naturally.

01 A: ______________ 끝났는데 주말에 무슨 계획 있어요?
(컨퍼런스도; 시험도)

02 B: 이번 주말에 ______________ 에 한 번 가 볼까 하는데,[II.1] 교통편은 뭐가 좋을까요?
(전주; 부산)

Choose option (1) or (2) to continue the conversation.

Option (1): 전주

03 A: KTX를 타면 ______________ 고 ______________ 지만
(빠르다; 조용하다; 운행 시간이 정확하다; 화장실을 언제든지 이용할 수 있다; 무선 인터넷을 무료로 사용할 수 있다; ...)

04 저는 고속버스 타는 걸[II.2] 선호하는 편이에요.

05 B: 고속버스는 오래 걸리지 않나요?

06 A: 그렇긴 하지만 ______________ 거든요.
(요금이 싸다; 휴게소에서 지역의 유명한 음식을 먹어 볼 수 있다; 천천히 바깥 경치를 즐길 수 있다; 좌석 마다 개인 모니터도 있고 뒤로 누울 수 있는 편한 프리미엄 버스도 있다; …)

07 B: 아~ 그럼, ______________ (으)니까[II.3]
(요금이 싸다; 휴게소에서 그 지역의 유명한 음식을 먹어 볼 수 있다; 천천히 바깥 경치를 즐길 수 있다; 누워서 편안하게 여행할 수 있다; …)

고속버스를 타야겠네요.

Option (2): 부산

03 A: 고속버스를 타면 ______ 고 ______ 지만
(요금이 싸다; 휴게소에서 그 지역의 유명한 음식을 먹어 볼 수 있다; 천천히 바깥 경치를 즐길 수 있다; …)

04 저는 KTX 타는 걸[II.2] 선호하는 편이에요.

05 B: KTX는 비싸지 않나요?

06 A: 그렇긴 하지만 ______ 거든요.
(빨라서 서울에서 부산까지 2시간 30분이면 가다; KTX안에서도 음식을 사 먹을 수 있다; 운행 시간이 정확하다; 조용하다; 화장실을 언제든지)

07 B: 아~ 그럼, ______ (으)니까[II.3]
(빠르다; 여행 중에 음식을 먹을 수 있다; 운행시간이 정확하다; 조용하다; 화장실을 언제든지 이용할 수 있다; 무선 인터넷을 무료로 사용할 수 있다; …)

KTX를 타야겠네요.

08 B: ______ 씨는 계획 없어요?

09 A: 저는 친구들하고 ______ 에 가 볼까 해요.
(DMZ, 춘천; 광주; 대구; …)

10 B: ______ 까지 어떻게 갈 거예요?
(DMZ, 춘천; 광주; 대구; …)

11 A: 제가 운전할 줄 아니까[II.3,4] 차를 렌트해서 가려고요.

(Switch roles and continue to practice.)

useful expressions

L03 운행 시간이 정확하다 operation schedule/hour is accurate;
무선 인터넷 wireless internet
L04 선호하다 to prefer
L06 그렇긴 하지만 it is so but … 바깥 경치 scenery outside;
좌석마다 per seat 개인 모니터 individual monitor;
뒤로 눕다 to lie back

Present the conversation above in front of the class. Try not to look at your paper!

VI. Spontaneous Conversation

This is your chance to have a realistic interaction with your classmates in Korean. You can practice writing, speaking with your classmates, and presenting in front of the class!

You and your classmate are planning to travel together to a city in Korea or in the US. Decide where to go and how to get there. Include the information (in the table below) in your conversation. Create a meaningful conversation with your partner similar to the one that you practiced in the Guided Conversation!

- Place or city to travel (For a place in Korea, you may choose one from Section III. in Lesson 2.)
- Transportation to get there (For a transportation option in Korea, refer to Section III. Culture)
- Reasons why you choose that transportation option

Write down the conversation you had with your partner in Step 1.

Step 3

A friend of yours is coming to Korea from the US and wants to visit some cities in Korea. Your friend asked you about available public transportation. Write a letter to your friend, introducing Korean transportation options for the trip and make a recommendation with your reasons. Use the ~아 speech style or the ~는다 speech style.

Present what you wrote in Step 3 in front of the class. Try not to look at your paper!

VII. Listening

Listen to the conversation between two friends and mark each statement T(rue) or F(alse). 43

1. ______ The man did not sign up for the event because he couldn't go.
2. ______ It was hard to make pottery.
3. ______ The woman bought a cup for the man as a gift.
4. ______ The woman has never studied about Korean pottery before.
5. ______ There is no bus going directly to 이천 from their school.

Listen to the following announcement by a group leader of a school field trip and mark each statement T(rue) or F(alse). 44

6. ______ This bus is arriving at the destination soon.
7. ______ They should use the restroom quickly because the bus will depart soon.
8. ______ They can eat various snacks here, but cannot have a meal.
9. ______ There is a museum at this rest area.
10. ______ They should return to the bus after spending some time at this rest area.

Words & Expressions

01-05 도자기 porcelain; ceramic

06-10 간식 light snacks 확인하다 to confirm

VIII. Reading

이천도자기축제 (Icheon Ceramics Festival)

New Message

To: all students

Subject:

학생 여러분,

공부하느라 바쁘시지요?

다음 주 토요일에 있을 도자기 체험 행사에 대해 알려 드리겠습니다.

이 행사는 도자기로 유명한 이천에서 한국의 도자기에 대해서 배우고 직접 도자기도 만들어 볼 수 있는 행사입니다. 다음 주 토요일 아침 9시에 학교 앞에서 버스로 출발해서 오후 5시에 돌아올 예정입니다. 참가비는 3만 원이고 이번 주까지 신청하면 됩니다.

많이 참가해 주시기 바랍니다.

한국 대학교 한국어 교육원

1. 왜 이 글을 썼는지 맞는 것을 고르십시오.
   ① 도자기 체험 행사에 참가하려고.
   ② 도자기 체험 행사 소식을 알리려고.
   ③ 도자기 체험 행사에 필요한 돈을 받으려고.
   ④ 도자기 체험 행사를 도와줄 사람을 찾으려고.

2. 위의 글의 내용과 같은 것을 고르십시오.
   ① 한국어 교실에서 도자기를 만들 것이다.
   ② 이천은 도자기로 유명하다.
   ③ 학생들은 도자기에 대해서 배웠다 .
   ④ 학교는 이천에 있다.

Words & Expressions

01-02 도자기 porcelain 이천 (City of) Icheon 예정 schedule 신청하다 to apply, register

천안 호두과자 (Cheonan Walnut Cookies)

고속도로 휴게소나 기차역에서 인기 있는 간식 중 하나가 호두과자이다. 호두과자는 호두 모양으로 생긴 일종의 작은 케이크인데 안에는 팥과 호두가 들어있다. 호두과자는 여행할 때 간식이나 선물용으로도 인기가 많다. 호두과자는 충청남도 천안에서 처음 만들어지기 시작했기 때문에 천안 호두과자가 제일 유명하다. 예전부터 천안에는 호두 나무가 많았는데 한 제과점에서 만들어진 호두과자가 천안역에서 팔리면서 전국으로 퍼져 나갔다고 한다. 천안역은 옛날부터 교통의 중심지였기 때문에 많은 사람들이 천안역을 지나가다가 호두과자를 사 먹게 되었고 ____㉠____ 천안을 대표하는 명물이 되었다.

3. ㉠에 들어갈 알맞은 말을 고르십시오.
   ① 전국적으로 유명해진 호두과자는
   ② 천안의 맛있는 호두는
   ③ 호두과자를 만든 제과점은
   ④ 교통의 중심지인 천안역은

4. 위의 글의 내용과 다른 것을 고르십시오.
   ① 호두과자는 천안에서만 살 수 있다.
   ② 고속도로 휴게소에서 호두과자를 살 수 있다.
   ③ 호두과자는 호두처럼 생겼다.
   ④ 호두과자는 천안에서 처음 만들었다.

03-04 호두 walnut 호두 모양으로 생기다 to resemble the shape of a walnut 일종의 a kind of 팥 red bean 선물용 as a gift 팔리다 to be sold 전국으로 around the country 퍼져 나가다 to spread out 명물 specialty 교통의 중심지 hub of transportation 대표하다 to represent

5 한국시리즈 경기 봤어?

Did you watch the Korean series game?

- Talking about popular sports in Korea
- Reporting the questions and suggestions of others

01 너, 어제 한국 시리즈 경기 봤어?
02 보고 싶었는데 일이 있어서 못 봤어요. 누가 이겼어요?

03 삼성이 이겼어. 끝까지 마음 졸이면서 봤어.
04 왜요? 어땠는데요?

05 9회까지 두산이 3대 0으로 이기고 있었거든.
06 그런데 삼성이 마지막에 만루 홈런을 쳐서 역전을 했어

07 아! 이번에는 두산이 이길 줄 알았는데… 정말 안타깝네요.
08 넌 두산 팬이니?

09 네. 형은 삼성 팬이죠?
10 당연하지! 내 고향이 대구잖아.

11 우리 이번 주 토요일 결승전 경기는 같이 볼까요?
12 그래! 우리 집에 와. 안 그래도 내가 민지한테 같이 보자고 했거든.

13 그럼 제니한테도 올 수 있냐고 물어볼까요?
14 좋지!

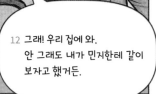

Preparation & Practice	I. New Words & Expressions II. Patterns, Expressions & Practice 1. ~거든 Indicating that you plan to continue talking 2. Reported question: ~냐고 하다 3. Reported proposal: ~자고 하다

	III. Culture 1. Baseball in Korea 2. Soccer in Korea
Conversation Activities	IV. Listen & Discuss V. Guided Conversation VI. Spontaneous Conversation
TOPIK Preparation	VII. Listening • Conversation • Interview
	VIII. Reading • Traffic announcement during the Korean Series final match • Popular sports in Korea

I. New Words & Expressions

 **Study the words and expressions along with the audio.** 

NOUN

9회	the 9th inning
결승전	final match
경기	game; match
대구	Daegu (the name of a city)
두산	Dusan (the name of a baseball team)
마지막	the last; end
만루 홈런	grand slam
삼성	Samsung (the name of a baseball team)
역전	turn around
팬	fan
한국시리즈	Korean Series (baseball league championship)

VERB

역전(을) 하다	to turn something around
이기다	to win (a person/team) *(a person; team) 을/를 이기다

ADJECTIVE

안타깝다	to be sad, regrettable, pitiful or pathetic

EXPRESSION

·(마음을 졸이)면서	while (I) am being anxious	* ~(으)면서 while ~ ing
·끝까지	to the very end	
·당연하지!	Of course.	
·안 그래도	actually; as a matter of fact	

Listen to the audio and fill in the blanks. 

1. A: 너 어제 ______________ 봤니?

   B: 보고 싶었는데, 다른 일이 있어서 못 봤어. 근데 어느 팀이 이겼어?

2. A: 삼성이 이겼는데, ______________ 마음 졸이면서 봤어.

   B: 그렇게 재미있었어? 누가 이겼는데?

3. A: 삼성이 마지막에 만루 홈런을 쳐서 ______________을 했어!

   B: 너 끝까지 마음 졸이면서 봤겠다.

4. A: 아! 이번에는 진짜 두산이 이길 줄 알았는데.

   B: 넌 두산 팬이지? 어제 경기는 정말 ________________.

5. A: 바빠서 어제 경기를 못 봤는데, 누가 ____________?

   B: 삼성이 ____________. 근데 끝까지 마음 졸이면서 봤어.

Exercise 2

Choose the best word to complete the sentences.

1. 9회말에 삼성이 __________을/를 치면서 역전을 했다.

   ① 결승전 ② 경기 ③ 만루 홈런 ④ 마지막

2. __________이/가 이번 주 토요일인데 우리 집에 와서 같이 보자.

   ① 9회 ② 역전 ③ 팬 ④ 결승전

3. 이번 __________은/는 정말 끝까지 마음 졸이면서 봤는데, 결국 삼성이 이겼다.

   ① 지역 ② 경기 ③ 관광 안내 ④ 교통편

4. 9회 초까지는 두산이 3대 0으로 이기고 있었는데, 9회말에 삼성이 만루 홈런을 치면서 ______________.

   ① 운전했다 ② 추천했다 ③ 이겼다 ④ 역전을 했다

5. 어제 한국시리즈 __________경기가 있어서 친구들하고 같이 경기장(stadium)에 가서 봤다.

   ① 역전 ② 일정 ③ 만루 홈런 ④ 마지막

II. Patterns, Expressions & Practice

1. ~거든 Indicating that you plan to continue talking

Usage

Use ~거든 when you begin telling a story and indicate that the story will continue. By raising the intonation of ~거든 slightly up, you can signal that you aren't finished speaking yet, and a new piece of information will follow. The new information indicated by this pattern is often unexpected or surprising. Thus, using ~거든, you can draw the listener's attention.

Form

Dictionary form (Word base + 다)	Present tense (word base + 았/었 + 거든)	Present tense (word base + 거든)	Future tense (word base+ 을/ㄹ 거 + 거든)
Verb/Adjective (가다/좋다)	갔거든/좋았거든	가거든/좋거든	갈 거거든/ 좋을 거거든
NOUN이다 • NOUN (ending in a consonant) 이다 • NOUN (ending in a vowel)다	대학생이었거든 친구였거든	대학생이거든 친구거든	대학생일거거든 친구일 거거든

Look at the following examples.

- 9회까지 두산이 이기고 있었거든. 근데 삼성이 역전을 한 거야!

  두산 was winning the game until the 9th inning but (surprisingly) 삼성 turned the game around!

- 저번에 부산 갈 때 KTX를 탔거든요. 그런데, 기차 안에 자판기가 있더라고요.

  I took the KTX last time when I went to 부산 and (I noticed) there were vending machines in the train.

- 우리 동네에 한국 식당이 하나도 없었거든요. 근데 작년에 2개나 생겼어요.

  There wasn't even a single Korean restaurant in my town but (surprisingly) two restaurants were opened last year.

- 내가 분명히 가방 안에 핸드폰을 넣었거든. 근데 아무리 찾아도 없는 거야.

  I'm sure I put my cell phone in the bag but (surprisingly) despite how hard I tried to find it, I couldn't.

useful expressions

(2개)나 about (two)

*NOUN(이)나 as many/much/long as NOUN, about NOUN, no less than NOUN

You can also use ~거든 when you provide a reason, justification, or clarification for what has already been said or what follows. (Refer to Beginning 2: Lesson 18, II.6.)

- A: LA Dodgers 팬이세요?
  B: 네. L.A.가 제 고향이**거든요**.
  Yes. Because L.A. is my hometown.

- A: 한국에서 여행할 때 어떤 교통편이 좋을까?
  B: 나는 버스보다 기차 타는 걸 더 좋아해. 훨씬 빠르**거든**.
  I prefer riding a train to a bus when traveling. It's much faster.

- A: 다음 학기에 들을 수업 정했어?
  B: 내가 역사에 관심이 많**거든**. 그래서 다음 학기에 한국 역사 수업을 들을까 해.
  I'm very interested in history, so I'm thinking of taking a Korean history class.

Your friend is making a suggestion or asking you a favor. Turn down the suggestion or request with a reason, using ~거든.

1. A: 내일 우리 집에 점심 먹으러 올래?
   B: 미안해, 못 갈 거 같아.
   ______________________________.
   (to visit grandparents; to have other plans; ...)

2. A: 이번 주말에 이사하는데, 좀 도와줄 수 있어?
   B: 어떡하지? 주말에는 시간이 없는데.
   ______________________________.
   (to visit grandparents; to have other plans; ...)

3. A: 한국 시리즈 시합이 있는데, 같이 야구 보러 갈래?
   B: 글쎄... ______________________________.
   (to not know about baseball; to not like baseball; to be a fan of soccer; ...)

4. A: 내일 민수 생일 파티가 있다던데, 같이 안 갈래?
   B: 글쎄... ______________________________.
   (to need to write a paper; to be not close with 민수; to not know him well; to have lots of things to do; ...)

5. A: 백화점 세일 한다던데, 같이 쇼핑 갈까?
   B: 미안해. 다른 친구한테 물어봐.

   나는 ____.

   (to not like crowded places; to usually do shopping online; to have spent all the money already; ...)

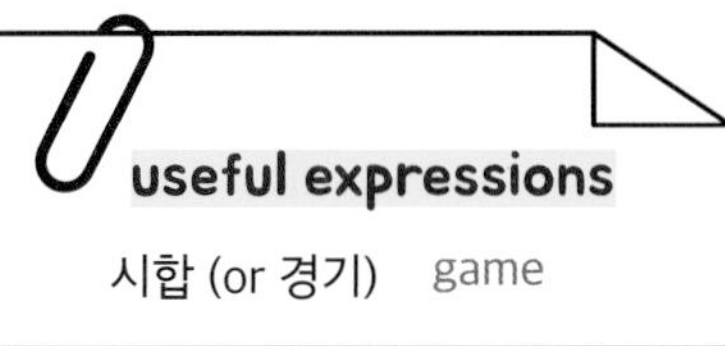

Complete each dialogue, using ~거든(요) to provide a reason.

1. A: 집에서 고양이를 키우기로 했어요. ______________________.
   B: 고양이를 좋아하는 줄 몰랐어요.

2. A: 저는 커피를 못 마셔요. 커피를 마시면 ______________________.
   B: 카페인 없는 커피를 마시면 괜찮을 거예요.

3. A: 내 룸메이트가 정말 청소하는 걸 싫어하거든. 그래서 ______________________.
   B: 너 혼자 하지 말고 룸메이트한테 같이 하자고 얘기해 봐.

4. A: 졸업하고 나서 한국에서 일하고 싶거든요. 그래서 ______________________.
   B: 그래요? 제 친구도 졸업하고 한국에서 일하려고 한국어 수업 듣고 있어요.

5. A: 이번 방학에 한국에 가요. ______________________.
   B: 잘 됐네요. 축하해요.

6. A: 지금 기숙사에 사는데, 내년에는 아파트로 이사할까 해요.

   ____.

   B: 맞아요. 혼자 사는 게 편하지요.

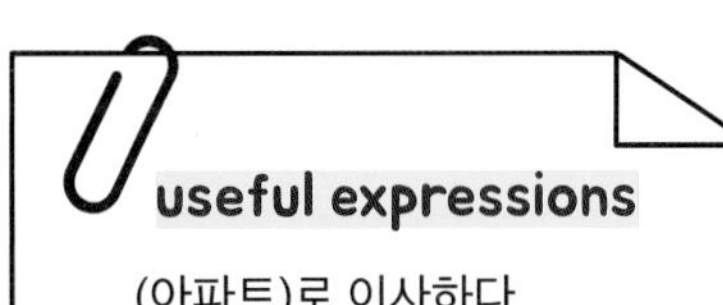

useful expressions
(아파트)로 이사하다
to move (to an apartment)

You're telling your friend what happened to you. Make your story interesting or surprising by providing information you recently discovered.

1. A: 제가 어제 학교에 가려고 버스를 탔거든요.

   ____.

   B: 아~, 박 선생님도 그 버스를 타시는군요.

2. A: 친구 생일이라서 저녁 먹으러 같이 중국 식당에 갔거든요.

   ____.

   B: 어머, 그럼 어디서 저녁 먹었어요?

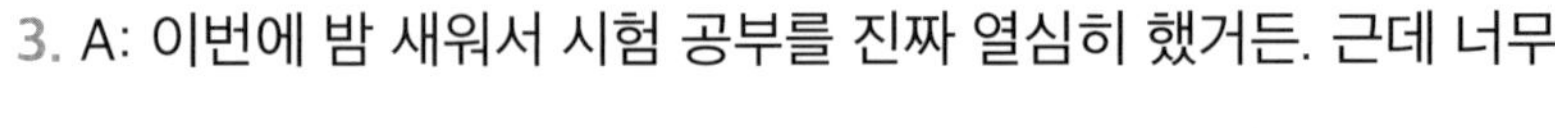

3. A: 이번에 밤 새워서 시험 공부를 진짜 열심히 했거든. 근데 너무

   졸려서 ____.

   B: 시험 보기 전에는 푹 자는게 더 도움이 돼.

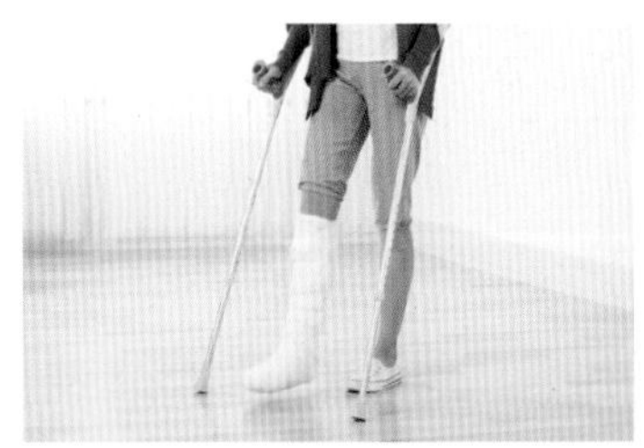

4. A: 어제 오랜만에 등산을 했거든요.

   ____.

   B: 저런! 병원은 갔다 왔어요?

5. A: 내가 부산에 가다가 화장실에 가려고 휴게소에 들렀거든. 근데,

   ____.

   B: 맞아. 고속도로 휴게소에는 맛있는 음식이 아주 많지.

useful expressions

밤새우다	to stay up all night; keep awake all night
푹 자다	to have a sound sleep; sleep well
병원	hospital

Listen to the dialogue and answer the questions. 

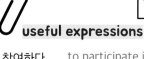

1. Why is the man not going to participate in the basketball game?

____.

2. What is the woman going to do and why?

____.

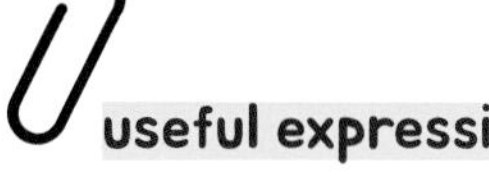

useful expressions

참여하다	to participate in
응원을 하다	to root for
다치다	to get injured

Listen to the dialogue and answer the question. 48

Why is the man so busy?

____.

useful expressions

심리학 시험 psychology exam

2. Reported question: ~냐고 하다

Usage Use **~냐고 하다** when you report a person's question (e.g., what was asked in the past).

You (Reporter): Person-이/가 (WHO (subject)) [what was asked ~냐]고 (WHAT (object)) 하다. (SAY (verb))

"A person asks/asked if/whether/who ~."

*The expression in [ ] is called "reported question." Let's use [ ] to mark the boundary of reported statement.

Form Use the ~냐 form of the verb/adjective in the reported question, as shown below.

<Present tense>

▶ [··· Verb/Adjective base + 냐]고 하다: 가냐고 하다/ 예쁘냐고 하다

▶ [··· Noun (이)냐]고 하다 : 학생이냐고 하다. 가수냐고 하다

<Past tense>

▶ [… Verb/Adjective base + 았냐/었냐]고 하다: 갔냐고 하다/ 예뻤냐고 하다

▶ [… Noun 이었냐/였냐]고 하다 : 학생이었냐고 하다, 가수였냐고 하다

Dictionary form	Present/ Past	Reported statement	
		Full form	Reduced form
Verb (가다)	가다 갔다	가냐고 해요 갔냐고 해요	가냬요 갔냬요
Adjective (예쁘다)	예쁘다 예뻤다	예쁘냐고 해요 예뻤냐고 해요	예쁘냬요 예뻤냬요
Consonant-ending Noun (학생이다)	학생이다 학생이었다	학생이냐고 해요 학생이었냐고 해요	학생이냬요 학생이었냬요
Vowel-ending Noun (가수다)	가수다 가수였다	가수냐고 해요 가수였냐고 해요	가수냬요 가수였냬요

Look at the following examples.

- 제임스: 마크가 어제 뭐라고 했어?
  스티브: [금요일 모임에 가냐]고 했어. or 금요일 모임에 가냬.
  (Mark) asked (me) if I would go to Friday's meeting.

- (민지 and 제니 are looking at a photo.)
  민지: 피터가 뭐라고 했어?
  제니: [여기가 전주한옥마을이냐]고 했어요. or 여기가 전주한옥마을이냬.
  (Peter) asked (me) if it is called 전주한옥마을.

- A: 레베카가 나한테 [이 선물을 어디에서 샀냐]고 했어.
  or 레베카가 나한테 이 선물을 어디에서 샀냬.
  B: 그래? 그래서, 뭐라고 했니?
  Rebecca asked (me) where I bought this gift.

Note

In reported questions, 하다 in ~다고 하다 means "to say" and can be replaced with such verbs as 묻다/물어보다 (to inquire/ask), 질문하다 (to ask a question).

A: 마크가 나한테 [금요일 모임에 가냐]고 물어봤어.
B: 근데, 마크는 간대? 안 간대?
Mark asked me if I would go to Friday's meeting.

Tell your classmate what someone else said to you. The icon in each question indicates what you were told in the past.

1. 브라이언: 요즘 바쁘세요?
Classmate: 브라이언이 뭐라고 했어요?
You: ______________________________.

2. 현수: 마크는 어느 대학교 학생입니까?
Classmate: 현수가 뭐라고 했어요?
You: ______________________________.

3. 민서: 저 사람은 누구니?
Classmate: 민서가 뭐라고 했어요?
You: ______________________________.

4. 샤오밍: 너 지난 번 소개팅 때 바람 맞았지?
Classmate: 샤오밍이 뭐라고 했어요?
You: ______________________________.

5. 에이미: 스티브 생일 파티에 갈 거야?
Classmate: 에이미가 뭐라고 했어요?
You: ______________________________.

Listen to the conversation and answer the questions in Korean, using a reported question.

1. What does the woman say to the man?

   여자는 남자에게 ______________________________.

2. What does the man say to the woman?

   남자는 제시카에게 ______________________________.

3. What does the woman say to the man?

   ______________________________.

4. What does the man ask the woman?

   ______________________________.

5. What does the man ask the woman?

   ______________________________.

Exercise 8

Listen to the conversation between two friends (윌, 민지) and mark each statement T(rue) or F(alse). 50

1. ______ Alex, Minji, Will, and Nick will go to Busan Film Festival together.
2. ______ Alex told Minji that they can go to Busan Film Festival together.
3. ______ Minji asked Nick to go to the Busan Film Festival together.
4. ______ Will's major is Film Studies.

useful expressions

급한 일	urgent matter
(-이/-가) 생기다	(for something) to come up

3. Reported proposal: ~자고 하다

Usage

Use **~자고 하다** when you report a person's proposal (e.g., what a person proposed in the past).

You (Reporter): Person-이/가 [what was proposed ~자]고 하다.
WHO (subject) WHAT (object) SAY (verb)

"A person **proposes/proposed** ~ing."
"A person **suggests/suggested** ~ing."

*The expression in [ ] is called "reported proposal." Let's use [ ] to mark the boundary of reported proposal.

Form

Use the ~자 form of the verb in the reported proposal, as shown below.

▶ [··· Verb base + **자]고 하다** : **가자고 하다, 먹자고 하다**

* The reduced form of 가자고 해요 is 가재요.

Look at the following examples.

- 테드: 우리 KTX 타고 갈까요?
  미영: 마크 씨는 [고속버스 타자]고 **하던데요**. or 마크 씨는 고속 버스를 타 **재는데요**?
  Ted suggested taking an express bus.

- 아버지: 민지야, 우리 주말에 등산 갈까?
  민지 : 친구가 [같이 영화 보자]고 **했는데** or (친구가 같이 영화 보**잿는데**) 다음 주말에 가면 안 돼요?
  My friend suggested watching a movie. Can't we go next weekend?

- 민수: 마크가 오늘 저녁에 자기 집에서 게임하**재**.
  윤기: 다음 주가 시험이잖아. 정신 좀 차리라고 해! ㅎㅎ
  Mark suggested playing the game at his house tonight.

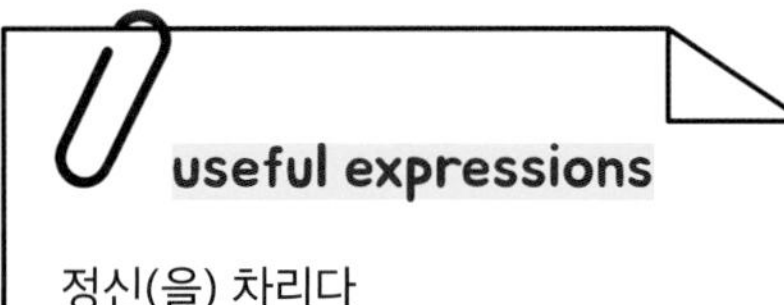
useful expressions

정신(을) 차리다
to come to one's senses; to get one's act together

Patterns, Expressions & Practice

Note 1

As mentioned previously, the literal meaning of the verb "하다" in ~자고 하다 is "to do." In the context of a reported proposal, it carries a general meaning "to propose/suggest doing." Thus, you can use a more specific verb than 하다 to report someone's proposal in a specific way, such as **제안하다** (to propose; suggest).

- A: (마크가) (나한테) [금요일 영화 클럽에 한번 같이 가 보자]고 **제안했어**.
  B: 그래? 나도 같이 가면 안 돼?
  (Mark) suggested (me) going to Friday's movie club meeting.

Note 2

When you report a person's proposal that has a suggestive meaning, such as ~**(으)ㄹ래요**? "Would you like to...?," ~**(으)ㄹ까요**? "Shall we...?," **(같이) ~하는 게 어때요**?, you should also use ~**자고 하다**. In the examples below, the (parenthesis) indicates what was suggested in the past.

- (피터: 같이 도서관에서 공부**할래요**?)
  Ann: 저랑 같이 영화 보러 갈까요?
  You: 미안해요. 피터가 [같이 도서관에서 공부하자]고 **했어요**. 지금 도서관에 가야해요.

- (민수: 오늘 새로 나온 영화 보러 **갈까요**?)
  Ann: 저랑 같이 도서관에 공부하러 갈래요?
  You: 미안해요. 민수가 저한테 [오늘 새로 나온 영화 보러 가자]고 **했어요**.

- (제니: 도서관 대신에 서점에서 만나는 게 어때요?)
  How about meeting at the bookstore instead of the library?
  Ann: 제니가 도서관에서 만나자고 했어요?
  You: 아뇨, [도서관 대신에 서점에서 만나자]고 **했어요**.

The icon in each question indicates what 안젤라 proposed to you in the past, and the classmate wants to know what 안젤라 proposed to you. Complete each conversation with a reported proposal.

1. 안젤라: 이번 금요일에 같이 코리아타운에 가서 저녁 먹을까?

   classmate: 안젤라 씨가 너한테 뭐라고 했어?

   You: ______________________________.

2. 안젤라: 내일이 발렌타인데이니까, 남자 친구한테 줄 초콜렛 사러 같이 가자!

   classmate: 안젤라 씨가 뭐라고 했어?

   You: ______________________________.

3. 안젤라: 여행하면서 휴게소에 들러서 그 지역 유명한 음식도 먹어 보고 싶어요. KTX 대신에 고속버스 타는 게 어때요?

   classmate: 안젤라 씨가 뭐라고 했어?

   You: ______________________________.

4. 안젤라: 이번 추석엔 고향에 내려가지 말고 저하고 같이 여행 가요.

   classmate: 안젤라 씨가 뭐라고 했어?

   You: ______________________________.

5. 안젤라: 우리 같이 나가서 한국 식당에서 점심 먹어요!

   classmate: 안젤라 씨가 뭐라고 했어?

   You: ______________________________.

The following script comes from the conversation that Jenny had with Minsoo at a blind date last weekend.

Minsoo: 대학교 3학년이세요?
Jenny : 아니요, 저 2학년인데요.
Minsoo: 아, 그래요? 저는 3학년인데, 저하고 같은 학년인 줄 알았어요.
저는 사회학을 전공하는데, 제니 씨는 전공이 어떻게 되세요?
Jenny : 동양학을 전공하고 있어요.
Minsoo: 그럼, 한국어 말고 일본어나 중국어도 할 줄 아세요?
Jenny : 일본어는 모르고, 중국어는 조금 해요.
Minsoo: 고향은 어디세요? 저는 시애틀에서 왔어요.
Jenny : 어! 저도 시애틀에서 왔어요.
Minsoo: 그래요? 정말 반가워요. 시간 있을 때는 보통 뭐 하세요?
Jenny : 저는 한국 노래를 좋아해서 K-pop을 자주 듣고, 콘서트에도 가끔 가요.
Minsoo: 다음 주말에 한국 가수 콘서트가 있는데, 시간 되면 같이 갈까요?

Now Sandy, Jenny's roommate, is curious about her blind date. Complete the following conversation between Jenny and Sandy, based on the above script.

01 Sandy: 어제 소개팅 어땠니? 무슨 얘기했어?
02 Jenny: 나한테 ____________________ 고 물어서, 내가 2학년이라고 했어.
03 자기는 3학년인데, 나하고 ____________________고 하더라구.
04 Sandy: 어, 그래? 또 무슨 얘기했어?
05 Jenny: ____________________고 물어봤어. 내가 동양학을 전공한다고 하니까,
06 한국어 말고 ____________________고 물어보더라.
07 Sandy: 그 사람 전공은 뭔데?
08 Jenny: ____________________대.
09 참, 그 사람 고향도 ____________________래.
10 Sandy: 진짜? 너랑 같네. 재밌다.
11 Jenny: 내가 ________________________________고 하니까,
12 다음 주말에 ________________________________재.
13 Sandy: 그래서? 같이 갈까야?

Exercise 11

Listen to the conversations and answer the questions in Korean, using a reported proposal. 51

1. What does the man suggest to the woman?

____.

2. What does the man suggest to the woman?

____.

3. What does the man suggest to the woman?

____.

4. What does the woman suggest to the man?

____.

Exercise 12

Listen to the conversation between two friends (윌, 민지) and answer the questions in Korean. 52

1. What did Will suggest he and Minji do for Alex?

____.

2. Why is Will's house not available next weekend?

____.

3. Which place did Minji suggest gathering at and Why?

____.

4. What did Minji suggest Will buy for Alex and why?

____.

III. Culture

1. 한국의 야구

야구 is one of the most popular sports in Korea. **대한민국 야구 국가대표팀** (South Korea's national baseball team) is considered one of the best national teams in the world. The team regularly participates in the World Baseball Classic and won the Gold Medal at the 2008 Olympic games. **KBO** (Korea Baseball Organization), Korea's professional baseball league, has been in operation since 1982. Currently, there are 10 teams in KBO.

Cheering is a culture unto itself at Korean baseball games, with each team having its own method of **응원** (cheering). Korean baseball fans are very collective and enthusiastic. Each team and individual player has an **응원가** (fight song). Also, each team has a group of cheerleaders, who often start cheering with the team's **응원가**. Baseball fans love to watch games while singing **응원가** and eating. The most popular baseball stadium meal is **치맥**, which is fried **치킨** (chicken) and **맥주** (beer).

Team	City	Logo
Hanhwa Eagles 한화 이글스	대전	
Kia Tigers KIA 타이거스	광주	
LG Twins LG 트윈스	광주	
NC Dinos NC 다이노스	창원	
Kiwoom Heroes 키움 히어로즈	서울	
Doosan Bears 두산 베어스	서울	
kt Wiz kt 위즈	수원	
Lotte Giants 롯데 자이언츠	부산	
Samsung Lions 삼성 라이온즈	대구	
SK Wyverns SK 와이번스	인천	

2. 한국의 축구

Along with **야구**, **축구** is also a very popular sport in Korea. Like **야구**, there is a **대한민국 프로 축구 리그** (Korea Professional Football League), but its games are not as popular as those of the **KBO**. However, the international matches that **대한민국 축구 국가대표팀** (South Korea National football team) plays in are by far more popular than the international matches of any other sport. **대한민국 축구 국가대표팀** is considered one of the strongest Asian teams, and they have qualified for the FIFA World Cup nine consecutive times since 1986. At the 2002 FIFA World Cup, co-hosted by Korea and Japan, the team did especially well, coming in 4th place. At that time, Koreans all over the country took to the streets during 한국팀's matches to cheer them on. The victories of the **한국팀** have given extreme joy and hope to the **한국 사람**, and united them in **애국심** (patriotism).

IV. Listen & Discuss

현수 and 웨이 are passing by the school grounds where some students are practicing baseball. 현수 begins chatting with 웨이 about a Korean series game.

First, listen to the conversation. With your classmates, discuss the answers to the questions that follow. Finally, write each answer in a full Korean sentence in the space provided.

1. 어제 야구 경기에서 어느 팀이 이겼습니까?

2. 웨이는 어느 팀을 응원합니까?

3. 현수는 어느 팀을 응원합니까? 왜 응원합니까?

4. 이번 주말에 현수와 웨이는 어디서 무엇을 할 겁니까?

Script

현수 and 웨이 are passing by the school grounds where some students are practicing baseball. 현수 begins chatting with 웨이 about a Korean Series game.

01 현수: 너, 어제 한국 시리즈 경기 봤어?
02 웨이: 보고 싶었는데 일이 있어서 못 봤어요. 누가 이겼어요?
03 현수: 삼성이 이겼어. 끝까지 마음 졸이면서 봤어.
04 웨이: 왜요? 어땠는데요?
05 현수: 9회까지 두산이 3대 0으로 이기고 있었거든.[II.1]
06 그런데 삼성이 마지막에 만루 홈런을 쳐서 역전을 했어.
07 웨이: 아! 이번에는 두산이 이길 줄 알았는데… 정말 안타깝네요.
08 현수: 넌 두산 팬이니?
09 웨이: 네. 형은 삼성 팬이죠?
10 현수: 당연하지! 내 고향이 대구잖아.
11 웨이: 우리 이번 주 토요일 결승전 경기는 같이 볼까요?
12 현수: 그래! 우리 집에 와. 안 그래도 내가 민지한테 같이 보자고 했거든.[II.2]
13 웨이: 그럼 제니한테도 올 수 있냐고 물어 볼까요?[II.3]
14 현수: 좋지!

01 현수: Did you watch the Korean series game yesterday?
02 웨이: I wanted to watch, but I couldn't because I had some other stuff to do. Who won the game?
03 현수: 삼성 did. I was so anxious the whole time, until the very end.
04 웨이: Why? How was it?
05 현수: 두산 was winning 3-0 until the 9th inning,
06 so I thought the game was over, but a grand slam home run from 삼성 turned the game around.
07 웨이: My god! I thought 두산 would win this time. Too bad.
08 현수: Are you a fan of 두산?
09 웨이: Yes. You're a fan of 삼성, aren't you?
10 현수: Of course! You know, my hometown is 대구.
11 웨이: Shall we watch the final match together this Saturday?
12 현수: Great! Come to my place. Actually, I also asked 민지 to watch.
13 웨이: Then, I will ask 제니 if she could also come.
14 현수: Nice!

V. Guided Conversation

Keeping in mind the organization of the model conversation in Listen & Discuss (Script), practice the modified conversation below with your partner.

Two friends are talking about yesterday's sports game.

Practice the following conversation with your partner, using the prompts in (parenthesis) to fill in the blanks and make the conversation flow naturally.

01 A: 어제 한국시리즈 경기 봤어?

02 B: 보고 싶었는데 ______________ 아서/어서 못 봤어. 누가 이겼어?
(시험이 있다; 아르바이트 하다; 친구 생일 파티에 가다; ...)

03 A: ______________ 이/가 이겼어. 근데 어제 경기 정말 ______________ 더라.
(삼성; 롯데; 두산; ...) (재미있다; 장난 아니다; 흥미진진하다;...)

완전 끝까지 마음 졸이면서 봤어.

04 B: 왜? 어땠는데?

05 A: 처음에 ______________ 이/가 ______________ (으)로 이기고 있었거든.[II.1]
(삼성; 롯데; 두산; ...) (3:0; 8:5; ⋯)

06 근데, 마지막에 ______________ 이/가 만루 홈런을 치면서 역전을 했어.
(삼성; 롯데; 두산; ...)

07 B: 아 ~아쉽다! 이번에는 ______________ 이/가 이길 줄 알았는데⋯.
(삼성; 롯데; 두산; ...)

08 A: 넌 ______________ 팬이냐?
(삼성; 롯데; 두산; ...)

09 B: 응. 너는 ______________ 팬이지?
(삼성; 롯데; 두산; ...)

Guided Conversation

10 A: 당연하지! 내 고향이 ____________ (대구; 부산; 서울; ...) (이)잖아.

11 B: 다음 경기는 경기장에서 같이 볼까?

12 A: 그래! 다음 경기는 ____________ (우리 집, 경기장) 에서 보자.

안 그래도 내가 민지한테 ____________ (같이 보다; 같이 가다;...) 자고 했거든.[II.3]

13 B: 아~ 그래? 그럼 내가 마크한테도 ____________ (올 수 있다; 갈 수 있다) 냐고 물어볼게.[II.2]

14 A: 그래, 좋아! 이번에는 우리 내기 할까?

15 B: 좋지! 자기가 응원하는 팀이 지면 ____________ (치맥 사다; 피자 사다; 저녁 사다; 술 사다; ....) 기로 하자!

(Switch roles and continue to practice.)

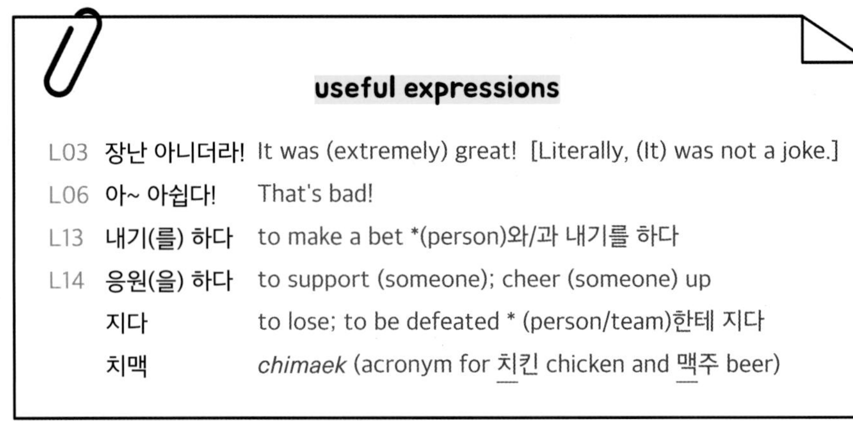

useful expressions

L03	장난 아니더라!	It was (extremely) great! [Literally, (It) was not a joke.]
L06	아~ 아쉽다!	That's bad!
L13	내기(를) 하다	to make a bet *(person)와/과 내기를 하다
L14	응원(을) 하다	to support (someone); cheer (someone) up
	지다	to lose; to be defeated * (person/team)한테 지다
	치맥	*chimaek* (acronym for 치킨 chicken and 맥주 beer)

Present the conversation above in front of the class. Try not to look at your paper!

VI. Spontaneous Conversation

This is your chance to have a realistic interaction with your classmates in Korean. You can practice writing, speaking with your classmates, and presenting in front of the class!

You and your classmate are talking about your favorite sports and sports teams. (You can use US sports teams or refer to Section III. Culture for Korean teams.) Include the information in the table below in your conversation. Create a meaningful conversation with your partner similar to the one that you practiced in the Guided Conversation!

- Your favorite sports and teams you cheer for (Refer to Section III.)
- Any specific game you particularly enjoyed watching and its results
- Make a plan to watch a game together
- Make bets on the outcome of the game

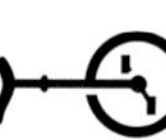

Write down the conversation you had with your partner in Step 1.

Step 3

Write a short essay about your favorite sports team and a game you enjoyed watching, based on the conversation in Step 2. (Use the ~는다 speech style.)

Present what you wrote in Step 2 in front of the class. Try not to look at your paper!

VII. Listening

Listen to the following conversation between two friends and answer the questions. 54

1. Why does the woman think that Korean people love soccer?

____.

2. Why does the man recommend going to the baseball stadium to the woman?

____.

Listen to the following conversation and mark each statement T(rue) or F(alse). 55

3. ______ 한국에는 미국처럼 야구 팬들이 많지 않다.
4. ______ 미국에서는 야구 경기를 할 때 치어리더들이 응원을 한다.
5. ______ 미국에서는 많은 사람들이 가족들과 같이 야구를 보러 간다.
6. ______ 한국에서는 야구장에서 맛있는 음식을 먹을 수 있다.

Words & Expressions

01-02 밤(을) 새우면서 staying up all night; keeping awake all night
응원(을) 하다 to support (someone); cheer (someone) up
기회가 있으면 if (you) have an opportunity 특별한 응원 문화 unique cheering culture
응원가를 부르다 to sing a fight song 경기장 stadium
03-06 프로 야구 professional baseball 치어리더들 cheerleaders
비슷한 점들 similarities [Literally, points that are similar]

VIII. Reading

한국 시리즈 결승전 교통 안내 (Traffic announcement during the Korean Series final match)

한국 시리즈 결승전

11월 20일 (일), 오후 6:30

잠실 야구장 주변 교통 안내

한국 시리즈 결승전이 시작되기 2시간 전인 4시 30분부터 잠실 야구장 근처에는 주차를 할 수 없습니다. 야구 경기를 보러 오시는 분들은 지하철이나 버스를 이용해 주시면 감사하겠습니다. 주차를 하실 분은 불편하시더라도 잠실 한강공원 주차장을 이용해 주시기 바랍니다.

1. 위의 글의 내용과 같은 것을 고르십시오.
   ① 야구 경기는 4:30에 시작한다.
   ② 잠실 야구장에 가는 지하철이 있다.
   ③ 잠실 한강공원 주차장은 잠실 야구장 근처에 있다.
   ④ 한국 시리즈 결승전은 2시간 동안 한다.

Words & Expressions

01 주변 surroundings 주차장 parking lot 이용하다 to use, make use of ~더라도 even though…

한국에서 인기있는 스포츠 (Popular sports in Korea)

한국인이 가장 즐겨 보는 스포츠는 야구와 축구인 것으로 조사됐다. 조사 결과에 따르면 응답자의 35%가 야구 경기를 보는 것을 가장 좋아한다고 대답했다. (㉠) 축구(33.6%), 골프(15.9%), 농구(10.2%)가 그 뒤를 이었다. 직접 하는 운동이나 스포츠 중에서 가장 좋아하는 것은 축구(21.3%)로 조사됐다. 그 다음으로는 등산(17.5%), 수영(11%), 농구(8.4%), 테니스(5.7%), 요가(3%) 순으로 나타났다. 조사 결과에 따르면 5년 전에 비해 축구나 농구를 하는 여자들이 많아졌고 테니스와 요가를 하는 사람들이 많아지고 있다고 한다.

2. ㉠에 들어갈 알맞은 말을 고르십시오.

① 하지만 ② 그래서 ③ 그러니까 ④ 그 다음으로

3. 이 글의 내용과 같은 것을 고르십시오.

① 한국 사람들은 야구경기를 하는 것을 제일 좋아한다.
② 한국에는 축구를 하는 것을 좋아하는 사람들이 많이 있다.
③ 여자들은 축구를 하지 않는다.
④ 수영 경기를 보는 사람들이 많아지고 있다.

02-03 즐겨 보다 to enjoy watching 조사되다 to be discovered, to be surveyed
조사 결과에 따르면 according to the survey result 응답자 respondent 뒤를 잇다 to follow
...순으로 in order ...에 비해 compare to ...

6 드라마 때문에 밤을 새웠다고?

Did you say you stay up all night watching a drama?

-Talking about one's favorite dramas and movies
-Places and events related to Korean dramas

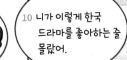

01 제니야,
너 오늘 좀 피곤해 보인다?

02 어, 오빠. 어제 드라마 보느라고 밤을 새워서요.
03 드라마 때문에 밤을 새웠어?

04 네. 보고 싶은 드라마가 있었는데, 그동안 시험 공부 하느라고 계속 못 봤거든요.
05 어제 밤 새워서 한꺼번에 다 봐 버렸어요.

06 근데, 어떤 드라마야?
07 조선 시대가 배경인 역사 드라마예요.

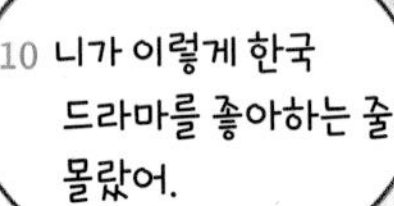
08 아, 요즘 주말에 하는 그 사극 말이야?
09 왕으로 나오는 남자 주인공이 진짜 잘 생겼어요. 배우들이 다 연기도 너무 잘 하구요.
10 니가 이렇게 한국 드라마를 좋아하는 줄 몰랐어.
11 저 사실 한국 드라마 때문에 한국어를 공부하기 시작했거든요.

12 드라마 보면서 한국어도 공부하고, 한국 역사도 배우고, 좋네.
13 자막 없이 내용을 다 이해할 수 있을 만큼 한국어를 잘 하고 싶어요.

Preparation & Practice	I. New Words & Expressions II. Patterns, Expressions & Practice 1. ~ 느라(고) "because of ~ ing" 2. ~아/~어 버리다 Declaring that an action has been completed 3. ~을/~ㄹ 만큼 "to the extent that ~"		III. Culture 1. Korean Dramas 2. Famous K-drama filming locations
		Conversation Activities	IV. Listen & Discuss V. Guided Conversation VI. Spontaneous Conversation
		TOPIK Preparation	VII. Listening • Conversation • Interview
			VIII. Reading • Historical drama festival • Reasons for foreigners to learn Korean

I. New Words & Expressions

 **Study the words and expressions along with the audio.** 

NOUN

내용	content(s); story
배경	background
배우	actor/actress
사극	historical drama
역사 드라마	historical drama
연기	acting; performance
왕	king
자막	caption; subtitle
조선 시대	the Joseon Dynasty
주인공	protagonist; main character

VERB

나오다	to star (as a character) *(a character)으로/로 나오다
밤새우다	to stay up all night (= 밤을 새우다)

ADVERB

사실	in fact
한꺼번에	at once

EXPRESSION

·(피곤해) 보인다	You look (tired) *~아/~어 보이다: (for a person/thing) to look/appear ~
·(그 사극) 말이야?	Are you talking about (that historical drama)?

Listen to the audio and fill in the blanks. 

1. A: 제니, 너 오늘 좀 ____________?

   B: 어, 오빠. 어제 밤 늦게까지 드라마 봤어요. 그래서 잠을 많이 못 잤거든요.

2. A: 뭐? 밤 늦게까지 드라마를 봤다고?

   B: 보고 싶은 드라마가 있었는데, 어제 저녁에 ____________ 다 봤어요!

3. A: 그 드라마가 요즘 인기가 많더라.

   B: 응, 이야기도 재미있고 특히 ____________이 연기를 진짜 잘 하더라고.

4. A: 앞으로는 ______________ 없이 드라마 내용들은 다 이해할 수 있으면 좋겠어요.

   B: 이번 학기에 매일 한국어 수업을 들으니까 그렇게 될거야!

5. A: 어떤 드라마인데, 잠도 안 자고 밤 늦게까지 봤어?

   B: 조선 시대가 배경인 ______________ 예요. 오빠도 보기 시작하면,

   너무 재미있어서, 계속 보게 될 거예요.

Exercise 2

Choose the best word to complete the sentences.

1. 요즘 내가 보는 주말 드라마는 왕으로 나오는 ____________ 이/가 진짜 잘 생기고 연기도 너무 잘 해서 사람들에게 인기가 많다.

   ① 내용　② 연기　③ 사극　④ 주인공

2. 어제 내가 밤을 새워서 본 드라마는 조선 시대를 ____________ (으)로 한 역사 드라마인데, 내가 좋아하는 여배우가 나와서, 첫 편부터 지금까지 계속 보고 있다.

   ① 계획　② 연기　③ 반전　④ 배경

3. 이 역사 드라마는 내용도 좋고 배우들이 모두 다 ______________ 도 잘 해서 내가 제일 즐겨보는 드라마이다.

   ① 예고　② 연기　③ 난　④ 명

4. 이번에 새로 시작하는 드라마에서는 내가 좋아하는 남자 배우가 주인공으로 ______________.

   ① 운이 좋다　② 역전을 한다　③ 이긴다　④ 나온다

5. 이번에 한국 역사 수업을 들어서, 요즘은 가족 드라마보다 __________ 을 더 자주 본다.

   ① 내용　② 자막　③ 배경　④ 사극

II. Patterns, Expressions & Practice

1. ~느라(고) "because of ~ ing"

Usage

Use ~**느라(고)** when you indicate that the action in the first clause is the reason or excuse for the consequence in the second clause. Generally, the consequence is negative or unexpected. ~**느라(고)** can be attached only to verbs, not to adjectives.

Look at the following examples.

- A: 어제 밤 새웠어?
  B: 어, 드라마 보**느라고** 시간 가는 줄 몰랐어.
  I lost track of time because I was absorbed in watching a drama.

- A: 요즘 어떻게 지내세요?
  B: 취직 준비 하**느라고** 정신이 없어요.
  I'm busy preparing to get a job.

- A: 마이클은 주말에도 바쁜 것 같아요.
  B: 학비를 버**느라고** 주말에도 아르바이트를 한대요.
  I heard that he works a part-time job even on weekends to earn his tuition.

Note 1

~**느라(고)** cannot be used to justify suggestions, requests, or commands. In those situations, use ~**(으)니까**.

1. 이 영화에는 내가 좋아하는 배우가 나오**니까** 꼭 보고 싶다.
   My favorite actor stars in this movie, so I really want to watch it.

2. 곧 시험이 있**으니까**, 드라마 그만 보고 공부해라.
   You have an exam soon, so stop watching dramas and study.

Note 2

~**(으)니까**, ~**아서**/~**어서**, and ~**느라(고)** are all expressions that allow you to offer a reason for something. However, while the clauses connected by ~**(으)니까** and ~**아서**/~**어서** can have different subjects, ~**느라(고)** should have the same subject in both clauses.

1. 시카고에서 친구가 **와서**, 친구를 만나러 공항에 나갔다.
   A friend of mine came from Chicago, so I went out to the airport to meet her.

2. 친구가 곧 도착하**니까**, 빨리 저녁을 준비하자.
Since our friend is arriving soon, let's prepare dinner quickly.

3. 친구하고 같이 시간을 보내**느라고**, 숙제를 다 못했다.
I spent time with my friend and couldn't finish my homework.

Column A lists actions that you can use as a reason or excuse for the consequences in Column B. Match each clause in Column A with the best suitable clause in Column B and write a complete sentence, as in the first example.

A	B
1. 어젯밤에 친구하고 이야기하다	a. 9시 수업에 늦다
2. 오늘 아침에 숙제하다	b. 전화 소리를 못 듣다
3. 샤워하다	c. 친구를 만날 시간이 없다
4. 지난 학기에 다섯 과목을 듣다	d. 늦게 자다
5. 아르바이트하다	e. 돈을 다 쓰다
6. 한국 가는 비행기 표를 사다	f. 힘들다

1. 어젯밤에 친구하고 이야기하느라 늦게 잤어요 ______.
2. ______.
3. ______.
4. ______.
5. ______.
6. ______.

Choose the appropriate form from the options in the parenthesis.

1. A: 요즘도 농구하세요?

   B: (수영하느라고, 수영해서) 농구 할 시간이 없어요.

2. A: 어제 골프 치셨어요?

   B: (비가 오느라고, 비가 와서) 못 쳤어요.

3. A: 아까 전화했는데 왜 안 받았어요?

   B: 운동하면서 (음악을 듣느라고, 음악을 들어서) 못 들었어요.

4. A: 어제 어디 갔어요?

   B: 친구가 보스톤에서 (오느라고, 와서) 같이 영화 보러 갔어요.

5. A: 요즘 왜 이렇게 바쁘세요?

   B: 한국말 (공부하느라고, 공부해서) 다른 것은 못 해요.

Complete the following conversations by providing your reason or excuse for the consequence.

1. A: 돈 있으면 5만 원만 빌려줄 수 있어?

   B: 미안. ____________________ 남은 돈이 없어.

2. A: 요즘 많이 바빠요?

   B: 네, ____________________ 바빠요.

3. A: 피곤해 보이네요.

   B: 어제 ____________________ 밤을 새웠어요.

4. A: 뭐 하느라고 전화도 안 받아?

   B: 미안해. ____________________ 전화 온 줄 몰랐어.

5. A: ____________________ 힘들죠?

   B: 좀 힘들지만 재미있어요.

useful expressions

인턴십 internship

6. A: 왜 이렇게 점심을 늦게 먹어?

   B: 2시까지 ____________________ 밥 먹을 시간이 없었어.

Listen to the short dialogues and answer the questions. 

1. Why did the man have a hard time?

   ____.

2. Why is the woman busy?

   ____.

3. Why did the man lose his voice?

   ____.

useful expressions

길이 막히다	(for a road) to be jammed
정신이 없다	to be out of mind
목소리	voice
예약하다	to make an appointment

2. ~아/~어 버리다 Declaring that an action has been completed

Usage

Use **~아/~어 버리다** to indicate that an action is completed and it cannot be undone. Though **버리다** literally means "to throw away," in this pattern, it means "to complete." You can use this pattern with verbs only, not adjectives.

Form

▶ Verb base (ending in 아 or 오) + **아 버리다** : 팔 + **아 버리다** → 팔**아 버리다**

▶ Verb base (ending in other vowels) + **어 버리다** : 먹 + **어 버리다** → 먹**어 버리다**

Look at the following examples.

- A: 머리 자르셨네요?
  B: 네, 날씨가 더워서 짧게 **잘라 버렸어요**.
  Yes, the weather was hot, so I got my hair cut short.

- A: 엄마, 돈을 다 **써 버렸어요**. 용돈 좀 더 주세요.
  B: 다음부터 돈 좀 아껴 써라.

useful expressions

머리를 자르다	to get a hair cut
용돈	allowance
아껴 쓰다	to use something sparingly

This pattern often expresses that an action ended with a result that the speaker did not expect or does not like.

- 우리 개가 제 음식을 **먹어 버렸어요**.
  My dog ate my food.
- 주말이 다 **지나가 버렸어요**.
  The weekend is all over.

Note 2

In some cases, this pattern indicates that something ended and the speaker is experiencing a feeling of relief or satisfaction.

- 숙제를 다 **해 버려서** 너무 기분이 좋아요.
  I feel really good because I finished my homework.
- 무더운 여름이 다 **지나가 버렸어요**.
  The hot and muggy summer has passed.

Note 3

잊어버리다 "to forget" and 잃어버리다 "to lose" were originally derived from this pattern, but they have become single words in contemporary Korean.

- A: 혹시 교실에서 지갑 못 보셨어요? 제가 지갑을 **잃어버렸어요**.

  Did you see a purse in the classroom by any chance? [Literally, Couldn't you have seen a purse ...?] I've lost mine.

  B: 못 봤는데요. 1층 분실물 센터에 가서 물어보세요.

  I didn't. Ask Lost & Found on the first floor.

- A: 선생님, 숙제를 깜빡 **잊어버리고** 안 했는데 내일 내도 될까요?

  B: 알았어요. 내일은 꼭 내세요.

Exercise 5

Complete the dialogues, using the ~아/~어 버리다 pattern.

1. A: 이 책을 벌써 다 읽었어요?

   B: 네, 너무 재밌어서 어제 밤에 다 ________________.

2. A: 혹시 100달러만 빌려줄 수 있어? 내일 갚을게.

   B: 미안해. 어제 아파트 렌트비 내느라고 돈을 다 ________________.

   그래서 나도 돈이 없어.

3. A: 오늘 왜 이렇게 늦었어요?

   B: 어제 너무 늦게 자서 오늘 아침에 ________________.

4. A: 숙제가 너무 많은데 정말 하기 싫다.

   B: 빨리 ________________! 그리고 나서 나랑 놀러 가자.

5. A: 어제 쇼핑 갔다가 이 옷을 ________________.

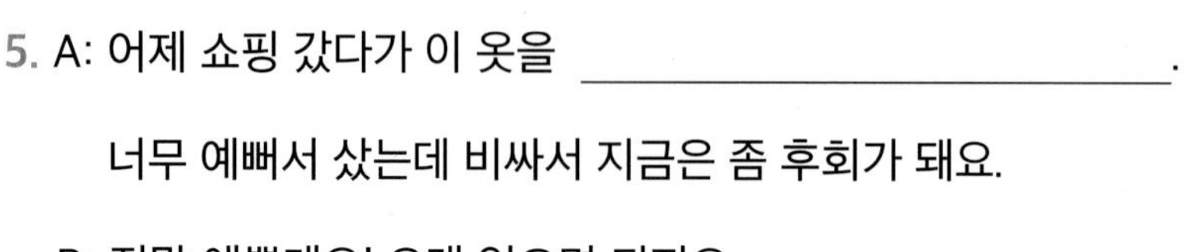

   너무 예뻐서 샀는데 비싸서 지금은 좀 후회가 돼요.

   B: 정말 예쁜데요! 오래 입으면 되지요.

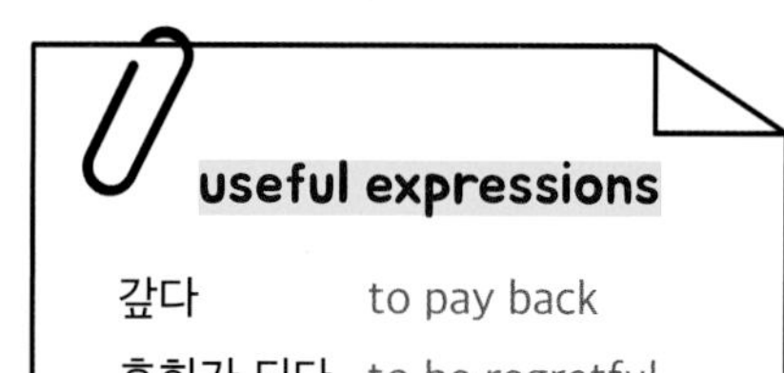

갚다	to pay back
후회가 되다	to be regretful

Choose the option from the parentheses that is most appropriate in the given context.

1. A: 곧 수업이 시작되는데, 지금 어딜 가요?
   B: 어제 학교에서 핸드폰을 (잊어버려서, 잃어버려서) 찾고 있는데,
   이 건물에는 분실물 센터가 어디 있어요?

2. A: 숙제를 (잊어버리고, 잃어버리고) 안 했어요.
   B: 다음부터 매일 매일 스케줄을 확인하세요.

3. A: 한국 갈 준비 다 하셨어요?
   B: 다른 준비는 다 됐는데 제가 여권을 (잊어버렸어요, 잃어버렸어요).
   그래서 새로 만들어야 해요.

4. A: 한국어 단어를 매일 외우는데 자꾸 (잊어버려요, 잃어버려요).
   어떻게 해야 단어를 잘 외울 수 있지요?
   B: 매일 연습하는 방법밖에 없어요.

5. A: 여자 친구랑 헤어져서 마음이 너무 아파요.
   B: 나쁜 일들은 빨리 (잊어버리고, 잃어버리고) 좋은 일들만 기억하세요.

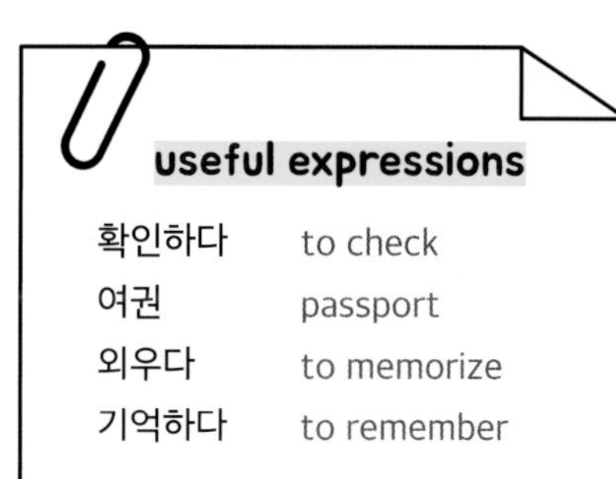

useful expressions
확인하다 to check
여권 passport
외우다 to memorize
기억하다 to remember

Listen to the conversation and mark each statement T(rue) or F(alse). 59

1. _____ The woman came to school late.

2. _____ The woman came to school by bus today.

3. _____ There was homework in today's class.

4. _____ The man already finished the homework.

Listen to the conversation and mark each statement T(rue) or F(alse). 60

1. _____ The man did do well on the test.

2. _____ The man studied hard yesterday.

3. _____ The man slept at home yesterday.

4. _____ The woman took the test well.

3. ~을/~ㄹ 만큼 "to the extent that ~ "

Usage

Use **~을/~ㄹ 만큼** to express that the extent or quantity in question is similar to what comes before.

Form

▶ Verb base (ending in a consonant)	+ 을 만큼	: 먹을 만큼	→ 먹을 만큼
▶ Verb base (ending in a vowel)	+ ㄹ 만큼	: 볼 만큼	→ 볼 만큼
*Verb base (ending in ㄹ)	+ 만큼	: 놀 만큼	→ 놀 만큼
*Past tense: ~았/~었	+ 을 만큼	: 먹었을 만큼	→ 먹었을 만큼

Note

"ㄷ-ending" irregular verbs conjugate as follows:

걷다 → 걷 + **을 만큼** → 걸 + 을 만큼
듣다 → 듣 + **을 만큼** → 들 + 을 만큼

Look at the following examples.

- A: 한국어를 공부한 지 2년밖에 안 됐는데, 참 잘하시네요.
  B: 아직 많이 부족해요. 저는 자막 없이 드라마를 이해할 수 있**을 만큼** 한국어를 잘하고 싶어요.
  I'm still not enough. I want to speak Korean well to the extent that I can understand Korean dramas without subtitles.

- A: 일본은 한국에서 가깝죠?
  B: 네, 어떤 섬은 날씨가 좋을 때 부산에서 보**일 만큼** 가까워요. *섬 island
  Yes, some islands (of Japan) are close enough (to Korea) that you can see them from Busan when the weather is clear.

- A: 물리학 시험이 그렇게 어려웠어?
  B: 응, 학생들 대부분이 C를 받**을 만큼** 어려웠어.
  Yes, it was difficult enough that most students got a C.

Complete the following sentences using ~을/~ㄹ 만큼.

1. A: 요즘 날씨가 많이 춥지요?

   B: 네, 길거리에 걸어 다니는 사람이 ______________________ 추워요.

2. A: 그 식당이 그렇게 인기가 많아요?

   B: 네, 예약 안 하고 가면 ______________________ 인기가 많대요.

3. A: 민지하고 수지가 그렇게 친한 줄 몰랐어.

B: 어, 수업도 같이 듣고, 아르바이트도 같이 ______________ 친해.

4. A: 취미가 등산이세요?

B: 네, 저는 아무리 바빠도 일주일에 적어도 한 번은 ______________ 등산을 좋아해요.

Exercise 10

Complete the following sentences using ~을/~ㄹ 만큼.

1. A: 그 영화가 그렇게 재밌니?

B: 응, ______________ 그 영화를 좋아해.

(to buy a DVD; to watch as many as 3 times at a theater; to visit the filming location)

2. 수지: 헨리 씨는 한국 음식을 정말 좋아하는 것 같아요.

헨리: 네, 저는 ______________ 한국 음식을 좋아해요.

(to go to a Korean restaurant at least once a week; to cook Korean food at home)

3. A: 한국에 관심이 많으시네요.

B: 네, ______________ 관심이 많아졌어요.

(to change my major to Korean studies; to take a Korean history class; to watch news about Korea everyday)

4. A: 한국어를 얼마나 하십니까?

B: 저는 한국어로 ______________ 합니다.

(to be able to write a letter; to be able to read a short story; to be able to understand Korean news; to be able to tell the story of my favorite movie)

Listen to the conversations and mark each statement T(rue) or F(alse). 

1. ______ The man is going to study in the library because he has an exam next week.

2. ______ The woman found out that no seats were available in the library.

Listen to the conversations and mark each statement T(rue) or F(alse). 

1. ______ The man was sick because he didn't sleep well.

2. ______ The man is feeling well enough now to go to work.

III. Culture

1. 한국 드라마 (K-drama)

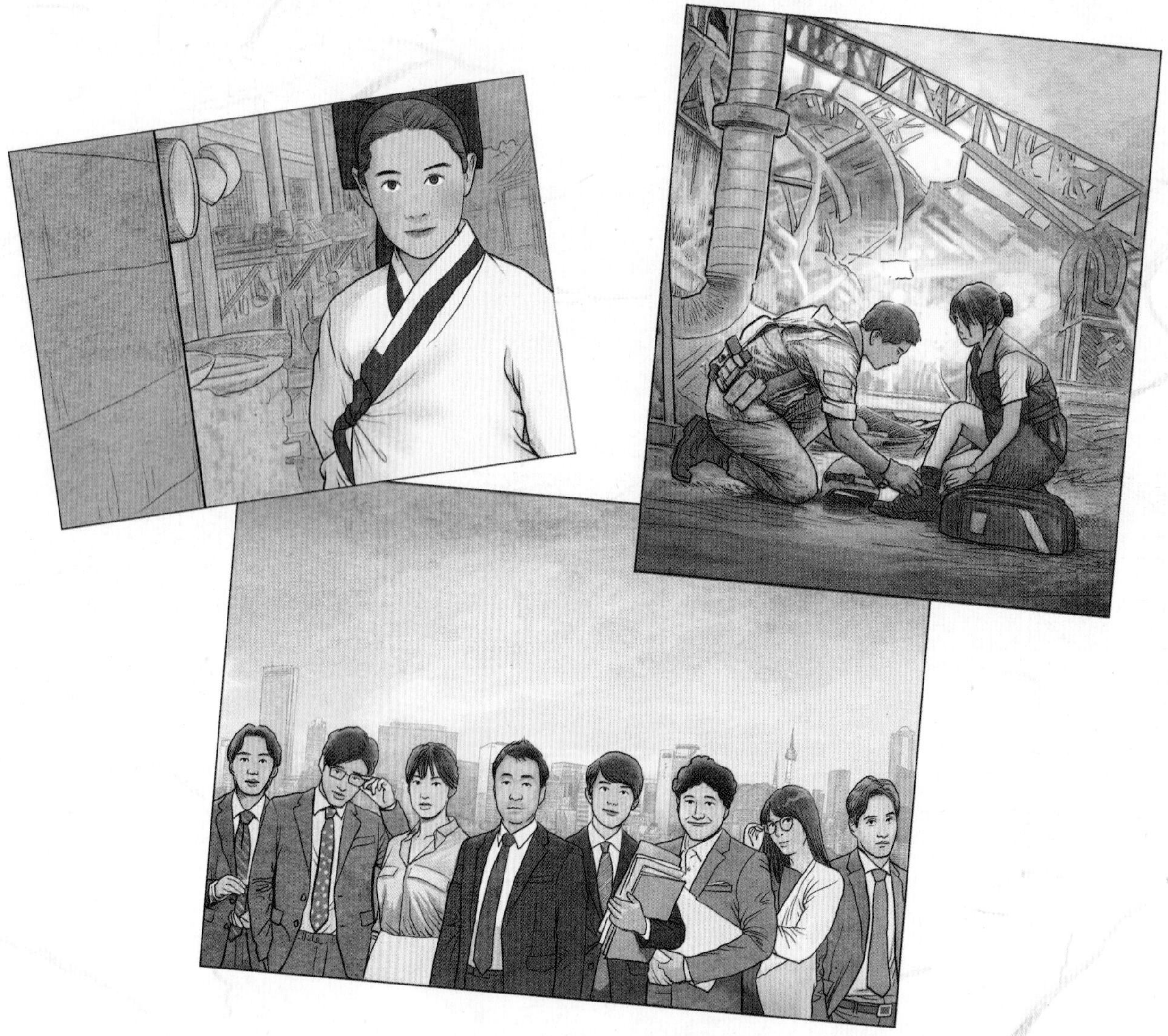

한국 드라마 (K-dramas), along with K-pop, are key driving forces of **한류** (the Korean Wave). **한국 드라마** started gaining popularity in the late 1990s, and now people enjoy **한국드라마** all over the world. For example, **역사 드라마** (historical drama) **대장금** (Jewel in the Palace) was sold to 91 countries. **한국 드라마** are generally less sexual and violent than **서양 드라마** (Western dramas). Most **한국 드라마** portray traditional **유교적 가치** (Confucian values) of **가족 관계** (family relationships), **윗사람에 대한 공경** (respect for elders), **우정** (friendships), and **사랑** (love). These values, though traditional, have universal appeal—especially when combined with the Western materialism and individualism popular among modern audiences.

2. Famous K-Drama Filming Locations

한국 드라마 have gained worldwide recognition over the last decade, and many foreigners visiting Korea want to visit places they have seen in their favorite dramas. The following places are popular filming locations **한국 드라마,** where many K-drama fans visit.

Culture

경복궁

경복궁 (Gyeongbokgung Palace) was the royal palace of the **조선 왕조** (Joseon Dynasty). It was the official residence and workplace of the kings of **조선 왕조**. **경복궁** is located in the center of **서울,** and it often appears in the background of many **역사 드라마** (historical dramas). There is a small entrance fee to **경복궁**, but if your wear **한복**, your visit is free. There are many **한복** rental places near **경복궁**.

용인 민속촌

용인 민속촌 (Yongin folk village) is a replica of a village from the late **조선 시대** (Joseon period). Many historical movies and dramas have been filmed here. Here, tourists can experience life of the people of **조선 왕조**. In **용인 민속촌**, there are also traditional restaurants, a traditional market, and various workshops showcasing all the traditional Korean crafts, among other attractions. **용인 민속촌** is also home to a Folk Museum, an Art Museum, and performances of traditional dance.

북촌 한옥마을

북촌 한옥마을 (Bukchon Hanok Village) is a traditional village located in the center of Seoul. 북촌 literally means "north village," which refers to the village's location north of 경복궁. The 한옥 at 북촌 were the residences of the high-officials of 조선 시대, but these days the village is a popular tourist attraction for those wanting to experience traditional Korean culture.

남산, 서울 타워

Located on top of 남산, N서울타워 is 236.7 meters high and 497.7 meters above sea level. The restaurant on the 7th floor revolves 360°, and you can see 서울 시내 (downtown Seoul) at a glance. Since the night view is especially beautiful, many dramas have been shot here, and many couples go here on dates.

여의도 한강 공원

여의도 한강 공원 is where couples in many dramas go on dates. At the park, various events such as the 여의도 벚꽃 축제 (Yeouido Spring Cherry Blossom Festival) and the 서울 국제 불꽃 축제 (Seoul International Fireworks Festival) are held throughout the year. Many people (or couples) take the 한강 유람선 (Han river ferry) at 여의도 to have a romantic date while enjoying the view of 한강.

IV. Listen & Discuss

제니 and 현수 are chatting in a coffee shop.

First, listen to the conversation. With your classmates, discuss the answers to the questions that follow. Finally, write each answer in a full Korean sentence in the space provided.

1. 제니는 오늘 왜 피곤해 보입니까?

2. 왜 제니는 좋아하는 드라마를 그동안 보지 못했습니까?

3. 제니가 본 드라마는 어떤 드라마입니까?

4. 제니는 어떻게 이 드라마를 좋아하게 된 것 같습니까?

5. 제니가 한국어 공부를 시작하게 된 이유는 무엇입니까?

6. 제니는 한국어를 얼마만큼 잘하고 싶어합니까?

Script

☞ 제니 (2학년) and 현수 (4학년) are chatting in a coffee shop.

01 현수: 제니야, 너 오늘 좀 피곤해 보인다?

02 제니: 어, 오빠. 어제 드라마 보느라고[II.1]밤을 새워서요.

03 현수: 드라마 때문에 밤을 새웠어?

04 제니: 네. 보고 싶은 드라마가 있었는데, 그동안 시험 공부 하느라고[II.1] 계속 못 봤거든요.

05 어제 밤 새워서 한꺼번에 다 봐 버렸어요.[II.2]

06 현수: 근데, 어떤 드라마야?

07 제니: 조선 시대가 배경인 역사 드라마예요.

08 현수: 아, 요즘 주말에 하는 그 사극 말이야?

09 제니: 왕으로 나오는 남자 주인공이 진짜 잘생겼어요. 배우들이 다 연기도 너무 잘 하구요.

10 현수: 니가 이렇게 한국 드라마를 좋아하는 줄 몰랐어.

11 제니: 저 사실 한국 드라마 때문에 한국어를 공부하기 시작했거든요.

12 현수: 드라마 보면서 한국어도 공부하고, 한국 역사도 배우고, 좋네.

13 제니: 자막 없이 내용을 다 이해할 수 있을 만큼[II.3] 한국어를 잘하고 싶어요.

01 현수: You look a little tired today, Jenny.

02 제니: I stayed up all night watching a drama.

03 현수: You stayed up all night because of a drama?

04 제니: Yes. There was a drama I wanted to watch, but because I needed to study for a test, I couldn't keep

05 watching. I just finished watching all the episodes last night.

06 현수: Which drama is it?

07 제니: It's a historical drama with 조선 시대 as its setting.

08 현수: Oh, you're talking about the historical drama that airs on weekends these days.

09 제니: The male main character who plays the King is really handsome. The actors and actresses give great performances.

10 현수: I didn't know that you like dramas so much.

11 제니: I actually began studying Korean because of Korean dramas.

12 현수: While watching the drama, you study Korean and also learn Korean history. That's nice.

13 제니: I want to be able to speak Korean well so that I can understand the story of the drama without subtitles.

V. Guided Conversation

Keeping in mind the organization of the model conversation in Listen & Discuss (Script), practice the modified conversation below with your partner.

Two people are talking about their favorite dramas.

Practice the following conversation with your partner, using the prompts in (parenthesis) to fill in the blanks and make the conversation flow naturally.

01 A: 너 오늘 좀 피곤해 보인다?

02 B: 어제 드라마 보느라고[II.1] 밤을 새워서요.

03 A: 뭐라구? 드라마때문에 밤을 새웠다고?

04 B: 네. 보고 싶은 드라마가 있었는데, ________ 느라고 계속 못 봤거든요.
(시험공부하다; 페이퍼를 쓰다; 아르바이트 하다; ...)

05 ________ 아서/어서 한꺼번에 다 봐 버렸어요.[II.2]
(어제 시험이 끝나다; 어제 페이퍼를 끝내다; 어제 아르바이트를 그만두다; ...)

06 A: 어떤 드라만데?

07 B: ________ 인 ________ 예요.
(조선 시대가 배경/역사 드라마; 서울에 있는 병원이 배경/의학 드라마; 그리스가 배경/로맨스 드라마; ...)

Guided Conversation

Choose (1) or (2) to continue the conversation.

Option (1)

08 A: 아~ 요즘 ________ 에 하는 그 ________ 말이야?
(월.수; 화.목; 금.토; 주말;..) (사극; 드라마)

09 B: 네.

10 A: 밤 새워서 볼 만큼[II.3] 그렇게 재미있어?

11 B: 네. ________ (으)로 나오는 ________ 배우가 ________ 거든요.
(왕;주인공; 주연; ...) (남자; 여자) (잘 생기다; 예쁘다; 멋있다; 연기를 잘 하다; …)

12 A: ㅎㅎ 너 그 ________ 에/한테 아주 푹 빠져 있구나!
(드라마; 배우; ...)

Option (2)

08 A: 아~ 요즘 ________ 에 하는 그 ________ 말이야?
(월.수; 화.목; 금.토; 주말;..) (사극; 드라마)

09 B: 네, 지난 주 예고에서 ________ 아서/어서 이번 주가 너무 기다려져요.
(진짜 엄청난 반전이 있다; 왕/주인공/조연이 위험해 지다; 왕/주인공/조연이 사랑에 빠지다;;...)

10 A: 니가 이렇게 ________ 를 좋아하는 줄 몰랐네.
(드라마; 그 배우)

11 B: 저 사실 ________ 때문에 한국어를 공부하기 시작했거든요.
(한국 드라마; 그 배우)

12 A: 어, 진짜?

13 B: ________ 만큼 한국어를 잘 하고 싶어요.
(자막 없이 드라마를 알아듣다; 한국 전통 문화를 이해하다; 한국 사회를 잘 이해하다; 한국어로 팬레터를 보내다; ...)

14 A: 드라마 보면서 한국어도 공부하고 좋네.

(Switch roles and continue to practice.)

useful expressions

L05 그만두다 to quit

L07 의학 medical

(Option 1)

L11 주연 starring role

L12 푹 빠져 있구나 to get hooked on

(Option 2)

L09 예고 preview, trailer; 반전 twists (in a story); 조연 supporting actor[actress]; 위험해지다 to get in danger; 사랑에 빠지다 to fall into love

L13 팬레터 fan letter

Present the conversation above in front of the class. Try not to look at your paper!

VI. Spontaneous Conversation

This is your chance to have a realistic interaction with your classmates in Korean. You can practice writing, speaking with your classmates, and presenting in front of the class!

You and your classmate are talking about your favorite dramas.Include the information (in the table below) in your conversation. Create a meaningful conversation with your partner similar to the one that you practiced in the Guided Conversation!

- Which drama you enjoyed watching recently
- Describe your favorite drama briefly, including the setting and airtime
- Who the main characters are and what they are like
- What aspects of the drama you particularly like
- Any cultural differences you noticed in the drama

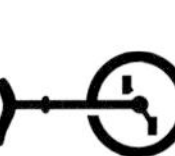

Write down the conversation you had with your partner in Step 1.

Step 3

Based on the conversation in Step 2, write a short paragraph which introduces your favorite drama. Use the ~는다 speech style.

Present what you wrote in Step 2 in front of the class. Try not to look at your paper!

VII. Listening

Listen to the conversation and mark each statement T(rue) or F(alse). 64

1. ______ 여자는 N서울타워를 안 좋아한다.

2. ______ 여자는 어제 피곤할 만큼 공부를 했다.

3. ______ 여자는 저녁도 못 먹을 만큼 피곤하다.

4. ______ 남자는 집에 가고 싶다.

5. ______ 남자와 여자는 오늘 치맥을 먹을 것이다.

Listen to the conversation and answer the following questions in Korean. 65

6. 남자는 왜 한국에 오게 됐습니까?

____.

7. 여자는 왜 한국어를 공부하게 됐습니까?

____.

VIII. Reading

사극 드라마 축제 (Historical drama festival)

※ Read the following passage and mark if the statement is T(rue) or F(alse).

11월 3일부터 12월 1일까지 용인 민속촌에서 사극 드라마 축제가 열린다. 행사기간 동안 관람객들은 민속촌 내에서 진행되는 영화나 드라마 촬영 현장을 구경할 수 있다. 그리고 드라마 속 특수분장 체험하기, 사극 의상 체험하기 등 체험 행사도 제공된다. 11월 10일에는 '대한민국 사극을 빛낸 스타 시상식'이 열릴 예정으로 관람객들은 '스타 핸드프린팅'과 '팬 사인회'에 참여하여 사극 배우들과 시간을 보낼 수 있다. 그리고 행사 기간 동안 '난타와 전통무용', '태권도 시범', 'B-boy' 등 화려한 공연도 준비되어 있다. 자세한 행사 내용과 스케줄은 한국민속촌 홈페이지(www.koreanfolk.co.kr)에서 확인할 수 있다.

1. ______ 관람객들은 영화나 드라마찍는 것을 볼 수 있다.
2. ______ 관람객들은 드라마에 직접 나올 수도 있다.
3. ______ 행사 기간동안 관람객들은 배우들을 만날 기회가 있다.
4. ______ 행사 기간 후에는 공연이 있다.

Words & Expressions

01-04 열리다 to be held 행사 기간 event period 관람객 visitor 진행되다 (something) goes on 현장 site 특수분장 special makeup 의상 costumes 제공되다 to be provided 예정 schedule 화려한 splendid 자세한 detailed 확인하다 to check

외국인들이 한국어를 배우는 이유 (Reasons for foreigners to learn Korean)

※ (5-6) 다음 글을 읽고 물음에 답하십시오.

최근 한국에서 한국어를 공부하는 외국인들이 늘어나고 있다. (㉠) 외국인들이 한국어를 배우는 이유를 알아보기 위해 한 신문사에서 한국에서 공부하는 외국인 대학생들 1,000명에게 설문 조사를 하였다. (㉡) 그리고 자국에서 취업(27%), 한국에서 대학원 진학(23%), K-pop, K-drama 등 한류 콘텐츠를 즐기기 위해(18%), 한국 친구를 사귀기 위해(11%) 등이 뒤를 이었다. (㉢) 한국어를 공부하는 효과적인 방법으로는 한국인과의 대화, 드라마나 예능 프로그램 보기, 노래듣기, 매일 일기쓰기 등 다양한 답변이 있었다. (㉣)

5. 다음 문장이 들어갈 곳을 고르십시오.

조사 결과에 따르면 한국에서 취업(38%)이 외국인들이 한국어를 공부하는 가장 큰 이유로 나타났다.

① ㉠ ② ㉡ ③ ㉢ ④ ㉣

6. 이 글의 내용과 같은 것을 고르십시오.

① 한국어를 배워서 한국에서 일하고 싶어하는 외국인들이 많다.
② 한국어를 배우는 가장 큰 이유는 한류이다.
③ 조사를 한 외국인들은 대학에 가기 위해 공부하는 학생들이다.
④ 대부분 사람들이 한국 드라마를 보면서 한국어를 공부한다.

05-06 늘어나다 to increase 신문사 newspaper publishing company 설문 조사 survey
자국 one's own country 취업 getting a job 진학 entering into a higher level of school
뒤를 잇다 to follow 효과적인 effective 방법 method; 대화 conversation 일기 diary
다양한 diverse 답변 response

7 인터넷으로 집 알아보고 있었어요.

I was searching for a house on the internet.

-Talking about housing options for college students
-Talking about pros and cons

Preparation & Practice	
	I. New Words & Expressions II. Patterns, Expressions & Practice 1. ~은/~는 편이다 "to tend to ~; It is more the case of~ than the other" 2. ~보다 (더/덜) "(more/less) ... than ~" 3. ~아야/어야 할지 모르다 "to not know whether ... have to ~"

	III. Culture 1. Housing options for college students 2. Apartment in Korea
Conversation Activities	IV. Listen & Discuss V. Guided Conversation VI. Spontaneous Conversation
TOPIK Preparation	VII. Listening • Conversation 1 • Conversation 2
	VIII. Reading • Looking for a room • Housing options for college students

I. New Words & Expressions

 **Study the words and expressions along with the audio.** 

NOUN

가구	furniture
방값	room rent
보증금	security deposit
부동산(사무소)	real estate office
화장실	bathroom; restroom

VERB

구하다	to find (something)
나오다	to come out (from a place); move out (from a place) *(a place)에서 나오다
알아보다	to search (a thing)
옮기다	to move (to a place) *(a place)으로/로 옮기다

ADJECTIVE

안전하다	to be safe

PRONOUN

니 you (as in 니가 used in the subject position of a sentence)

*니 is a variant of the standard counterpart 너. Note that when 너 is used in the subject position in a sentence, 네가 (not 너가) is correct.

EXPRESSION

·그렇겠네요! That must be so!

Listen to the audio and fill in the blanks. 

1. A: 저 지금 인터넷으로 집 ____________________고 있어요.

   B: 왜? 이번 학기 마치고 기숙사에서 나오려고?

2. A: 기숙사에서 룸메이트하고 같이 방 쓰는 게 불편해서 다음 학기부터는 혼자 살아 보고 싶어요.

   B: 우리 집 근처에 원룸이 하나 있는데, 같이 한번 ____________________?

3. A: 오빠가 살고 있는 원룸은 방값이 얼마예요?

   B: 한달에 50만 원이야. 근데 ____________________1,000만 원이 있어.

4. A: 원룸이 좀 비싸지만, 필요한 ______________ 들도 다 있고 화장실을 혼자 쓰니까 그게 제일 좋더라구.

B: 그렇겠다. 근데 오빠는 그 집 어떻게 ______________?

5. A: 내가 살고 있는 동네는 ______________ 좋아.

B: 혹시 그 동네에 빈 방 있어요?

Exercise 2

Choose the best word to complete the sentences.

1. 어떤 학생들은 1학년 때 기숙사에서 살다가 혼자 생활하기 편한 원룸으로 ______________.

① 구한다 ② 나온다 ③ 안전하다 ④ 옮긴다

2. 대학교 근처 원룸에는 필요한 ______________ 이/가 다 있어서 혼자 생활하는 데 불편한 게 없다.

① 방값 ② 부동산 ③ 연기 ④ 가구

3. 대학교 기숙사는 학교 안에 있어서 학교 다니기 편하고 ______________.

① 안타깝다 ② 쉽지 않다 ③ 안전하다 ④ 운이 좋다

4. 한국 대학생들은 인터넷으로 집을 알아보기도 하지만, 시간이 없을 때는 부동산에서 집을 ______________.

① 안타깝다 ② 쉽지 않다 ③ 이사간다 ④ 알아본다

5. 졸업하기 전에 학교 근처에 있는 원룸에서 살아 보고 싶은데, ______________ 이/가 너무 비싸서 그냥 학교 기숙사에서 계속 살기로 했다.

① 화장실 ② 자막 ③ 배경 ④ 보증금

II. Patterns, Expressions & Practice

1. ~은/~는/~ㄴ 편이다 "… tend to ~ ; It is more the case of ~ than the other"

Usage

Use "**~은/~는/~ㄴ 편이다**" to express "tend to ~" or "It is more the case of ~ than the other." "**편**" is a noun, meaning "side; team." Thus, "**~은/~는/~ㄴ 편이다**" literally means "to be on the side/team."

Form

present noun-modifying form NOUN

- ▶ Verb base + 는 편이다 : 이해하는 **편이다**
- ▶ Adjective base (ending in consonants) + 은 편이다 : 많은 **편이다**
- Adjective base (ending in vowels) + ㄴ 편이다 : 비싼 **편이다**

Note

"Conjugate ㄹ/ㅂ-ending" irregular verbs and adjectives as follows.

- 알-다 (verb) → 아 +는 편이다 → 아는 편이다
- 멀-다 (adjective) → 머 +ㄴ 편이다 → 먼 편이다
- 춥-다 (adjective) → 추 + 우 + ㄴ 편이다 → 추운 편이다

For the conjugation rule of "ㄹ" irregular verbs/adjectives, see Appendix V,2.
For the conjugation rule of "ㅂ" irregular verbs/adjectives, see Appendix V,3.

Look at the following examples.

- A: 한국 대학생들은 어떻게 집을 찾아요?
  B: 주로 인터넷으로 집을 알아보**는 편이에요**.
  They tend to search for housing on the internet.
- A: 저는 여행 가면 사진을 많이 찍**는 편이에요**.
  I tend to take lots of pictures while traveling.
  B: 저도 여행은 좋아하는데, 사진 찍는 건 싫어해서 사진이 별로 없어요.
- A: 새로 이사한 동네는 어때?
  B: 동네가 조용하고 안전**한 편이라서 좋아**.
  I like it because it tends to be quiet and safe.

● A: 내 룸메이트는 주말에 집에 없는 **편이야**.

My roommate tends not to be at home on weekends.

B: 좋겠다. 나도 가끔 혼자 있고 싶은데, 내 룸메이트는 항상 집에 있어.

Using ~은/~는/~ㄴ 편이다, answer the questions.

1. A: 영화 보는 거 좋아하세요?

   B: ____.
   (to like; to watch often; to not like very much…)

2. A: 요즘 샌프란시스코 날씨는 어때요?

   B: ____.
   (to be warm; to be cloudy; to rain often; to be cold)

3. A: 주말에 시간 있으면, 보통 뭐 하세요?

   B: ____.
   (to walk at a park; to make bread; to watch dramas…)

4. A: 새로 오신 한국어 선생님은 어떤 분이세요?

   B: ____.
   (to be tall; voice is nice; to be kind…)

Exercise 2

Using ~은/~는/~ㄴ 편이다, answer the questions.

1. A: 저녁은 어디서 먹어요?

   B: 가끔 식당에서 사 먹기도 하는데, ______________________________.

2. A: 나도 다음 학기에 들을까 하는데, 수학 수업은 어때?

   B: 음... ______________________________지만, 시험은 그렇게 어렵지 않아.

3. A: 학교 갈 때 어떤 옷을 자주 입어요?

   B: ____________________어/아서 ______________________________.

4. A: 지금 사는 동네는 어때요?

B: 다 좋은데, ____.

5. A: 어떤 음악을 자주 들으세요?

B: 저는 ____.

Exercise 3

Listen to the conversation between two friends and mark each statement T(rue) or F(alse). 68

1. ______ The man usually eats at home.

2. ______ The woman suggests to the man to watch a cooking channel on Youtube.

useful expressions

집밥	homemade meal
동영상	video clip

Exercise 4

Listen to the conversation between two friends and mark each statement T(rue) or F(alse). 69

1. ______ The woman usually watches a baseball game on TV.

2. ______ The man suggests to the woman to watch the final match at home together.

useful expressions

결승전	final match

Exercise 5

Listen to the dialogue and answer the questions in Korean. 70

1. What are the woman's eating habits like?

____.

2. Why does the woman not have lunch?

____.

2. NOUN + 보다 (더/덜) ~ "(more/less) ~ than + NOUN"

Usage Use "NOUN +보다 (더/덜) ..." to compare one item (i.e., NOUN 1) in a higher/lower degree to the other (i.e., NOUN 2).

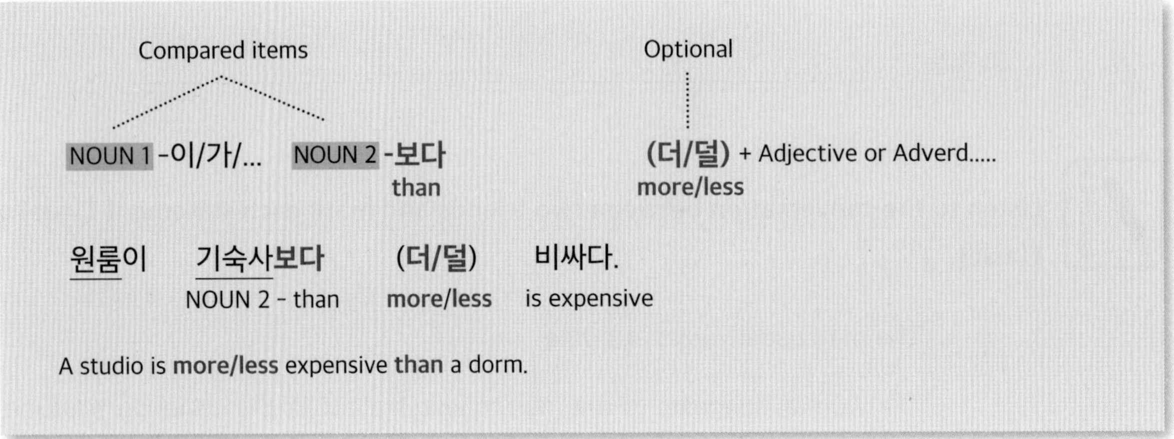

Look at the following examples.

● A: 나는 역사 드라마가 로맨틱 드라마보다 더 재미있어.
NOUN 1 NOUN 2
I am more interested in historical dramas than romantic dramas.

B: 진짜? 나는 좀 지루하던데.

● A: 너, 오늘 집 알아보러 부동산사무소에 들를 거지? 언제 나갈 거야?

B: 부동산보다 인터넷으로 집을 알아보는 편이 더 편해서, 오늘은 하루 종일 집에 있을 계획이야.
NOUN 2 NOUN 1

It is more convenient to search for a house on the Internet than in a real estate office, so I will be home all day.

*You can switch NOUN 1 and NOUN 2. However, make sure to attach the marker "보다" after NOUN 2.

● A: 이번 한국시리즈에서는 두산이 삼성을 이기겠지?

B: 뭐? 나는 삼성이 야구를 더 잘 한다고 들었는데? 말도 안 돼!
NOUN 1

What? I heard that 삼성 plays baseball better (than 두산). No way!
NOUN 1 NOUN 2

*In B's reply, NOUN 2 is dropped because it is understood from A's sentence.

● A: 나는 주중보다 주말에 잠을 덜 자.
NOUN 1 NOUN 2

I sleep less on weekends than on weekdays.

B: 너, 주말마다 한국 드라마 보느라고 못 자는 거지?

Compare two items, using either -보다 더/덜, as shown in example (1).

1.

$200
(구두)

$50
(운동화)

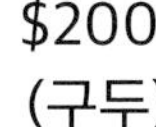

운동화**보다** 구두가 **더** 비싸다 .

(*Use your own words for the adjective/adverb and, if needed, other parts of the sentence.)

2.

(로스엔젤레스)

(시애틀)

______________________________.

3.

(a dormitory)

(an apartment)

______________________________.

4.

(driving a car)

(taking a bus)

____.

5.

(high school)

(college)

____.

6.

(a library)

(a restaurant)

____.

Using the information given below, complete the sentences to compare 우리 원룸, with 서울 원룸.

서울 원룸	우리 원룸
•학교까지 걸어서 5분 •세탁기, 냉장고, 침대 •월 53만/ 보증금 500만	•학교까지 걸어서 10분 •세탁기, 냉장고, 침대, 에어컨, 인터넷, 케이블 TV •월 60만/ 보증금 350만

1. 우리 원룸의 월세는 ______________________________.

2. 보증금은 ______________________________.

3. 학교까지는 ______________________________.

4. 가구는 ______________________________.

Describe the difference between two rooms and the persons who use them, using the target expression (either -보다 더 or 보다 덜) and the information in the (parenthesis).

(현수 방)

(제니 방)

1. (지저분해 보이다 to look unclean)
현수 방은 제니 방보다 더 지저분해 보여요. or 제니 방은 현수 방보다 덜 지저분해 보여요.

2. (물건들이 많다 there are many items)
______________________________.

3. (바쁜 것 같다 to seem busy)
______________________________.

4. (비싸 보이다 to look expensive)
______________________________.

5. (부지런해 보이다 to look diligent)
______________________________.

Listen to the conversation between two friends and mark each statement T(rue) or F(alse). 71

1. ______ The man's rent is cheaper than the woman's.

2. ______ The man's security deposit was cheaper than the woman's.

3. ~아야/~어야 할지 모르다 "to not know whether ... have to ~"

Usage

Use **~아야/~어야 할지 모르다** when you express that you do not know what to do in a given context. This pattern is often used with a question word such as 뭐 (what), 언제(when), 어떻게 (how), 어디(where).

This pattern consists of two expressions:(1) **~아야/~어야 하다** (have to ~) which is used to express the speaker's obligation, and (2) **~을/ㄹ지 모르다** (don't know whether ~) which is used to express a speaker's uncertainty about what will happen in the future.

Form

- ▶ Verb base (ending in 아 or 오) + **아야 할지 모르다** (e.g., 팔**아야 할지 모르다**)
- ▶ Verb base (ending in other vowels) + **어야 할지 모르다** (e.g., 먹**어야 할지 모르다**)

Look at the following examples.

- 내일이 마크 생일인데 무슨 선물을 줘**야 할지 모르겠어요**.
  Tomorrow is Mark's birthday, but I don't know what present I should give him.

- 학생: 다음 학기에 무슨 수업을 들**어야 할지 몰라서** 선생님께 여쭤 보고 싶습니다.
  I don't know what class I should take, so I want to ask you.
  선생님: 좋아요. 1시에 오피스로 올래요?

- A: 생일 축하해. 선물이야.
  B: 어머, 너무 고맙습니다. 이렇게 좋은 선물을.... 어떻게 감사드**려야 할지 모르겠어요**.
  I don't know how to thank you.

Fill in the blanks to make the dialogues natural, using ~아야/~어야 할지 모르다.

1. A: 오늘 영화를 보러 가면 어떨까요?
   B: 좋아요. 그런데 요즘 재미있는 영화가 많아서 ______________.

2. A: 제가 새 전화기를 사고 싶은데 갤럭시하고 아이폰 중에서 ______________.
   B: 인터넷에 리뷰가 많으니까 잘 읽어 보고 결정하세요.

3. A: 우리 집에서 파티를 하는데 어떤 음식을 ______________________.

   B: 그냥 친구들한테 음식을 조금씩 가지고 오라고 하세요.

4. A: 남자 친구가 결혼을 하자고 하는데 ______________________.

   B: 축하해요! 고민하지 말고 그냥 결혼하세요.

5. A: 서울에 사흘 동안 여행을 가는데 ______________________.

   B: 시간이 많이 없지만 역사를 좋아하시니까 경복궁이랑 국립 박물관에는 꼭 가 보세요.

Exercise 11

Complete each dialogue, using ~아야/~어야 할지 모르다 to express the information in the parenthesis.

1. (Situation: You don't know what you have to wear for tomorrow's interview.)

   You: ______________________.

   Your friend: 단정한 정장을 입고 가세요.

2. (Situation: You don't know what you should buy for your friend's birthday.)

   You: ______________________.

   Your friend: K-pop 콘서트 티켓은 어떨까요?

3. (Situation: You are in a restaurant and you are not sure what food you should eat.)

   You: ______________________.

   Your friend: 이 식당은 비빔밥이 맛있으니까 비빔밥을 먹어 봐.

4. (Situation: You used up all your money and don't know what to do.)

   You: ______________________.

   Your friend: 그냥 엄마한테 돈을 달라고 하세요.

5. (Situation: You don't know what to do after graduation.)

   Your friend: 졸업하고 나서 뭐 할지 정했어요?

   You: 글쎄요. 아직 ______________________.

6. (Situation: You don't know if you should take a summer course.)

Your friend: 이번 여름학기에도 수업 들을 거죠?

You: 글쎄요. 아직 ______________________________.

Listen to the conversations and mark each statement T(rue) or F(alse). 

1. ______ The woman is currently living in a dorm.
2. ______ The woman wants to move to a dorm.
3. ______ The studio apartments near the school are not very expensive.
4. ______ The man is living in a studio apartment.

Listen to the conversation between two friends and mark each statement T(rue) or F(alse).

1. ______ The woman decided what to wear.
2. ______ The woman is thinking of wearing a red dress.
3. ______ Today's gathering is a formal one.
4. ______ The man will wear jeans and a t-shirt.

III. Culture

1. 대학생들의 주거 형태 (Housing options for college students)

Many Korean college students live with their parents, but if their homes are far from school, they have to find somewhere to live near school. The most popular types of residence for Korean college students are **하숙집**, **고시원**, and **오피스텔/원룸**.

하숙집

In **하숙집**, or boarding house, you can have your own room but share the **부엌** (kitchen) and **화장실** (bathroom). **하숙집** provides you with two meals a day (**아침** and **저녁**) and some places even do your **빨래** (laundry) for you. **하숙집** used to be a very popular housing option because it was the most affordable, but students nowadays prefer a more private lifestyle.

고시원 (고시텔)

고시원 or **고시텔** is a building with lots of small rooms for rent. **고시원** room has a structure similar to a university dorm. Depending on the quality of **고시원**, you can have a private or shared **화장실**. The kitchen may also be shared, and is equipped with basic appliances. Some **고시원** provide their tenants with free **밥** and **김치**.

오피스텔, 원룸

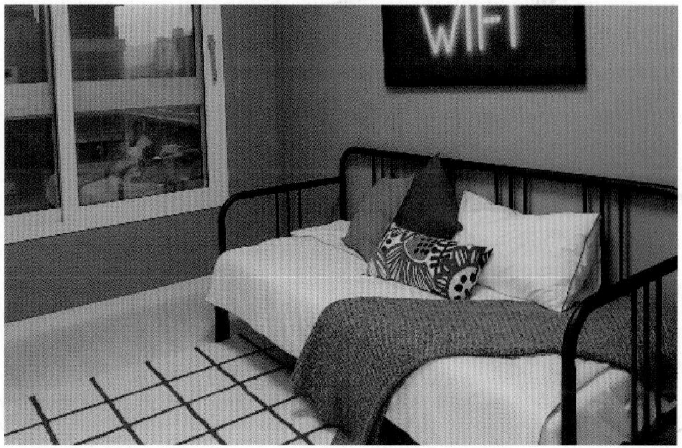

오피스텔 (Officetel) is a multi-purpose building for residential or commercial use. It is similar to **원룸** (one room), which is a type of a studio apartment. Renting **오피스텔** or **원룸** is burdensome because you have to put down a big **보증금** (security deposit), ranging from approximately $5,000 ~ $15,000, in addition to paying **월세** (monthly rent) ($300~$500) and utilities.

Culture

2. 한국의 아파트 (Apartments in Korea)

The most common and preferred type of residence in Korea is **아파트**. **아파트** is a loan word that comes from the English word "apartment," and it refers to common housing with five stories or more. The Korean **아파트** is more likes a condominium in America, where each unit is privately owned by a household. In big cities like **서울** and **부산**, **아파트** are concentrated and organized into **아파트 단지**(residential and commercial complexes), which are very convenient to live in because they generally include many facilities such as supermarkets, convenience stores, fitness centers and even daycare centers. Since many people want to live in such apartments, more and more high-rise apartment complexes have emerged recently in metropolitan areas.

IV. Listen & Discuss

현수 finds 제니 sitting alone on a bench on campus and starts talking to her.

First, listen to the conversation. With your classmates, discuss the answers to the questions that follow. Finally, write each answer in a full Korean sentence in the space provided.

1. 제니는 지금 무엇을 하고 있습니까?

2. 제니는 어떤 집을 알아보고 있습니까?

3. 현수가 사는 곳은 어떻습니까?

4. 현수는 원룸이 기숙사보다 어떤 점이 좋다고 생각합니까?

5. 현수는 왜 제니와 부동산에 같이 가려고 합니까?

Script

현수 finds 제니 sitting alone on a bench on campus and talks to her.

01 현수: 제니야, 여기서 뭐해?

02 제니: 어, 현수 오빠. 인터넷으로 집 알아보고 있었어요.

03 현수: 왜? 기숙사에서 나오려고?

04 제니: 네, 학교 근처 원룸으로 옮기려고요. 오빠가 사는 원룸은 어때요?

05 현수: 학교까지 걸어서 10분밖에 안 걸리고, 동네가 안전한 편이라서 좋아.[II.1]

06 제니: 방값은 얼마나 해요?

07 현수: 한 달에 50만 원이야. 보증금 1,000만 원 하고.

08 제니: 보증금이 뭔데요?

09 현수: security deposit같은 거야.

10 제니: 아~. 가구는 다 있어요?

11 현수: 응. 그리고 원룸이 기숙사보다 좀 비싸지만,[II.2]화장실을 혼자 쓰니까 그게 제일 좋더라구.

12 제니: 그렇겠네요. 근데, 오빠는 그 집 어떻게 구했어요?

13 현수: 학교 앞에 부동산이 있는데, 거기서 구했어. 너도 거기 한번 가 볼래?

14 제니: 네. 근데 거기 가서 뭘 물어봐야 할지 잘 모르겠어요.[II.3]

15 현수: 걱정 마. 내가 도와줄게. 오늘 수업 끝나고 같이 가 보자.

01 현수: What are you doing here, Jenny?

02 제니: Oh, Hyunsoo. I was searching for a house on the Internet.

03 현수: Why? Do you intend to move out of the dorm?

04 제니: Yes, I plan to move to a studio near our school. How do you like your studio?

05 현수: It's good because it takes only ten minutes to walk to school and my neighborhood tends to be safe.

06 제니: How much is the room price?

07 현수: It's 500,000 a month. 보증금 is ₩10,000,000.

08 제니: What is 보증금?

09 현수: It is kind of a security deposit.

10 제니: Oh~. Is it furnished?

11 현수: Yes. My studio is a little more expensive than a dorm, but I feel it's much better to have my own bathroom.

12 제니: You bet. How did you find that studio anyway?

13 현수: There's a real estate office in front of our school. I found it there. Will you go there, too?

14 제니: Yes. But I don't know what questions I should ask there.

15 현수: Don't worry. I'll help you. Let's go together after class today.

V. Guided Conversation

Keeping in mind the organization of the model conversation in Listen & Discuss (Script), practice the modified conversation below with your partner.

Sitting on a bench alone, Speaker B is searching for something on his/her phone. Speaker A, passing by, strikes up a conversation.

Practice the following conversation with your partner, using the prompts in (parenthesis) to fill in the blanks and make the conversation flow naturally.

01 A: 너 여기서 뭐 하고 있니?

02 B: 집 알아보려고 인터넷 보고 있어.

03 A: 왜? __________ 려고?
(학교/회사 기숙사에서 나오다; 학교/회사 기숙사에서 이사하다)

04 B: 응, __________ 아서/어서
(방을 같이 쓰는 게 불편하다; 공용 화장실을 사용하는 게 불편하다; 비싸다; 요리하기가 싫다; ...)

05 __________ 근처 __________ 으로/로 옮기려고 해.
(학교; 회사) (원룸/오피스텔; 고시원/하숙집; ...)

06 니가 사는 __________ 은/는 어때?
(원룸/오피스텔; 고시원/하숙집; ...)

07 A: __________ 고 __________ 아서/어서/(이)라서 좋아.
(학교/회사까지 걸어서 10분밖에 안 걸리다; 동네가 안전한 편이다; 화장실을 혼자 쓰다; 동네가 조용한 편이다; 식사를 제공해 주다; 교통이 편한/좋은 편이다; 필요한 가구가 다 있다; 싼 편이다; ...)

Guided Conversation

08 B: 방값은 얼마나 해?

09 A: ______________ 보다 좀 비싼 편인데[II.1,2]
(학교 기숙사; 회사 기숙사)

10 한 달에 ______________ 만 원이야. 보증금 ______________ 만 원하고.
(50; 40; 30) (천; 백; 오십;...)

11 B: 그렇구나. 근데, 너는 그 집 어떻게 구했어?

12 A: ______________ 에서 구했어.
(학교 앞 부동산; 인터넷)

13 B: ______________ 고 싶은데/고 있는데, ______________ 지 모르겠어.[II.3]
(나도 부동산에 가 보다; 나도 지금 인터넷에서 알아보다) (가서 뭘 물어 봐야 하다; 어떻게 찾아야 하다)

14 A: 걱정마. 내가 도와줄게. 오늘 수업 끝나고 ______________ 자.
(같이 가 보다; 같이 알아보다)

(Switch roles and continue to practice.)

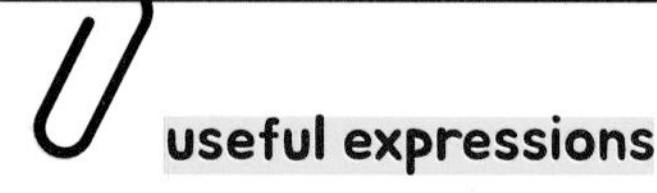

L04 공용 화장실 shared bathroom;
요리하기가 싫다 to hate cooking
L07 식사를 제공해 주다 to provide meals

Present the conversation above in front of the class. Try not to look at your paper!

VI. Spontaneous Conversation

This is your chance to have a realistic interaction with your classmates in Korean. You can practice writing, speaking with your classmates, and presenting in front of the class!

You and your classmate currently live in different types of housing. You live in a dorm, while your classmate lives in another housing close to campus. Recently you are thinking about changing your housing situation. After comparing the conditions of your dorm with those of your classmate's housing, decide either to move out from your dorm or to stay.
Create a meaningful conversation with your partner similar to the one that you practiced in the Guided Conversation!

- Ask your classmate what type of housing (s)he currently lives in.
  (Refer to III. Culture for various housing types for college students.)
- Tell your classmate why you plan to move out from your dorm.
- Compare various conditions of your dorm with those of your friend's type of housing, such as rent, security deposit, available appliances, roommate, distance from campus, and transportation.
- Discuss the best way to find your housing (e.g., getting help from your classmate or a realtor).
- Try to include **~은/~는/~ㄴ 편이다; -보다 (더/덜), ~아야/~어야 할지 모르다** in your conversation.

Write down the conversation you had with your partner in Step 1.

Step 3

Now you are living in Seoul and your American friend is coming to Korea next semester as an exchange student. S/he needs your advice for housing. Based on the conversation in Step 2, write a letter to your friend providing information s/he may need when choosing between different housing options. Finally, recommend a type of housing to him/her. Use the ~아 speech style.

Present what you wrote in Step 2 in front of the class. Try not to look at your paper!

VII. Listening

Listen to the conversation between two friends and answer the questions. 75

1. 다음 중 남자의 중심생각(main point)으로 맞는 것을 고르십시오.
   ① 학교 앞 원룸은 비싸다.
   ② 남자의 집이 학교에서 멀어서 불편하다.
   ③ 자취하는 것은 힘들다.
   ④ 부모님께 감사해야 한다.

2. 윗 글의 내용과 같은 것을 고르십시오.
   ① 여자는 부모님과 함께 살고 있다.
   ② 남자는 싼 곳으로 이사하고 싶다.
   ③ 여자의 집은 학교 앞에 있다.
   ④ 남자는 자취하는 것을 좋아한다.

Listen to the following conversation and answer the questions. 76

3. 남자가 살고 있는 오피스텔은 어떻다고 했습니까?

   ______________________________.

4. 여자는 왜 오피스텔로 이사하고 싶어하지 않습니까?

   ______________________________.

5. 여자는 왜 하숙집이 더 좋다고 했습니까?

   ______________________________.

Words & Expressions

01-02 구하다 to look for, seek 자취(를) 하다 to live apart from one's own family; to board oneself
지방 the provinces outside of metropolitan area 떨어진 곳 remote place
자유롭게 freely

VIII. Reading

방 구하기 (Looking for a room)

2호선 신촌역 근처 원룸 있습니다

- ■ 신촌역 1번 출구에서 걸어서 5분 거리
- ■ OO쇼핑센터, XX마트 근처
- ■ 방 2개, 욕실 1개, 넓은 거실
- ■ 에어컨 설치
- ■ 세탁실 공용
- ■ 보증금 1,200만 원/월세 50만 원 (인터넷 포함)

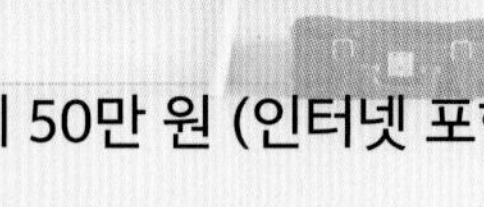

1. 윗 글의 내용과 다른 것을 고르십시오.

   ① 이 원룸은 지하철 역에서 가깝다.

   ② 이 원룸에 살면 쇼핑하러 가기에 편리하다.

   ③ 자기 원룸에서 빨래를 할 수 있다.

   ④ 이 원룸에 살면 인터넷 요금은 따로 안 내도 된다.

---

01 출구 exit 욕실 bathroom 거실 living room 설치 installation 세탁실 laundry room
공용 common use 월세 monthly rent 포함 included

서울 고시원

홍대역 5분, 버스 정류장 1분 거리

개인 화장실, 샤워 시설

각 방 텔레비전 설치

인터넷, 에어컨 포함

남녀 층 분리

공용 부엌, 휴게실, 세탁실

1인실: 월 30만 원, 2인실: 월 50만 원

2. 윗 글의 내용과 다른 것을 고르십시오.

① 이 고시원은 교통이 편리하다.

② 이 고시원은 방마다 욕실이 있다.

③ 인터넷 요금은 따로 내야 한다.

④ 이 고시원에서는 두 사람이 방을 같이 쓸 수 있다.

Words & Expressions

02 개인 private, individual 시설 facilities 분리 separation 휴게실 lounge 1인실 room for one person 2인실 room for two persons

대학생들의 주거 형태 (Housing options for college students)

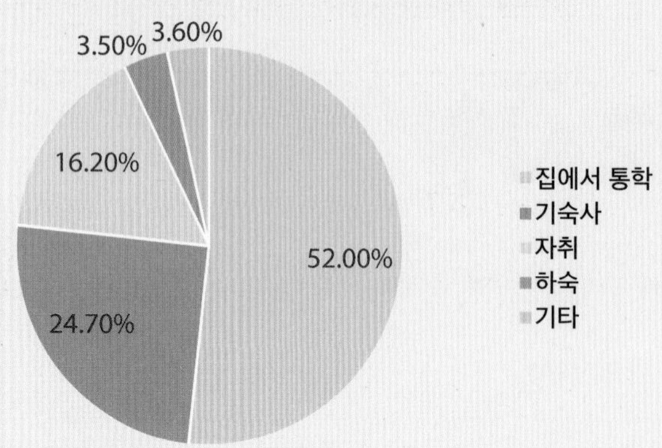

한국대학교 대학 신문의 설문 조사 결과에 따르면 한국 대학교 학생 중 절반 정도가 집에서 통학을 하고 24.7%가 기숙사에 사는 것으로 나타났다. 2년 전 설문 조사에서는 자취를 하는 학생이 21%, 하숙집에 사는 학생이 7.5%였지만, 이번 조사에서는 각각 16.2%, 3.5%로 줄어들었다. 한 학생에 따르면 많은 학생들이 혼자 살기를 원하지만 원룸이나 오피스텔의 보증금과 월세가 계속 비싸지기 때문에 실제로 자취를 할 수 있는 학생은 많지 않다고 답했다. 그리고 하숙은 개인 생활을 중요시하는 요즘 대학생들이 선호하지 않는 것으로 나타났다.

3. 위의 글의 내용과 같은 것을 고르십시오.

① 자취를 하는 학생들이 늘어나고 있다.

② 자취를 하려면 돈이 많이 든다.

③ 집에서 통학을 하는 학생들이 줄어들고 있다.

④ 하숙이 싸서 하숙을 하는 학생들이 많아지고 있다.

03 주거 형태 residence type 설문 조사 survey 결과 result ~에 따르면 according to ~ 절반 half
통학 commute to school 나타나다 to appear 각각 each; respectively 줄어들다 to decrease
실제로 in reality 개인 생활 private life 중요시하다 to consider something important
선호하다 to prefer

Answer keys
&
Appendices

Answer keys

Lesson 1

I. New Words & Expressions (P.13)

Exercise 1

1. 사회학과 2. 이쪽 3. 도와줄 거예요 4. 인사하세요
5. 반 년 6. 유학생 7. 도움

Exercise 2

1. ② 2. ④ 3. ④ 4. ④ 5. ②

II. Patterns, Expressions & Practice (P.15)

Exercise 1

Answers may vary.
1. 지호: 김지호라고 해요. or 김지호라는 사람이에요.
   린다: 린다 존슨이라고 해요. or
   린다 존슨이라는 사람이에요.
2. 그 스포츠는 태권도라고 해요. or
   태권도라고 하는 스포츠예요.
3. 김세훈이라고 하는 컴퓨터 프로그래머
4. 된장국이라고 하는or 된장국이라는; 순두부찌개라고 하는 or 순두부찌개라는; 비빔밥이라고 하는 or 비빔밥이라는 ; 해물파전이라고 하는 or 해물파전이라는

Exercise 2

2. 요리사라고 합니다. or 요리사라고 해요.
3. 취미라고 합니다. or 취미라고 해요.
4. 기자라고 합니다. or 기자라고 해요.
5. 이틀이라고 합니다. or 이틀이라고 해요.
6. 유학생이라고 합니다. or 유학생이라고 해요.

Exercise 3

Answers may vary.
1. "name of food"(이)라고 하는 or "name of food"(이)라는
2. "학생회"라고 하는 or "학생회"라는
3. "서촌"이라고 하는 or "서촌"이라는
4. "a professor's name"(이)라고 하는 or
   "a professor's name"(이)라는
5. "name of library"라고 하는 or "name of library"라는

Exercise 4

1. F 2. T 3. T

Exercise 5

Answers may vary.
2. 들은 지/배운 지 1년이 됐어요.
3. 쓴 지 6개월 (or 반 년, 여섯 달)이 됐어요.
4. 본 지 2주가 됐어요.
5. 산 지 한 달이 됐어요.
6. 들은 지 (or 듣기 시작한 지) 3년이 됐어요.

Exercise 6

Answers may vary.
2. B: 졸업한 지 2년 됐어요.
3. B: 가 본 지 1년 정도 됐어요.
4. B: 한국어 수업을 들은 지 1년 반 됐어요.
5. B: 웨이 씨를 안 지 거의 5년 됐어요.
6. B: 한국에 산 지 8년이 다 됐어요.

Exercise 7

1. F 2. F

Exercise 8

1. 세 권밖에 없어요.
2. 여동생밖에 없어요.
3. 천 원밖에 없어요.
4. 세 과목밖에 안 들어요.
5. 밖에 몰라요.

Exercise 9

1. T 2. F

Exercise 10

1. F 2. F

Exercise 11

Answers may vary.
2. 수업에 가기 전에 숙제를 했어요. or
   숙제한 후에 수업에 갔어요.
3. 약을 먹기 전에 식사를 했어요. or 식사 후에 약을 먹었어요.
4. 수영을 하기 전에 준비 운동을 했어요. or
   준비 운동을 한 후에 수영을 했어요.
5. 졸업을 하기 전에 취직을 했어요. or
   취직한 후에 졸업을 했어요.
6. 자기 전에 양치질을 했어요. or
   양치질 한 후에 잤어요.

Exercise 12

Answers may vary.

Exercise 13

1. T 2. T 3. F 4. F

IV. Listen & Discuss (P.31)

Answers may vary.
1. 현수는 선배이고 웨이는 후배입니다. or
   현수는 웨이(의) 선배입니다. or
   웨이는 현수(의) 후배입니다.
2. 한국에 온 지 일주일밖에 안 됐습니다.
   (or 일주일 전에 왔습니다.)
3. 한국에 온 지 일 년이 됐습니다.
   (or 일 년 전에 왔습니다.)
4. 웨이가 도와줄 거예요.

VII. Listening (P.39)

1. ④ 2. T 3. F 4. T 5. F

VIII. Reading (P.40)

1. ④ 2. ③ 3. ②

Lesson 2

I .New Words & Expressions (P.43)

Exercise 1

1. 견학; 보령머드축제 2. 전주 한옥 마을 3. 한옥; 생각보다
4. 공연 5. 어울려

Exercise 2

1. ② 2. ③ 3. ③ 4. ④ 5. ④

II. Patterns, Expressions & Practice (P.45)

Exercise 1

1. (1) 어땠니/어땠냐? (2) 알았니/알았냐?
2. (1) 오니?/오냐? (2) 봐라 (3) 사자
(4) 얼마니?/얼마냐? (5) 가자

Exercise 2

(1) 하기로 했다 (2) 갔다 (3) 만날 것이다 (4) 기다려진다

Exercise 3

웨이: 전주한옥마을에서 재미있었어?
제니: 네, 한옥들도 예쁘고 맛집도 많이 있어서 너무 좋았어.
→ 응 (or 어)
웨이: 잠은 어디서 잤어?
한옥 마을에 호텔도 있었습니까?
→ 있었어? (or 있었니? 있었냐?)
제니: 아뇨. 그런데 호텔처럼 돈을 내고 묵을 수 있는 한옥들이
→ 아니
있어서 한옥에서 묵었어.
웨이: 아~ 그랬어요? 어땠어?
→ 그랬어? (or 그랬니?그랬냐?)
제니: 첫째 날은 좀 불편했는데, 둘째 날부터는 괜찮았어.
그리고 아침 식사도 나왔는데,
정말 맛있었습니다.
→맛있었어. (or 맛있었다.)
웨이: 저도 한번 가 보고 싶다.
→ 나
제니: 서울에도 한옥 마을이 있는데, 같이 가요!
→가 (or 가자!)
웨이: 그럼 그럽시다.
→ 그래 (or 그러자) *그러-다 "to do so"

Exercise 4

2. 디즈니랜드에서 롤러코스터를 타봤는데 되게 무섭더라고.
3. 저번에 에이미 남자 친구를 만났는데 진짜 잘생겼더라고.
4. 뉴스를 봤는데, 뉴욕에 눈이 많이 왔더라고.
5. 파티에서 떡볶이를 먹어 봤는데 엄청 맵더라고.
6. 학교 앞 식당에 가 봤는데 메뉴에 한국 음식이 있더라고.

Exercise 5

Answers may vary.

2. 뉴욕에 갔는데 차가 정말 많이 막히더라고.
3. 블랙 프라이데이에 쇼핑을 했는데, 텔레비전이 진짜 싸더라고.
4. 한국어 수업을 듣는데 쉽더라고.
5. 영화 배우를 만났는데, 정말 잘생겼더라고.

Exercise 6

Answers may vary.

1. 룸메이트가 저녁을 만들어 줬는데
2. 7월 4일에 시내에 나갔는데
3. 룸메이트하고 방을 같이 쓰는데
4. 제임스는 나이가 많은데도
5. 공부를 많이 했는데도

Exercise 7

1. T 2. T

Exercise 8

1. T 2. F

Exercise 9

1. F 2. F

Exercise 10

1. T 2. F

Exercise 11

Answers may vary. You can also use the reduced form "~(는)군" in your answers.

1. 너 핸드폰 샀구나.or 핸드폰 바꿨구나.
2. 내일 시험이 있구나.
3. 서울에서 전주한옥마을이 정말 가깝구나.
4. 요리를 잘 하는구나.
5. 제니하고 소피아가 룸메이트구나. or 룸메이트였구나.

Exercise 12

Answers may vary. You can also use the reduced form "~(는)군" in your answers.

1. 정말 재미있었겠구나.
2. 스트레스가 많겠군요.
3. 정말 슬프겠군요.
4. 축하해요! 결혼 준비 때문에 바쁘겠군요.
5. 한국어를 많이 배우겠구나./공부하겠구나.

Exercise 13

1. T 2. T 3. T 4. F

IV. Listen & Discuss (P.61)

Answers may vary.

1. 민지는 보령 머드 축제에, 웨이는 DMZ에, 제니는 전주 한옥 마을에 갔다 왔습니다.
2. 사람들이 걸어 다니는 것이 다 보입니다.
3. 머드축제에 가서 K-pop공연을 봤습니다.
4. 한복을 입고 사진도 찍고, 온돌방에서 잤습니다.
5. 제니가 생각한 것보다 편했습니다.

VII. Listening (P.69)

1. T 2. F 3. T 4. F 5. T 6. F 7. T 8. F

VIII. Reading (P.70)

1. ① 2. ② 3. ①

Lesson 3

I .New Words & Expressions (P.73)

Exercise 1

1. 추석, 고향 2. 표, 표 3. 기차표, 연휴 4. 추석, 추석연휴
5. 송편

Exercise 2

1.② 2.③ 3.④ 4.④ 5.④

II. Patterns, Expressions & Practice (P.75)

Exercise 1

<Option 1> Answers may vary.

1. (브라이언 씨는 한국어를) 잘 못 한다고 했어요.
2. (마크는 어제) 자기/마크 집에서 친구들하고 같이 한국드라마 봤다고 했어. *자기 means 'self' that refers to 마크.
3. (민서는 지금) 열심히 공부하고 있는 중이라고 했어.

*~하는 중이다 → ~하는 중이라고
4. (샤오밍이 나한테) 마크가 파워블로거래.
5. (에이미는) 일주일에 한 번 정도 블로그에 글을 쓸 거라고 했어.
*~을/ㄹ 것이다 → *~을/ㄹ 것이라고; *~을/ㄹ 거다 → *~을/ㄹ거라고

<Option 2> Answers may vary.
You can use "present tense" for reporting verbs.
1. (브라이언 씨는 한국어를) 잘 못한다고 해요 (or 잘 못한대요).
2. (마크는 어제) 자기/마크 집에서 친구들하고 같이 한국 드라마를 봤다고 해 (or 봤대).
3. (민서는 지금) 열심히 공부하고 있는 중이라고 해 (or 열심히 공부하고 있는 중이래).
4. (샤오밍이 나한테) 자기가 파워블로거라고 해 (or 파워블로거래).
5. (에이미는) 일주일에 한 번 정도 블로그에 글을 쓸 거라고 해 (or 글을 쓸 거래).

Exercise 2

<Option 1> Answers may vary.
2. (제니퍼는) 한국에서 일주일 동안 한 여행이 재미있었다고 했어요.
3. (제니퍼는) 한국의 날씨가 생각보다 더웠다고 했어요.
4. (제니퍼는) 서울에서는 지하철하고 버스가 아주 편리해서 차가 필요 없었다고 했어요.
5. (제니퍼는) 자기/제니퍼 가족도 한강에서 치킨을 배달시켰다고 했어요.

<Option 2> Answers may vary. You can use "present tense" for reporting verbs.
2. 고등학교 졸업하고 나서, 가족들하고 같이 일주일 동안 한국을 여행했다고 해요.
3. 여행은 재미있었다고 해요. 그런데 날씨가 생각보다 더웠다고 해요.
4. 서울은 지하철하고 버스가 아주 편리해서 차가 필요 없다고 해요.
5. 한국에서는 공원에서 음식도 주문할 수 있다고 해요.
6. 자기/제니퍼 씨 가족도 한강에서 치킨을 배달시켰다고 해요.

Exercise 3

Your answer may vary.
1. 사람도 엄청 많고 끝내주게 재미있었다고 했어요.
2. 한복을 입고 사진도 찍고 한옥에서 잤다고 했어요.
3. 한국말을 아직 잘 못한다고 했어요.
*You don't need to report the reported speaker's knowledge status that is expressed with "네" in 잘하시네요.
4. 1년 더 일하고 대학원에 갈 거라고 했어요.
*~을/ㄹ 것이다 or ~을/ㄹ 거다 (reduced form) changes to ~을/ㄹ 거라고 하다.
5. 회사를 다녔는데도 아직 공부가 더 필요해서 대학원에서 경영학을 전공한다고 했어요.
6. 생일축하한다고 했어요.
7. 비빔밥하고 불닭이 맛있다고 했어요.

Exercise 4

Answers may vary.
1. (마크가) (저한테) 지금 빨리 가려면 버스 말고 지하철을 타라고 했어요/타랬어요.
2. (민준 씨는) 자기/민준 씨 친구가 되게 잘 생겼는데, (나한테) 한번 만나 보라고 했어요/만나 보래요.
*자기 means "self" that refers to 민준. Do not use ~(으)시 when you report about yourself. Thus, you should say 만나보라고 instead of 만나보시라고.
3. 이 근처에 새로 생긴 한국식당이 있는데 한 번 가 보라고 했어요/가 보래요.
4. 전주한옥마을에 가서, 한복도 입어 보고, 온돌방에도 한번 자 보라고 했어요/자 보랬어요.
5. 온라인 게임을 한번 해 보라고 했어요/해 보랬어요. 스트레스도 풀고 친구도 사귈 수 있는 좋은 기회라고 해요/기회래요.

Exercise 5

1. 옷을 따뜻하게 입고 모자하고 장갑도 가지고 가라고
2. 차를 빌리지 말고 지하철이나 버스를 타라고
3. 시간 있으면 제주도에 꼭 가 보라고

Exercise 6

1. 오후 2시쯤에 문자 보내라고 했어요/말했어요.
2. 자기 친구를 한 번 만나 보라고 했어요.
3. 생일 축하한다고 했어요. 생일 선물을 열어 보라고 했어요.
4. 김밥 좀 드시라고/먹으라고 했어요.
5. 떡볶이를 좀 먹어 보라고 했어요.
*Do not use "~(으)시" when you report about yourself.

Exercise 7

2. 많이 막히지 않았어요.
3. 자지 못 했어요.
4. 어울리지 않는
5. 덥지도 않, 춥지도 않 (or 춥지도 않, 덥지도 않)
6. 먹지 못해요.

Exercise 8

2. 갔다 오지 못했다
3. 참가 못했다
4. 보내지 못하신다
5. 보이지 않는다
6. 안 넘었다

Exercise 9

1. 부모님이 주말에 집에 오시기 때문이에요.
2. 웨이 룸메이트가 주말에 집에 없기 때문이에요.

Exercise 10

1. F 2. F

Exercise 11

1. 저는 밖에 비가 오는 줄 몰랐어요.
2. 저는 서울이 이렇게 추울 줄 몰랐어요.
3. 저는 대학 생활이 이렇게 힘들 줄 몰랐어요.
4. 저는 룸메이트가 자는 줄 알았어요.
5. 저는 오늘 비가 올 줄 몰랐어요.

Exercise 12

1. 도서관에 있는 줄 알았어요.
2. 20살인 줄 몰랐어.
3. 추운 줄 몰랐어. or 추울 줄 몰랐어.

4. 잘하는 줄 몰랐어요.
5. 있는 줄 알았

Exercise 13

1. T 2. F 3. F 4. T

Exercise 14

1. F 2. F 3. F 4. T

Exercise 15

1. T 2. F

IV. Listen & Discuss (P.97)

Answers may vary.

1. 추석 (명절)에 대해서 이야기하고 있다.
2. 표 사기가 쉽지 않다고 들었다.
3. 이번 주말에 내려 간다.
4. 고향에 내려가지 않고 친구들이랑 여행 가기로 했다.
5. 한국 사람들은 다 고향에 가는 줄 알았다.
6. 교수님 댁에 송편을 먹으러 갈 것이다.

VII. Listening (P.105)

1. F 2. T 3. T 4. F
5. 3 days
6. Because many people are going to their hometown
7. Food for 추석 and presents
8. Rice cake shop
9. Clear and cool

VIII. Reading (P.106)

1. ③ 2. ① 3. ③ 4. ④

Lesson 4

I . New Words & Expressions (P.109)

Exercise 1

1. 일정; 사흘 2. 고속버스 3. 지역 4. 교통편
5. 택시 기사님들

Exercise 2

1. ③ 2. ④ 3. ④ 4. ③ 5. ②

II .Patterns, Expressions & Practice (P.111)

Exercise 1

Answers may vary.

2. 테니스를 칠까 해요.
3. 떡국을 먹을까 해요.
4. 탈까 해요. or 타고 갈까 해요.
5. 입을까 해요. or 입어 볼까 해요.

Exercise 2

Answers may vary.

2. 생일카드하고 꽃을 (사) 드릴까 해.
3. 잡채를 만들까 해.
4. 한국 역사 (수업)을 들을까
5. 수영장에 갈까 (or 가 볼까).
6. 초대할까 하
7. 놀까 해 or 놀까 생각해.

Exercise 3

1. F 2. T

Exercise 4

1. F 2. F

Exercise 5

L02 것을 L03 것은 L05 것이

Exercise 6

2. 자는 게 3. 비싼 걸 4. 가는 게 5. 비싼 건

Exercise 7

L03 집에서 파티하는 것을/걸
L04 식당에서 만나는 것이/게 (or 식당에서 만나는 것은/건)
L05 식당 예약하는 것이/게 (or 식당 예약하는 것은/건)
L06 음악 듣는 것을/걸; 이어폰을 사는 것이/게 (or 이어폰을 사는 것은/건)

Exercise 8

1. a. going to Korean students' club
   b. watching Korean dramas
2. She feels uncomfortable when she talks with people she doesn't know.

Exercise 9

Answers may vary.

2. 날씨가 추우니까
3. 저 한국 식당이 맛있으니까
4. 지금은 차가 막히니까
5. 지난 번에 사셨으니까

Exercise 10

2. 제주도에 가 보니까
3. 전화해 보니까
4. 한국 역사 수업을 들어 보니까
5. 먹어 보니까

Exercise 11

1. 없으니까 2. 복잡하니까 3. 가서 4. 일요일이니까
5. 도와주셔서 6. 보니까

Exercise 12

1. T 2. F

Exercise 13

1. 재미있는 경험을 해 볼까 합니다.
2. a. 도서관에서 아르바이트를 해 보라고 합니다.
   b. 기차 여행을 해 보라고 합니다.
3. 방학에는 일하고 싶지 않기 때문입니다.

Exercise 14

Answers may vary.

1. 저는 한국어를 할 줄 알아요.
2. 아니요. 스키를 탈 줄 몰라요.
3. 기타를 칠 줄 알아요. 그리고 피아노를 칠 줄 알아요.
4. 아니요. 한국 음식을 만들 줄 몰라요.
5. 네, 조금 할 줄 알아요. 그런데 잘 못해요.

Exercise 15

Answers may vary.

Exercise 16

Answers may vary.

Exercise 17

1. F 2. F

Exercise 18

1. T 2. T

IV. Listen & Discuss (P.129)

Answers may vary.

1. 편하고 빠르다고 합니다.
2. (고속도로) 휴게소에서 그 지역의 유명한 음식을 먹어볼 수 있는 게 좋다고 했습니다.
3. 비행기를 타고 가려고 합니다.
4. 택시 기사님들이 관광 안내도 해 주는 게 좋다고 합니다.

VII. Listening (P.137)

1. F 2. F 3. F 4. T 5. T
6. F 7. F 8. F 9. T 10. T

VIII. Reading (P.138)

1. ② 2. ② 3. ① 4. ①

Lesson 5

I .New Words & Expressions (P.141)

Exercise 1

1. 한국시리즈 경기 2. 끝까지 3. 역전
4. 안타까웠어 5. 이겼어; 이겼어

Exercise 2

1.③ 2.④ 3.② 4.④ 5. ④

II . Patterns, Expressions & Practice (P.143)

Exercise 1

Answers may vary.

1. 할머니 댁에 가기로 했거든.
2. 그룹 프로젝트 때문에 반 친구들을 만나야 되거든.
3. 야구를 잘 모르거든.
4. 보고서를 써야 되거든.
5. 복잡한 곳을 안 좋아하거든.

Exercise 2

Answers may vary

1. 제가 고양이를 너무 좋아하거든요.
2. 잠을 못 자거든요.
3. 나 혼자 (or 내가) 청소해.
4. 지금 한국어 수업을 듣고 있어요.
5. 장학금을 받았거든요.
6. 혼자 방을 쓰고 싶거든요.

Exercise 3

Answers may vary.

1. 그런데, 버스에 박선생님이 앉아 계셨어요.
2.근데, 문을 닫았더라구요.
3. 시험을 잘 못 봤어.
4. 근데 다리를 다쳤어요.
5. 맛있는 음식을 많이 팔더라고.

Exercise 4

1. Because he has an important test on Monday.
2. She is going to root for the team because she got her leg injured while exercising.

Exercise 5

He thought that he had the psychology exam next Friday but found out that it's tomorrow.

Exercise 6

1. 요즘 바쁘냐고 했어/바쁘냬 or 바쁘냐고 물었어.
2. 마크는 어느 대학교냐고 했어요/ 냬요 or 어느 대학교냐고 물었어요.
3. 저 사람이 누구냐고 했어/누구냬 or 누구냐고 물었어.
4. 지난 번 소개팅 때 바람 맞았냐고 했어/맞았냬 or 맞았냐고 물었어.
5. 스티브 생일 파티에 갈 거냐고 했어/거냬 or 거냐고 물었어.

Exercise 7

1. 소개팅 한 거 어떻게 알았냐고 했어요/했냬요 or 물었어요.
2. 어떤 남자를 좋아하냐고 했어요/좋아하냬요 or 좋아하냐고 물었어요.
3. 민준 씨 친구가 한국 사람이냐고 했어요/한국 사람이냬요 or 한국 사람이냐고 물었어요.
4. 제시카 씨가 언제 졸업이냐고 했어요/졸업이냬요or 졸업이냐고 물었어요.
5. 이 근처 한국식당에 가 봤냐고 했어요/물었어요.

Exercise 8

1. F 2. F 3. T 4. F

Exercise 9

1. (안젤라가) 이번 금요일에 같이 코리아타운에 가서 저녁먹자고 했어/저녁먹쟤.
2. 내일이 발렌타인데이니까, 남자 친구한테 줄 초콜렛 사러 같이 가자고 했어/가쟤.
3. 여행하면서 휴게소에 들러서 그 지역 유명한 음식도 먹어 보고 싶다고 했어/싶대.(그래서) KTX대신에 고속버스 타자고 했어/타쟤.
4. 이번 추석엔 고향에 내려가지 말고 자기하고 여행가자고 했어요/가쟤요.
5. 같이 나가서 한국식당에서 점심 먹자고 했어요/가쟤요.

Exercise 10

L02 3학년이냐
L03 같은 학년인 줄 알았다
L05 전공이 뭐냐
L06 일본어나 중국어도 할 줄 아냐
L08 사회학을 전공한
L09 시애틀이
L11 한국 노래를 좋아해서 음악을 자주 듣고, 콘서트에도 가끔 간다
L12 한국 가수 콘서트가 있는데, 시간 되면 같이 가

Exercise 11

1. 부산에 한번 놀러 가자고 했어요.
2. 교수님 댁에 같이 가자고 했어요.
3. 다음에 다른 데 같이 한 번 가보자고 했어요.
4. 같이 해물 파전을 만들어 보자고 했어요.

Exercise 12

1. 생일 파티를 해 주자고 했다.
2. 룸메이트 부모님이 오신다고 했다.
3. 닉이 혼자 사니까, 닉 아파트에서 모이자고 했다.
4. 알렉스가 아마존에서 자주 쇼핑하니까, 아마존 기프트 카드를 사 주자고 했다.

IV. Listen & Discuss (P.159)

Answers may vary.
1. 삼성이 이겼습니다.
2. 두산을 응원합니다.
3. 고향이 대구라서 삼성을 응원합니다.
4. 현수 집에서 결승전을 같이 볼 겁니다.

VII. Listening (P.167)

1. People watched games without sleeping during the world cup.
2. Stress gets relieved if you sing rooster's songs while eating chicken and beer.

3. F 4. F 5.T 6. T

VIII. Reading (P.168)

1. ② 2. ④ 3. ②

Lesson 6

I . New Words & Expressions (P.171)

Exercise 1

1. 피곤해 보인다 2. 한꺼번에 3. 남자 주인공 4. 자막 5. 역사 드라마

Exercise 2

1.④ 2.④ 3.② 4.④ 5.④

II . Patterns, Expressions & Practice (P.173)

Exercise 1

2. 오늘 아침에 숙제하느라고 9시 수업에 늦었어요.
3. 샤워하느라고 전화 소리를 못 들었어요.
4. 지난 학기에 다섯 과목을 듣느라고 힘들었어요.
5. 아르바이트하느라고 친구를 만날 시간이 없어요.
6. 한국 가는 비행기 표를 사느라고 돈을 다 썼어요.

Exercise 2

1. 수영하느라고 2. 비가 와서 3. 음악을 듣느라고
4. 와서 5. 공부하느라고

Exercise 3

Answers may vary.
1. 여자 친구 생일 선물 사느라(고)
2. 인턴쉽 찾느라(고)
3. 보고서 쓰느라(고)
4. 점심 먹느라(고)
5. 아르바이트하느라(고)
6. 수업 듣느라(고)

Exercise 4

1. He drove on a snowy day.
2. She is busy because she is looking for a summer internship.
3. Because he cheered up his team loudly at the baseball stadium.

Exercise 5

Answers may vary.
1. 읽어 버렸어요.
2. 써 버렸어.
3. 늦잠을 자 버렸어요./늦게 일어나 버렸어요.
4. 해 버려/끝내 버려.
5. 사 버렸어요.

Exercise 6

1. 잃어버려서 2. 잊어버리고 3. 잃어버렸어요
4. 잊어버려요 5. 잊어버리고

Exercise 7

1. T 2. F 3. T 4. F

Exercise 8

1. T 2. F 3. F 4. F

Exercise 9

Answers may vary.
1. 없을 만큼/안 보일 만큼/적을 만큼
2. 자리가 없을 만큼/못 먹을 만큼
3. 할 만큼
4. 갈 만큼/할 만큼

Exercise 10

Answers may vary.
1. DVD를 살 만큼/극장에서 세 번이나 볼 만큼/촬영 장소까지 가 볼 만큼
2. 적어도 일주일에 한 번은 한국 식당에 갈 만큼/집에서 한국 음식을 만들 만큼
3. 전공을 한국학으로 바꿀 만큼/한국 역사 수업을 들을 만큼/매일 한국에 대한 뉴스를 볼 만큼
4. 편지를 쓸 수 있을 만큼/짧은 이야기를 읽을 수 있을 만큼/뉴스를 이해할 수 있을 만큼/좋아하는 영화의 줄거리를 말할 수 있을 만큼

Exercise 11

1. F 2. T

Exercise 12

1. F 2. T

IV. Listen & Discuss (P.187)

1. 어제 드라마 보느라고 밤을 새워서 피곤해 보인다.
2. 시험 공부하느라고 시간이 없어서 보지 못 했다.
3. 조선 시대가 배경인 역사 드라마다.
4. 왕으로 나오는 남자 주인공이 잘생겼고 배우들이 다 연기를 잘해서 좋아하게 된 것 같다.
5. 한국 드라마 때문이다.
6. 자막 없이 내용을 다 이해할 수 있을 만큼 잘하고 싶어한다.

VII. Listening (P.195)

1. F 2. T 3. F 4. F 5. T

6. 한국 룸메이트 덕분에 한국에 대해 알게 됐는데, 더 알고 싶어서 한국에 왔습니다.
7. 한국 음악을 좋아해서 듣다가 노래 내용을 이해하고 싶어서 공부하게 됐습니다.

VIII. Reading (P.196)

1. T 2. F 3. T 4. F 5. ② 6. ①

Lesson 7

Ⅰ. New Words & Expressions (P.199)

Exercise 1

1. 알아보 2. 알아볼까 3. 보증금 4. 가구; 구했어요
5. 안전해서

Exercise 2

1.④ 2.④ 3.③ 4.④ 5. ④

Ⅱ. Patterns, Expressions & Practice (P.201)

Exercise 1

Answers may vary.

1. 좋아하는 편이에요/자주 보는 편이에요/별로 안 좋아하는 편이에요
2. 따뜻한 편이에요/흐린 편이에요/비가 자주 오는 편이에요/추운 편이에요
3. 공원에서 자주 걷는 편이에요/빵을 만드는 편이에요/드라마를 보는 편이에요
4. 키가 큰 편이세요/목소리가 좋은 편이세요/친절한 편이세요

Exercise 2

Answers may vary.

1. 집에서 먹는 편이에요.
2. 어려운 편이
3. 요즘 날씨가 따뜻해져서, 반바지를 자주 입는 편이에요.
4. 좀 시끄러운 편이에요.
5. 클래식을 자주 듣는 편이에요.

Exercise 3

1. F 2. T

Exercise 4

1. T 2. F

Exercise 5

1. 아침을 많이 먹고, 점심은 안 먹고, 저녁은 일찍 먹는 편이다. (She has a big breakfast, skips her lunch and has an early dinner.)
2. 점심을 먹으면 졸리기 때문입니다. (It's because she feels sleepy after having lunch.)

Exercise 6

Answers may vary.

2. 로스앤젤레스가 시애틀보다 더 크다.
3. 기숙사에 사는 것이 아파트에 사는 것보다 덜 비싸다.
4. 나는 운전하는 것보다 버스 타는 것이 더 편하다.
5. 고등학교 때보다 대학교 때 더 많이 공부한다.
6. 도서관에서 아르바이트하는 것보다 햄버거 가게에서 아르바이트하는 게 더 재미있다.

Exercise 7

Answers may vary.

1. 우리 원룸의 월세는 서울 원룸보다 비쌉니다.
2. 보증금은 우리 원룸보다 더 비쌉니다.
3. 학교까지는 우리 원룸보다 더 가깝습니다. (or 시간이 더 걸립니다).
4. 가구는 서울 원룸보다 더 많습니다.

Exercise 8

Answers may vary.

2. 현수 방에 있는 물건들은 제니 방(에 있는 물건들)보다 더 많아요. or 제니 방에 있는 물건들은 현수 방(에 있는 물건들)보다 덜 많아요.
3. 현수는 제니보다 더 바쁜 것 같아요. or 제니는 현수보다 덜 바쁜 것 같아요.
4. 현수 방은 제니 방보다 더 비싸 보여요. or 제니 방은 현수 방보다 덜 비싸 보여요.
5. 제니는 현수보다 더 부지런한 것 같아요. or 현수는 제니보다 덜 부지런한 것 같아요.

Exercise 9

1. F 2. T

Exercise 10

Answers may vary.

1. 무슨 영화를 (or 뭘) 봐야 할지 모르겠어요.
2. 어느 전화기를 (or 뭘) 사야 할지 모르겠어요.
3. 준비해야 할지 모르겠어요.
4. (언제?) 결혼을 해야 할지 모르겠어요.
5. 어디를 가 봐야 할지 모르겠어요.

Exercise 11

Answers may vary.

1. 무슨 옷을 입어야 할지 모르겠어요.
2. 무슨 선물을 사야 할지 모르겠어요.
3. 무슨 음식을 먹어야 할지 모르겠어요.
4. 돈을 다 써 버렸는데, 어떻게 해야 할지 모르겠어요.
5. 뭘 해야 할지 모르겠어요.
6. 들어야 할지 모르겠어요.

Exercise 12

1. T 2. F 3. F 4. T

Exercise 13

1. F 2. F 3. F 4. F

Ⅳ. Listen & Discuss (P.213)

Answers may vary.

1. 인터넷으로 집을 알아보고 있다.
2. 원룸을 알아보고 있다.
3. 학교까지 걸어서 10분밖에 안 걸리고 동네도 안전한 편이다.
4. 화장실을 혼자 쓰는 것이 좋다고 생각한다.
5. 제니를 도와주려고 같이 가려고 합니다.

Ⅶ. Listening (P.221)

1. ③ 2. ①
3. 깨끗하고 조용하고, 학교도 가깝다고 했습니다.
4. 오피스텔은 보증금을 내야 되는데 큰 돈이 없기 때문입니다.
5. 여자는 요리를 못해서, 밥을 주는 하숙집이 더 좋다고 했습니다.

Ⅷ. Reading (P.222)

1. ③ 2. ③ 3. ②

Listening scripts (of I, II, IV, VII)

Lesson 1

I. New Words & Expressions (P.13)

Exercise 1

Listen to the audio and fill in the blanks.

1. A: 안녕하세요? 저는 제니 스미스예요.
   B: 네, 반갑습니다. 저는 사회학과 4학년 김현수입니다.

2. A: 서로 인사하세요. 이쪽은 미국에서 온 제니 씨예요.
   B: 아, 안녕하세요! 만나서 반가워요.

3. A: 저는 1주일 전에 미국에서 와서 한국은 아직 잘 몰라요.
   B: 걱정하지 마세요. 웨이 씨가 많이 도와줄 거예요.

4. A: 제 후배 웨이인데 서로 인사하세요.
   B: 만나서 반갑습니다.

5. A: 넌 한국에 온 지 벌써 반 년쯤 됐지?
   B: 네, 벌써 6개월이 됐네요.

6. A: 이번에 새로 온 유학생이죠?
   B: 네, 미국에서 온 제니 스미스입니다.

7. A: 도움이 필요하면 저한테 연락 주세요.
   B: 네~ 많이 도와주시면 감사하겠습니다.

II. Patterns, Expressions & Practice (P.15)

Exercise 4

Listen to the phone conversation between two friends and mark each statement T(rue) or F(alse).

M: 나 방금 학교 정문 들어왔는데, 오늘 신입생 환영회는 어디서 해?
W: 대강당인데, 지금 대강당 앞에서 너 기다리고 있어. 빨리 와.
M: 저기 학생회관이 보이네.
W: 그래? 그럼 다 왔네. 학생회관 옆에 "친구"라는 작은 커피숍에 있는데, 그 뒤에 대강당이 있어.

Exercise 7

Listen to the conversation between two friends and mark each statement T(rue) or F(alse).

W: 시험도 끝났는데, 내일 뭐 할 거예요?
M: 집에서 "Star Wars"나 보려구요.
W: 그 영화 아직 안 봤어요?
M: 본 지 너무 오래돼서 기억이 잘 안 나네요.

Exercise 9

Listen to the conversation between two friends and mark each statement T(rue) or F(alse).

W: 앤디 씨, 어디 가세요?
M: 핸드폰 하나 새로 사려구요.
W: 지금 쓰는 핸드폰도 좋아 보이는데요?
M: 산 지 1년밖에 안 됐는데, 벌써 고장이 나서요.

Exercise 10

Listen to the conversation between two friends and mark each statement T(rue) or F(alse).

M: 어떻게 한국어를 배우셨어요?
W: 2년 전부터 혼자 한국어를 공부하다가, 작년부터 한국어 수업을 들었어요.
M: 한국어 수업 들은 지 1년밖에 안 됐는데, 정말 잘 하시네요.
W: 고마워요.

Exercise 13

Listen to the phone conversation between two friends and mark each statement T(rue) or F(alse).

M: 왜 안 와? 우리는 벌써 식당에 왔어.
W: 지금 가고 있어.
M: 어딘데?
W: 식당 근처인데 10분쯤 후에 도착할 거야. 내가 도착하기 전에 내 것도 좀 주문해 줘.
M: 그래, 너는 뭐 먹을래?

IV. Listen & Discuss (P.31)

제니 is an international student who recently came to Korea to attend university. In the following conversation, she meets 현수 and 웨이 during freshman orientation. First, listen to the conversation. With your classmates, discuss the answers to the questions that follow. Finally, write each answer in a full Korean sentence in the space provided.

01 현수: 안녕하세요? 이번에 새로 온 유학생이죠?
02 제니: 네, 안녕하세요? 제니 스미스라고 해요.
03 현수: 저는 사회학과 4학년 김현수라고 해요.
04 제니 씨, 이쪽은 제 후배 웨이인데 서로 인사하세요.
05 제니: 안녕하세요? 만나서 반갑습니다.
06 웨이: 네, 반갑습니다. 왕웨이라고 합니다.
07 현수: 제니 씨, 한국에 온 지 얼마나 됐어요?
08 제니: 아직 일주일밖에 안 됐어요.
09 현수: 웨이, 넌 한국에 온 지 벌써 일 년쯤 됐지?
10 학기 시작하기 전에 제니 씨 좀 많이 도와줘.
11 웨이: 네~ 선배님!
제니 씨, 도움이 필요하면 언제든지 연락 주세요.
12 제니: 네~ 감사합니다.

VII. Listening (P.39)

1. Listen to the following conversation between a man and a woman during a freshman welcome party at a college in Korea. Then, answer the questions.

W: 안녕하세요? 저는 학생회에서 유학생들을 도와주고 있는 크리스티나라고 해요.
M: 아~ 네, 안녕하세요? 저는 이번 학기에 중국에서 유학 온 슈잉이라고 해요.
W: 그럼, 한국에 온 지 얼마 안 됐겠네요.
M: 네, 아직 삼 주밖에 안 됐어요.
W: 학기 시작하기 전에 도움이 필요하면 언제든지 저한테 연락 주세요. 여기 제 전화 번호예요.
M: 감사합니다!

2-5 Listen to the following announcement from a university broadcasting station and mark each statement T(rue) or F(alse).

안녕하세요. 20학번 신입생 여러분! 한국 대학교에 들어오신 것을 환영합니다. 총학생회가 준비한 2020년도 신입생 환영회가 이번 주 금요일 오후 5시부터 7시까지 학교 대강당에서 있습니다. 모두 참석하셔서 선배님들과 좋은 이야기 나누는 즐거운 시간이 되길 바랍니다. 학교 방송국에서 알려드렸습니다.

Lesson 2

I .New Words & Expressions (P.43)

Exercise 1

Listen to the audio and fill in the blanks.

1. A: 지난 주말에 어디로 견학 갔다 왔어?
   B: 보령머드축제에 갔다 왔어.
2. A: 이거 어디서 찍은 사진이야?
   B: 전주 한옥 마을에서 찍은 거야.
3. A: 그럼, 한옥에 묵었어?
   B: 응, 생각보다 편했어!
4. A: 난 거기서 K-pop 공연을 봤는데, 너는 뭐 했어?
   B: 나는 머드 축제에 갔어.
5. A: 한복이 너한테 정말 잘 어울려!
   B: 그래? 너도 다음에 한번 입어 봐.

II .Patterns, Expressions & Practice (P.45)

Exercise 7

Listen to the conversation between two friends and mark each statement T(rue) or F(alse).

M: 학교 앞에 한국 식당이 생겼다던데, 가 봤어?
W: 응. 어제 거기서 점심 먹었어.
M: 나도 오늘 가볼까 하는데, 어땠어?
W: 떡볶이를 먹었는데, 너무 **맵더라고**.
M: 그래? 내 친구는 맛있다던데.

Exercise 8

Listen to the conversation between classmates and mark each statement T(rue) or F(alse).

M: 다음 학기에 무슨 수업 들을 거야?
W: 글쎄, 경제학 수업을 듣고 싶은데, 어떨까?
M: 나는 작년에 들었는데, 재미가 **없더라고**.
W: 왜? 내 룸메이트는 재미있다던데?
M: 내 친구들도 다 재미있다던데, 나는 수학을 싫어해서 너무 **어렵더라고**.

Exercise 9

Listen to the conversation between classmates and mark each statement T(rue) or F(alse).

M: 어젯밤에 도서관에 있었어?
W: 아니, 공부하러 도서관에 갔는데, 사람이 너무 **많더라고**. 그래서 그냥 집에서 공부했는데, 왜?
M: 진짜? 전화했는데, 네 동생이 집에 없다던데.

Exercise 10

Listen to the conversation between classmates and mark each statement T(rue) or F(alse).

W: 시험이 끝나서 너무 기분 좋다! 뭐 재미있는 일 없을까?
M: 이번 주말에 시내에서 마라톤이 있다던데, 같이 안 갈래?
W: 마라톤? 나 운동 싫어하는데....
M: 나도 운동은 별로 안 좋아하는데, 작년에 한번 해 보니까, 별로 안 **힘들더라고**. 예쁜 티셔츠도 선물로 준다던데?
W: 글쎄.. 나는 그냥 집에서 쉬고 싶은데.
M: 그러지 말고 같이 가자.

Exercise 13

Listen to the conversation between two friends and mark each statement T(rue) or F(alse).

W: 가방 진짜 예쁘다! 어디서 샀니?
M: 온라인 쇼핑몰에서 샀어. 여기 봐. 여기 예쁜 가방이 많아.
W: 지금 세일을 하는**구나**! 나도 가방을 하나 사고 싶었는데, 한 번 찾아봐야겠다.
M: 세일이 이번 주까지야. 이 쇼핑몰은 세일을 자주 안 하니까, 빨리 사.

IV. Listen & Discuss (P.61)

제니 and 웨이 are chatting at a school cafeteria.
First, listen to the conversation. With your classmates, discuss the answers to the questions that follow. Finally, write each answer in a full Korean sentence in the space provided.

01 민지: 지난 주말에 다들 어디로 견학 갔다 왔어?
02 웨이: 전 DMZ에 갔다 왔어요.
03 제니: DMZ? 거기서는 북한이 정말 가깝게 보이니?
04 웨이: 어, 망원경으로 보니까 사람들이 걸어 다니는 것도 다 보이더라고.

05 제니: 와아~! 되게 가깝구나!
06 웨이: 민지 누나는 어디 갔었어요?
07 민지: 난 보령에 갔다 왔어!
08 웨이: 거기 머드 축제에 가 봤어요?
09 민지: 당연하지! K-pop 공연도 봤는데, 정말 재밌더라~.
10 제니: 전 전주 한옥 마을에 갔다 왔어요. 이거 거기서 찍은 사진이에요. (Showing a photo.)
11 민지: 와~ 너 한복이 참 잘 어울리는구나! 꼭 한국 사람같아!
12 제니: 그리고 한옥에서 묵었는데, 온돌방이 생각보다 편하더라구요.
13 민지: 와~! 모두 좋은 경험을 했구나!

VII. Listening (P.69)

1-4 Listen to the following conversation between a man and a woman and mark each statement T(rue) or F(alse).

M: 다른 애들은 지난 주에 전주한옥마을 견학 갔다 왔다던데, 우리만 못 갔네.
W: 서울에도 한옥 마을이 있는데, 주말에 같이 가 볼래?
M: 정말? 대중교통으로도 갈 수 있어?
W: 어, 지하철로도 갈 수 있는데, 역에서 좀 걸어야 되니까 그냥 버스로 가자. 학교 앞에서 버스를 타면 남산골한옥마을 앞까지 가.
M: 거기 밥 먹을 식당도 있니?
W: 식당도 많이 있는데, 요즘 날씨가 좋으니까 도시락 싸가지고 가서 밖에서 먹자.
M: 좋아, 도시락은 내가 준비할게. 참, 입장료는 얼마니?
W: 무료라던데.

5-8 Listen to the following announcement at a museum and mark each statement T(rue) or F(alse).

저희 박물관을 찾아 주셔서 감사합니다. 1층 어린이 박물관에서는 한국의 전통문화를 재미있게 배울 수 있는 행사가 진행되고 있습니다. 2층 전시실에서는 한복 전시를 하고 있습니다. 특히 한복을 입어볼 수 있는 체험 행사도 함께 하고 있으니 많은 참여 부탁드립니다. 3층에는 식당과 커피숍 등 편의 시설이 있습니다. 저희 박물관은 화요일부터 일요일까지 매일 아침 8시부터 오후 5시까지 방문하실 수 있습니다. 월요일은 문을 닫습니다. 그럼 즐거운 시간 되시기 바랍니다.

Lesson 3

I .New Words & Expressions (P.73)

Exercise 1

Listen to the audio and fill in the blanks.

1. A: 다음 주가 추석인데, 넌 무슨 요일에 고향에 내려가니?
   B: 화요일 저녁에 가. 너는?
2. A: 너 고향 가는 표는 샀니? 표 사기가 쉽지 않을 건데.
   B: 벌써 샀어.
3. A: 나는 일찍 기차표를 사서 이번 주말에 고향에 내려갈거야.
   B: 이번 추석은 연휴가 길어서 난 추석 하루 전에 갈거야.
4. A: 이번 추석에도 서울에서 부산으로 고향 가는 길은 엄청 복잡할 거야. 힘들겠다.
   B: 걱정해 줘서 고마워. 근데, 이번 추석연휴에는 부모님께서 서울로 올라오셔!
5. A: 이번 추석 어떻게 보냈니?
   B: 친구 집에 가서 송편도 먹고 추석 게임들도 하고 재미있게 보냈어.

II . Patterns, Expressions & Practice (P.75)

Exercise 3

Listen to each conversation and then answer the following question using a reported statement.

1.

M: 보령 머드 축제? 세계인의 축제라고 하던데 어땠어?
W: 사람도 엄청 많고 끝내주게 재미있었어.

2.

W: 전주한옥마을에서 뭐 했어?
M: 한복을 입고 사진도 찍고 한옥에서 잤어.

3.

M: 제시카 씨, "기자"라는 말도 알고, 한국말 참 잘 하시네요!
W: 아니에요. 아직 잘 못 해요.

4.

M: 저는 1년 더 일하고 대학원에 갈 거예요.
W: 아~ 뭐 전공하실 거예요?

5.

W: 졸업하고 뭐 하실 거예요?
M: 대학원에서 경영학을 전공하려고 해요. 회사를 다녔는데도 아직 공부가 더 필요해서요.

6.

W: 생일 축하해요!
M: 어! 제 생일 어떻게 알았어요?

7.

W: 그 음식점은 뭐가 맛있어요?
M: 비빔밥하고 불닭이 맛있어요.

Exercise 6

Listen to each conversation and then answer the question using a reported command.

1.

W: 이따가 오후 2시쯤에 문자 보내.
M: 그래. 알았어.

2.

M: 제 친구 한번 만나 보세요. 잘 나가는 자동차 엔지니어예요. 그리고 되게 잘 생겼어요.
W: 고마워요. 근데 ㅎㅎ 혹시 사진 있어요?

3.

W: 생일 축하해요!
M: 어! 제 생일 어떻게 알았어요?
W: 샤오밍한테 들었어요. 이거 별 거 아니지만... 선물이에요.
M: 와~ 고마워요! 지금 열어 봐도 돼요?
W: 그럼요~. 열어 보세요.
M: 우와! 핸드폰 케이스네요! 마침 필요했는데. 잘 쓸게요!

4.

W: 김밥 좀 드세요.
M: 어, 제시카 씨가 만들었어요?

5.

M: 제가 떡볶이를 만들었는데, 맛 좀 보세요.
W: (먹은 후) 음~ 맛있네요!! 여기는 뭐가 들어갔어요?
M: 떡하고, 설탕하고, 고추장하고... 아 참 그리고 양파요.

Exercise 9

민지 called 현수 but he didn't answer, so she left a message. Listen to her message and answer the following questions in Korean.

현수야, 나 민지야. 제니 생일 파티 때문에 전화했어. 우리 집에서 모이기로 했었잖아. 그런데, 이번 주말에 갑자기 부모님이 **오신다고 하셔서** 우리 집에서는 파티를 **하지 못할** 것 같아. 웨이 룸메이트가 이번 주말에 집에 **없을 거라고 하던데**, 웨이 집에서 모이면 안 될까?

Exercise 10

In this audio, two friends talk about a restaurant that recently opened. Listen to their conversation and mark each statement T(rue) or F(alse).

M: 학교 앞 한국 식당에 가 봤니?
W: 한국 식당이 생긴 줄 몰랐네. 음식은 맛있어?
M: 나도 아직 먹어보지 않아서 잘 모르겠어. 어제 저녁에 갔는데, 자리가 없어서 들어가지도 못했어. 근데, 스티브가 그러는데, 맛있대.

Exercise 13

In this audio, two friends are talking about where 제니 is. Listen to their conversation and mark each statement T(rue) or F(alse).

W: 제니가 어디에 있어요?
M: 방에 있을 거예요.
W: 방에 없는데요?
M: 그래요? 저는 제니가 나간 줄 몰랐어요.

Exercise 14

In this audio, two friends are talking about the weather. Listen to their conversation and mark each statement T(rue) or F(alse).

W: 오늘 너무 추워요.
M: 그렇죠. 그런데 왜 이렇게 짧은 치마를 입고 나왔어요?
W: 이렇게 추울 줄 몰랐어요.
M: 그래서 일기예보를 매일 봐야 해요. 어제 일기예보에서 오늘 춥다고 얘기하더라구요.

Exercise 15

In this recording, two classmates talk about taking a Chinese class. Listen to their conversation and mark each statement T(rue) or F(alse).

W: 지난 학기에 중국어 수업 들었지?
M: 듣지 않았는데, 왜?
W: 나는 네가 들은 줄 알았어.
M: 들으려고 했는데, 전공 수업하고 수업 시간이 같아서 듣지 못했어.
W: 그럼, 다음 학기에 나하고 같이 듣자. 나도 중국 문화에 관심이 많아.
M: 네가 중국 문화에 관심이 있는 줄 몰랐어.

IV. Listen & Discuss (P.97)

웨이, 현수, 민지 are talking to one another. First, listen to the conversation. With your classmates, discuss the answers to the questions that follow. Finally, write each answer in a full Korean sentence in the space provided.

01 웨이: 이번 추석에는 표 사기가 쉽지 않다고 들었어요. 형하고 누나도 고향에 가세요?
02 현수: 어, 나는 올해 기차표를 일찍 사서 이번 주말에 고향에 내려갈 거야.
03 민지: 고향에 가면 친척들도 만나고 재밌겠네.
04 현수: 민지 너는 언제 갈 거야?
05 민지: 난 이번 추석에는 고향에 내려가지 않고, 친구들이랑 여행가기로 했어.
06 웨이: 한국 사람들은 명절에 다 고향에 가는 줄 알았는데 ….
07 현수: 요즘은 명절에 여행을 하는 사람도 많아졌어.
08 웨이: 그렇구나. 명절 풍습도 조금씩 달라지는군요.
09 민지: 웨이야, 너는 추석 어떻게 보낼 거니?
10 웨이: 교수님께서 송편 먹으러 오라고 초대해 주셔서, 교수

님 댁에 갈 거예요.
11 현수: 잘 됐네. 그럼, 다들 추석 연휴 즐겁게 보내고, 다음 주에 봐.

VII. Listening (P.105)

1-4 In this audio, two friends discuss New Year's Day in Korea. Listen to their phone conversation and mark each statement T(rue) or F(alse).

M: 다음 주 수요일이 설날이네요. "새해 복 많이 받으세요!"
W: 고마워요. 그런데 지난 1월 1일에 벌써 새해 복 많이 받으라고 하셨잖아요? 벌써 한 이 주나 지났는데....
M: 아, 그거는 양력설이었죠. 다음 주 수요일이 한국의 전통적인 새해 첫 날인 설날이에요.
W: 아, 그럼 한국 사람들은 새해를 두 번 보내네요?
M: 맞아요. 설날에는 보통 고향에 가서 가족들과 함께 시간을 보내요. 그리고 떡국도 먹고 어른들께 절을 해요. 설날 아침 어른들께 절하는 것을 세배라고 해요.

5-9 Listen to the following news report and answer the questions in English.

내일부터 3일 동안 추석 연휴가 시작됩니다. 지금 기차역과 버스 터미널은 오래간만에 가족을 만나러 고향으로 내려가는 사람들로 복잡합니다. 그리고 많은 사람들이 추석 음식과 선물을 사러 시장에 나와 있는데요, 그 중에서도 떡집이 가장 바쁘다고 합니다. 이번 추석 연휴 동안 날씨는 계속 맑고 시원해서 가족들과 좋은 시간을 보낼 수 있을 것 같습니다. 시청자 여러분, 즐거운 한가위 보내시기 바랍니다.

Lesson 4

I .New Words & Expressions (P.109)

Exercise 3
Listen to the audio and fill in the blanks.

1. A: 테드 씨, 다음 일정은 어떻게 되세요?
   B: 사흘 후에 제주도에서 컨퍼런스가 있어요.
2. A: KTX를 타면, 빠르고 편해요. 두 세 시간밖에 안 걸려요.
   B: 맞아요. 근데 저는 고속버스를 타는 것도 좋아해요.
3. A: 고속버스를 타고 휴게소에 들르면, 그 지역의 유명한 음식들을 먹어 볼 수 있어요.
   B: 그럼 고속버스를 타야겠네요!
4. A: 부산에서 제주도까지 가는 교통편은 뭐가 좋을까요?
   B: 보통 비행기를 많이 타요.
5. A: 제주도에 가서는 어떻게 다니실 거예요?
   B: 택시를 타고 다니려구요. 택시 기사님들이 관광 안내도 해 준다고 들었어요.

II .Patterns, Expressions & Practice (P.111)

Exercise 3
Listen to the conversation between two friends and mark each statement T(rue) or F(alse).

M: 주말 잘 보냈니?
W: 오래간만에 영화를 볼까 해서 극장에 갔는데, 표가 없더라구.
M: 그래서 보지 못했구나?
W: 그냥 집에서 컴퓨터로 봤어.

Exercise 4
Listen to the conversation between two friends and answer the following questions.

M: 다음 주가 스티브 생일이잖아, 선물 샀어?
W: 뭐가 좋은지 몰라서 아직 못 샀어. 안 그래도 오늘 백화점에 구경하러 가볼까 하는데, 아직 안 샀으면 같이 갈래?
M: 난 벌써 샀어. 스티브가 핸드폰을 새로 사서, 핸드폰 케이스를 샀어.
W: 그거 괜찮네. 나는 뭘 사지?

Exercise 8
Listen to the conversation between two friends and answer the questions in English.

W: 요즘 한국어 수업이 너무 어려워졌어. 새 단어도 많아지고. 어떻게 공부하는 게 좋을까?
M: 음... 학교에 한국 학생 모임이 있는데, 나랑 같이 가 볼래?
W: 나는 처음 보는 사람하고 얘기하는 게 좀 불편하더라고.
M: 그래? 그럼, 한국 드라마 보는 건 어떨까?

Exercise 12
Listen to the conversation between two friends and mark each statement T(rue) or F(alse).

M: 혹시 민기 봤어?
W: 글쎄, 오늘 못 봤는데. 어제도 보니까 수업 끝나고 바로 집에 가더라고.
M: 매일 일찍 집에 가는 걸 보니까 요즘 많이 피곤한가 봐.
W: 아닐 거야. 요즘 늦게까지 컴퓨터 게임을 하더라고.

Exercise 13
Listen to the conversation between 현수 and 민지 and answer the questions in Korean.

현수: 다음 주가 벌써 겨울 방학이구나. 넌 무슨 계획 있니?
민지: 내가 벌써 4학년이잖아. 그래서 졸업하기 전에, 재미있는 경험을 해볼까 하는데, 뭘 하는 게 좋을까?
현수: 아르바이트 해 보는 건 어때? 학교 웹사이트에 보니까, 도서관에서 방학 동안 아르바이트 할 사람을 찾던데.
민지: 이번 방학에는 일하고 싶지 않아. ㅎㅎ
현수: 그럼, 졸업하면 시간이 많이 없으니까, 이번에 기차 여행을 해 보는 건 어때?
민지: 아, 그거 재밌겠다. 같이 할래?

Exercise 17

Listen to the conversation between 남자 and 여자 and mark each statement T(rue) or F(alse).

M: 이번 여름에 뭐 할 거예요?
W: 독일에 여행을 가려고요.
M: 좋겠네요! 독일어 할 줄 아세요?
W: 1년동안 독일어 수업을 들었어요. 잘 못하지만 간단한 말은 할 수 있어요.
M: 저는 할 줄 아는 외국어가 없는데 부럽네요.

Exercise 18

Listen to the conversation between 남자 and 여자 and mark each statement T(rue) or F(alse).

M: 민지 남자 친구가 어느 나라 사람이에요?
W: 글쎄요. 아마 캐나다 사람인 것 같아요.
M: 어제 인사했는데 한국말을 너무 잘 해서 놀랐어요.
W: 네, 그리고 한국 문화도 잘 알아요. 송편도 만들 줄 알더라구요.

IV. Listen & Discuss (P.129)

Directions: An American businessman (테드) visits Korea to attend two international conferences. After finishing the first conference, he is talking with his colleague (미영) who works at a branch of his company in Seoul.
First, listen to the conversation. With your classmates, discuss the answers to the questions that follow. Finally, write each answer in a full Korean sentence in the space provided.

01 미영: 테드 씨, 다음 일정은 어떻게 되세요?
02 테드: 제주도 컨퍼런스 전에 부산에 한번 가 볼까 하는데, 교통편은 뭐가 좋을까요?
03 미영: KTX를 타면 편하고 빠르지만, 고속버스 타는 걸 추천해요.
04 테드: 고속버스는 오래 걸리지 않나요?
05 미영: 그렇긴 하지만, 휴게소에서 그 지역의 유명한 음식들도 먹어 볼 수 있거든요.
06 테드: 다양한 음식을 먹어 보고 싶었는데, 그럼 고속버스를 타야겠네요.
07 미영: 부산에서 제주도는 어떻게 가실 거예요?
08 테드: 비행기를 탈까 해요.
09 미영: 아~네. 그럼 제주도에 가서는 어떻게 다니실 거예요? 차를 렌트하실 거예요?
10 테드: 제가 운전할 줄 몰라서 택시를 타고 다니려구요.
11 미영: 그것도 괜찮아요. 택시 기사님들이 관광 안내도 잘 해 주시니까요.
12 그럼 즐겁게 여행하세요!

VII. Listening (P.137)

1-5 Listen to the conversation between two friends and mark each statement T(rue) or F(alse).

01 M: 지난 주말 도자기 체험 행사는 재밌었어?
02 W: 어, 생각보다 훨씬 좋았어. 나는 너도 오는 줄 알았는데.
03 M: 사실 나도 신청했는데, 갑자기 급한 일이 생겨서 못 갔어.
04 도자기 만드는 건 어렵지 않았어?
05 W: 거기 선생님께서 잘 가르쳐 주셔서 별로 어렵지 않았어.
06 이게 내가 만든 커피잔인데 너한테 선물로 주려고 가지고 왔어.
07 M: 우와, 정말 고마워! 잘 쓸게.
08 W: 나는 도자기가 그렇게 예쁜 줄 몰랐어.
09 한국 도자기에 대해 더 공부해 보고 싶어졌어.
10 M: 아, 같이 못 가서 정말 아쉽다.
11 나중에 나도 꼭 한 번 가보고 싶은데, 거기까지 어떻게 가는지 가르쳐 줄 수 있어?
12 W: 어, 학교 앞에서 지하철 2호선을 타고 동서울터미널 역까지 가면,
13 거기에서 이천까지 바로 가는 버스가 있어.

6-10 Listen to the following announcement by a group leader of a school field trip and mark each statement T(rue) or F(alse).

여러분, 조금 있으면 우리 버스가 휴게소에 도착할 거예요. 휴게소에서 30분 동안 쉴 건데, 사람들이 많으니까, 화장실에 가고 싶은 사람은 먼저 화장실부터 빨리 가세요. 휴게소에는 다양한 맛있는 음식을 팔아요. 여러가지 간식들도 있고, 특히 이 휴게소는 우동하고 김치찌개가 맛있대요. 그리고 이 휴게소에는 도자기 박물관이 있다던데 한 번 가 보세요. 여기 버스가 아주 많으니까 우리 버스를 잘 확인하고 늦지 않게 오세요.

Lesson 5

I. New Words & Expressions (P.141)

Exercise 1

Listen to the audio and fill in the blanks.

1. A: 너 어제 한국시리즈 경기 봤니?
   B: 보고 싶었는데, 다른 일이 있어서 못 봤어. 근데 어느 팀이 이겼어?
2. A: 삼성이 이겼는데, 끝까지 마음 졸이면서 봤어.
   B: 그렇게 재미있었어? 누가 이겼는데?
3. A: 삼성이 마지막에 만루홈런을 쳐서 역전을 했어!
   B: 너 끝까지 마음 졸이면서 봤겠다.
4. A: 아! 이번에는 진짜 두산이 이길 줄 알았는데.
   B: 넌 두산 팬이지? 어제 경기는 정말 안타까웠어.
5. A: 바빠서 어제 경기를 못 봤는데, 누가 이겼어?
   B: 삼성이 이겼어. 근데 끝까지 마음 졸이면서 봤어.

II. Patterns, Expressions & Practice (P.143)

Exercise 4

Listen to the dialogue and answer the questions.

W: 토요일에 기숙사 농구 시합이 있는데, 너도 경기에 참가하니?
M: 이번 주 시합은 참가 못 할 거 같아. 월요일에 중요한 시험이 있거든. 너는?
W: 지난 주에 연습하다가 다리를 다쳤거든. 그래서 나도 이번에는 응원만 하기로 했어.

Exercise 5

Listen to the dialogue and answer the questions.

W: 점심 안 먹을 거야?
M: 미안. 시간 없으니까 너 혼자 먹어.
W: 왜 이렇게 바빠?
M: 심리학 시험이 다음 주 금요일인 줄 알았거든. 근데, 내일이더라구.

Exercise 7

Listen to the conversation and answer the questions in Korean, using a reported question.

1.

M: 참! 지난 번 소개팅은 어땠어요? 그 베트남 친구 말이에요.
W: 소개팅 한 거 어떻게 알았어요?

2.

M: 제시카 씨는 어떤 남자를 좋아하세요?
W: 글쎄요. 저는 성격이 좋은 남자가 좋아요.

3.

W: 민준 씨 친구는 한국 사람이에요?
M: 아뇨. 베트남계 미국인이에요. 근데 한국말을 진짜 잘 해요.

4.

M: 전 내년에 졸업하는데... 제시카 씨는 언제 졸업할 거예요?
W: 저도 내년에요.

5.

M: 이 근처 한국 식당에 가 봤어요?
W: '코리아 하우스' 말이에요?
M: 네.
W: 아뇨. 아직 안 가 봤어요.

Exercise 8

Listen to the conversation between two friends (윌, 민지) and mark each statement T(rue) or F(alse).

윌 : 어, 민지야.
민지: 이번 주 금요일, 우리 알렉스랑 부산국제영화제에 가기로 했잖아?
윌 : 응.
민지: 근데 알렉스가 갑자기 급한 일이 생겨서 같이 못 간다고 해서....
윌 : 그래? 우리 둘만 가면 재미없지 않을까?
민지: 그래서, 내가 닉한테 전화해서 같이 갈 수 있냐고 했더니 좋대. 알렉스 대신에 닉하고 같이 가도 괜찮겠지?
윌 : 물론이지! 닉 전공이 영화연구니까 잘 됐네. 이번 영화제에선 그냥 놀기만 하는 게 아니라 공부도 좀 하겠어. ㅎㅎ

Exercise 11

Listen to the conversations and answer the questions in Korean, using a reported proposal.

1.

테드: 미영 씨, 제주도 컨퍼런스는 사흘 후에 있어요. 그래서, 그때까지 시간이 좀 있는데, 부산에 한 번 놀러 가 볼까요?
미영: 그럴까요? 테드 씨가 가자고 하니까, 안 갈 수가 없네요.

2.

민지: 너는 추석 어떻게 보낼 거니?
마크: 교수님께서 송편 먹으러 오라고 초대해 주셔서, 교수님 댁에 갈 거예요. 누나도 같이 가요!
민지: 그럴까?

3.

M: 그럼... 너 한옥에서 묵은거야?
W: 네. 온돌방에서 자는 게 불편할 줄 알았는데, 생각보다 정말 편하고 잠도 푹 잤어요.
M: 와~! 좋은 경험을 했구나! 다음에는 우리끼리 다른 데 한번 가 보자!

4.

샤오밍: 어제 요리 블로그를 보다가 에이미 씨 글을 봤어요.
에이미: 어, 어떤 거요?
샤오밍: 해물파전 레시피요. 에이미 씨, 요리사 해도 되겠어요!
에이미: 고마워요. 샤오밍 씨, 언제 우리 같이 해물파전 만들어 볼까요?
샤오밍: 네. 에이미 씨가 만든 파전 꼭 한번 먹어 보고 싶어요.

Exercise 12

Listen to the conversation between two friends (윌, 민지) and answer the questions in Korean.

윌 : 민지야, 다음 주말이 알렉스 생일이잖아. 우리 생일 파티 해 줄까?
민지: 좋아, 근데 어디서 하지?
윌 : 우리 집에서 하고 싶은데, 주말에 룸메이트 부모님이 오신대.
민지: 닉이 혼자 살잖아. 닉 아파트에서 하는 게 어떨까?

윌 : 그래, 내가 닉한테 물어 볼게. 아마 괜찮다고 할 거야.
민지: 그런데, 생일 선물은 뭘 사 주지?
윌 : 알렉스 시계가 고장나서 새 시계가 필요하다고 했어.
민지: 그럼, 알렉스가 아마존에서 쇼핑을 자주 하니까, 아마존 기프트 카드를 사주는 건 어때?
윌 : 좋은 생각이야. 알렉스가 좋아하겠다.

IV. Listen & Discuss (P.159)

Directions: 현수 and 웨이 are passing by the school grounds where some students are practicing baseball. 현수 begins chatting with 웨이 about a Korean series game. First, listen to the conversation. With your classmates, discuss the answers to the questions that follow. Finally, write each answer in a full Korean sentence in the space provided.

01 현수: 너, 어제 한국 시리즈 경기 봤어?
02 웨이: 보고 싶었는데 일이 있어서 못 봤어요. 누가 이겼어요?
03 현수: 삼성이 이겼어. 끝까지 마음 졸이면서 봤어.
04 웨이: 왜요? 어땠는데요?
05 현수: 9회까지 두산이 3대 0으로 이기고 있었거든.
06 그런데 삼성이 마지막에 만루 홈런을 쳐서 역전을 했어.
07 웨이: 아! 이번에는 두산이 이길 줄 알았는데… 정말 안타깝네요.
08 현수: 넌 두산 팬이니?
09 웨이: 네. 형은 삼성 팬이죠?
10 현수: 당연하지! 내 고향이 대구잖아.
11 웨이: 우리 이번 주 토요일 결승전 경기는 같이 볼까요?
12 현수: 그래! 우리 집에 와. 안 그래도 내가 민지한테 같이 보자고 했거든.
13 웨이: 그럼 제니한테도 올 수 있냐고 물어볼까요?
14 현수: 좋지!

VII. Listening (P.167)

1-2 Listen to the following conversation between two friends and answer the questions.

W: 한국 사람들은 축구를 진짜 좋아하는 거 같아. 월드컵 때는 잠을 안 자고 경기를 보더라고.
M: 맞아. 나도 저번 월드컵 때 친구들이랑 밤새우면서 한국팀 응원했어.
W: 축구 말고 또 어떤 스포츠가 인기가 있어?
M: 야구도 정말 좋아해. 한국 시리즈 경기가 있을 때는 표를 사기도 어려워. 너도 기회가 있으면, 꼭 경기장에 한번 가 봐.
W: 그냥 텔레비젼으로 보면 되잖아.
M: 한국 야구장에는 특별한 응원 문화가 있어. 치맥을 먹으면서 다같이 응원가를 부르면 스트레스가 풀려.

3-6 Listen to the following conversation and mark each statement T(rue) or F(alse).

W: 한국 프로 야구는 미국 프로 야구하고 어떻게 다르다고 생각하세요?
M: 한국은 야구 팬들 문화가 재미있는 것 같아요. 미국 사람들도 야구를 좋아하지만, 한국 야구 팬들이 응원을 더 열심히 하는 것 같아요. 미국에서는 야구 경기에는 보통 치어리더들이 없는데, 한국에는 야구장에서 치어리더들이 응원을 하는 것이 아주 재미있더라구요.
W: 비슷한 점들도 있을 것 같은데요.
M: 그럼요. 가족이 함께 야구장에 가서 경기를 보는 모습을 볼 수 있어요. 그리고 야구장에서 맛있는 음식들도 많이 파는 것 같구요.

Lesson 6

I .New Words & Expressions (P.171)

Exercise 1

Listen to the audio and fill in the blanks.

1. A: 제니, 너 오늘 좀 피곤해 보인다?
   B: 어, 오빠. 어제 밤늦게까지 드라마 봤어요. 그래서 잠을 많이 못 잤거든요.
2. A: 뭐? 밤늦게까지 드라마를 봤다고?
   B: 보고 싶은 드라마가 있었는데, 어제 저녁에 한꺼번에 다 봤어요!
3. A: 그 드라마가 요즘 인기가 많더라.
   B: 응, 이야기도 재미있고 특히 남자 주인공이 연기를 진짜 잘 하더라고.
4. A: 앞으로는 자막없이 드라마 내용들은 다 이해할 수 있으면 좋겠어요.
   B: 이번 학기에 매일 한국어 수업을 들으니까 그렇게 될거야!
5. A: 어떤 드라마인데, 잠도 안 자고 밤늦게까지 봤어?
   B: 조선 시대가 배경인 역사 드라마예요. 오빠도 보기 시작하면, 너무 재미있어서, 계속 보게 될 거예요.

II. Patterns, Expressions & Practice (P.173)

Exercise 4

Listen to the short dialogues and answer the questions.

1.

W: 어서 오세요. 오늘 눈이 많이 왔죠?
M: 네, 눈 때문에 길이 많이 막히네요.
W: 눈 오는데 운전하시느라고 고생하셨어요.
M: 아니에요. 초대해 주셔서 감사합니다.

2.

M: 요즘 공부하면서 아르바이트까지 하느라 바쁘겠어요.
W: 아르바이트는 생각보다 재밌고, 그렇게 바쁘지는 않아요.

그런데, 여름 방학 인턴쉽 찾느라 정신이 없어요.
M: 아, 인턴쉽을 찾고 있군요.

3.

W: 목소리가 왜 그래? 감기 걸렸어?
M: 지난 주말에 야구 경기장에서 큰 소리로 응원하느라 이렇게 됐어.
W: 벌써 3일이나 지났는데, 아직도 목소리가 잘 안 나오네. 병원에 한번 가봐.
M: 안 그래도 오늘 오후에 예약했어.

Exercise 7

Listen to the conversation and mark each statement T(rue) or F(alse).

M: 오늘 왜 이렇게 늦게 왔어? 수업이 다 끝났는데.
W: 집에서 좀 늦게 나와서 버스를 놓쳐 버렸어. 그래서 그냥 걸어왔어. 오늘 수업은 어땠어? 숙제가 있었어?
M: 숙제가 있는데 교과서 몇 페이지를 해야 하는지 잊어버렸어.
W: 아니, 수업이 좀 전에 끝났는데 어떻게 벌써 잊어버려?

Exercise 8

Listen to the conversation and mark each statement T(rue) or F(alse).

W: 오늘 시험 잘 봤어요?
M: 사실 어제 공부를 하나도 못 해서 시험을 망쳐 버렸어요.
W: 어제 무슨 일이 있었어요?
M: 공부를 하려고 도서관에 갔었는데 너무 피곤해서 잠이 들어 버렸어요.
W: 그랬군요. 다음 번에는 잘 보면 되지요.

Exercise 11

Listen to the conversations and mark each statement T(rue) or F(alse).

M: 도서관에 간 줄 알았는데, 집에 일찍 왔네.
W: 도서관에 갔는데 자리가 없을 만큼 사람이 많더라구.
M: 다음 주가 시험이라서 그럴 거야.
W: 응, 그냥 내 방에서 공부해야겠어.

Exercise 12

Listen to the conversations and mark each statement T(rue) or F(alse).

W: 감기에 걸렸다고 하던데, 이제 좀 괜찮으세요?
M: 네, 지난 주에는 잠도 못 잘 만큼 많이 아팠거든요.
W: 정말요? 고생했겠네요.
M: 동생이 약을 사다 줘서, 먹고 나서 푹 잤어요.
W: 다행이네요.
M: 지금은 일하러 갈 수 있을 만큼 좋아졌어요.

IV. Listen & Discuss (P.187)

Directions: 제니 and 현수 are chatting in a coffee shop. First, listen to the conversation. With your classmates, discuss the answers to the questions that follow. Finally, write each answer in a full Korean sentence in the space provided.

01 현수: 제니야, 너 오늘 좀 피곤해 보인다?
02 제니: 어, 오빠. 어제 드라마 보느라고 밤을 새워서요.
03 현수: 드라마 때문에 밤을 새웠어?
04 제니: 네. 보고 싶은 드라마가 있었는데, 그동안 시험 공부하느라고 계속 못 봤거든요.
05 어제 밤 새워서 한꺼번에 다 봐 버렸어요.
06 현수: 근데, 어떤 드라마야?
07 제니: 조선 시대가 배경인 역사 드라마예요.
08 현수: 아, 요즘 주말에 하는 그 사극 말이야?
09 제니: 왕으로 나오는 남자 주인공이 진짜 잘 생겼어요. 배우들이 다 연기도 너무 잘 하구요.
10 현수: 니가 이렇게 한국 드라마를 좋아하는 줄 몰랐어.
11 제니: 저 사실 한국 드라마 때문에 한국어를 공부하기 시작했거든요.
12 현수: 드라마 보면서 한국어도 공부하고, 한국 역사도 배우고, 좋네.
13 제니: 자막 없이 내용을 다 이해할 수 있을 만큼 한국어를 잘 하고 싶어요.

VII. Listening (P.195)

1-5 Listen to the conversation and mark each statement T(rue) or F(alse).

M: 오늘 수업 끝나고 N서울타워에 갈래? 야경도 보고 저녁도 먹고.
W: 거기 가 보고 싶기는 한데 다음에 가자. 내가 어제 시험 공부하느라고 잠을 잘 못자서 좀 피곤해. 그냥 집에 가서 잠이나 잘까 하고 있었어.
M: 저녁도 못 먹을 만큼 피곤해? 잘 먹고 쉬어야지. 어디 가서 맛있는 거 먹고 한강 공원에서 산책이나 하자.
W: 그럼 치맥 먹으러 갈까? 내가 요즘 치킨이 먹고 싶었거든.
M: 그러자. 그럼 이따가 만나!

6-7 Listen to the conversation and answer the following questions in Korean.

리포터: 오늘은 서울의 한 대학교에서 열심히 한국어 수업을 듣고 있는 학생들을 만나서 이야기를 들어 보겠습니다. 안녕하세요? 어떻게 한국어 공부를 시작하게 되셨습니까?
M : 대학교 1학년 때 기숙사 룸메이트가 한국사람이었거든요. 그 친구 덕분에 한국에 대해 많이 알게 됐는데, 한국에 대해 더 알고 싶어서, 작년에 한국에 왔습니다.
W : 저는 고등학교 때 우연히 한국 음악을 듣고, 너무 좋

아서 계속 듣다가 노래 내용을 이해하고 싶어서 한국어를 배우게 됐습니다.

Lesson 7

I .New Words & Expressions (P.199)

Exercise 1

Listen to the audio and fill in the blanks.

1. A: 저 지금 인터넷으로 집 알아보고 있어요.
   B: 왜? 이번 학기 마치고 기숙사에서 나오려고?
2. A: 기숙사에서 룸메이트하고 같이 방 쓰는 게 불편해서 다음 학기부터는 혼자 살아 보고 싶어요.
   B: 우리집 근처에 원룸이 하나 있는데, 같이 한번 알아볼까?
3. A: 오빠가 살고 있는 원룸은 방값이 얼마예요?
   B: 한달에 50만 원이야. 근데 보증금 1,000만 원이 있어.
4. A: 원룸이 좀 비싸지만, 필요한 가구들도 다 있고 화장실을 혼자 쓰니까 그게 제일 좋더라구.
   B: 그렇겠다. 근데 오빠는 그 집 어떻게 구했어요?
5. A: 내가 살고 있는 동네는 안전해서 좋아.
   B: 혹시 그 동네에 빈 방 있어요?

II . Patterns, Expressions & Practice (P.201)

Exercise 3

Listen to the conversation between two friends and mark each statement T(rue) or F(alse).

M: 요리 자주 하세요?
W: 주말에는 친구들이랑 식당에 가기도 하는데, 보통 집에서 요리해서 먹는 편이에요.
M: 저도 집밥을 먹고 싶은데, 저는 요리를 잘 못해서 자주 사 먹는 편이에요.
W: Youtube에 요리 동영상이 많으니까 보면서 만들어 보세요.

Exercise 4

Listen to the conversation between two friends and mark each statement T(rue) or F(alse).

(Script)

W: 야구 보러 경기장에 가 본 적 있어요?
M: 그럼요! 제가 야구를 좋아해서 경기장에 한 달에 한 번은 꼭 가요.
W: 저도 야구 좋아하는데, 저는 그냥 TV로 보는 편이에요.
M: TV로 보는 거하고 완전 달라요. 이번 주말 한국 시리즈 결승전이 있는데, 같이 가 볼래요?
W: 진짜요? 너무 기대돼요. 고마워요.

Exercise 5

Listen to the dialogue and answer the questions in Korean.

M: 점심 먹었어요?
W: 저 보통 점심 안 먹어요. 대신 아침을 많이 먹는 편이에요.
M: 아니 왜 점심을 안 드세요? 다이어트 하세요?
W: 그런건 아니구요, 점심을 먹으면 오후 수업 시간에 졸리더라구요.
M: 저도 그렇긴 한데.. 근데 배 고프지 않아요?
W: 저녁을 좀 일찍 먹는 편이라서 괜찮아요.

Exercise 9

Listen to the conversation between two friends and mark each statement T(rue) or F(alse).

M: 네가 지금 살고 있는 원룸은 월세가 어떻게 돼?
W: 응, 43만 원인데, 네가 살고 있는 원룸은?
M: 학교 가까이 있어서 그런지, 좀 더 비싼데, 48만 원이야.
W: 그럼 보증금도 우리 원룸보다 비싸겠네? 난 1,200만 원 냈는데.
M: 아니, 난 850만 원 냈어.

Exercise 12

Listen to the conversations and mark each statement T(rue) or F(alse).

W: 다음 학기에는 기숙사에서 나가야 하는데 아직 어디로 이사가야 할지 모르겠어. 학교 앞 원룸들은 비싸지?
M: 어, 학교 앞은 비싼 편인데 버스타고 30분만 가면 괜찮은 원룸도 있어.
W: 그래? 네가 사는 원룸은 어때?
M: 많이 비싸지 않고 교통도 편하고 좋아. 한 번 가서 알아 볼래?

Exercise 13

Listen to the conversation between two friends and mark each statement T(rue) or F(alse).

W: 오늘 저녁 모임에 어떤 옷을 입어야 할지 모르겠어.
M: 이 빨간색 원피스는 어때?
W: 오늘은 친한 친구들끼리 모이는 편한 모임이라서 원피스는 안 어울려.
M: 그럼 흰 티셔츠에 청바지를 입어. 너는 그게 예뻐.

IV. Listen & Discuss (P.213)

Directions: 현수 finds 제니 sitting alone on a bench on campus and talks to her.
First, listen to the conversation. With your classmates, discuss the answers to the questions that follow. Finally, write each answer in a full Korean sentence in the space provided.

01 현수: 제니야, 여기서 뭐해?
02 제니: 어, 현수 오빠. 인터넷으로 집 알아보고 있었어요.
03 현수: 왜? 기숙사에서 나오려고?
04 제니: 네, 학교 근처 원룸으로 옮기려고요. 오빠가 사는 원룸은 어때요?
05 현수: 학교까지 걸어서 10분밖에 안 걸리고, 동네가 안전

한 편이라서 좋아.

06 제니: 방값은 얼마나 해요?
07 현수: 한 달에 50만 원이야. 보증금 1,000만 원 하고.
08 제니: 보증금이 뭔데요?
09 현수: security deposit같은 거야.
10 제니: 아~. 가구는 다 있어요?
11 현수: 응. 그리고 원룸이 기숙사보다 좀 비싸지만, 화장실을 혼자 쓰니까 그게 제일 좋더라구.
12 제니: 그렇겠네요. 근데, 오빠는 그 집 어떻게 구했어요?
13 현수: 학교 앞에 부동산이 있는데, 거기서 구했어. 너도 거기 한번 가 볼래?
14 제니: 네. 근데 거기 가서 뭘 물어봐야 할지 잘 모르겠어요.
15 현수: 걱정 마. 내가 도와줄게. 오늘 수업 끝나고 같이 가 보자.

VII. Listening (P.221)

1-2 Listen to the conversation between two friends and answer the questions.

W: 자취를 해 보고 싶은데, 네가 사는 원룸은 얼마야?
M: 내 원룸? 보증금 1,200만 원에 월세가 50만 원이야.
W: 1,200만 원? 그렇게 비싸?
M: 학교 앞은 비싼데, 좀 떨어진 곳으로 가면 1,000만 원 정도면 원룸을 구할 수 있을거야. 그런데 왜 자취를 하려고?
W: 집도 멀고 부모님하고 같이 사니까 불편해서 나도 혼자 살아보고 싶어.
M: 나는 집이 지방이라서 자취하는 거지만, 혼자 사는 거 생각보다 힘들어.
W: 그래도 자유롭게 살 수 있어서 좋지 않아?
M: 나도 그럴 줄 알았는데 돈도 많이 들고 밥 해 먹기도 귀찮아서 라면을 자주 먹었더니 요즘 건강이 많이 나빠졌어.
W: 그래도... 혼자 한 번 살아 보고 싶은데....
M: 집에서 다닐 수 있으면 부모님한테 감사하면서 그냥 집에서 살아.

3-5 Listen to the following conversation and answer the questions.

W: 혹시 하숙집에서 살아본 적 있어요?
M: 아니요, 저는 2년동안 학교 기숙사에서 살다가 지금은 오피스텔에 살고 있어요. 왜요? 하숙집 찾으세요?
W: 네, 저도 지금은 기숙사에 살고 있는데, 하숙집으로 옮길까 생각하고 있어요.
M: 하숙집은 여러 사람이 같이 사니까 불편하지 않을까요? 우리 오피스텔로 이사오세요. 깨끗하고 조용해요. 학교도 가까운 편이구요.
W: 저도 그러고 싶은데, 오피스텔은 보증금을 내야 되잖아요. 제가 그렇게 큰 돈이 없거든요.
M: 네, 좀 비싸기는 하죠.
W: 그리고, 제가 요리를 잘 못 해서 밥도 주는 하숙집이 저한테는 더 좋을 것 같아요.

Conversation samples, English translation (of V. Guided Conversation)

Lesson 1 (p. 33)

Step 1 **At an information session for international students at a college in Korea, two students (니샤 Nisha, 케빈 Kevin) are talking to each other.**

01 니샤: 안녕하세요? 이번에 새로 온 유학생이죠?
02 케빈: 네, 안녕하세요? 케빈이라고 합니다.[II.1] 미국에서 왔어요.
03 니샤: 저는 인도에서 온 니샤라고 해요.[II.1] 만나서 반갑습니다.
04 케빈: 저도 만나서 반갑습니다.
05 니샤: 케빈 씨는 한국에 온 지 얼마나 됐어요?[II.2]
06 케빈: 이 주일밖에[II.3] 안 됐어요.
07 니샤: 그럼, 아직 시차 적응도 못 했겠네요.
08 케빈: 아뇨, 이제 거의 다 했어요.
09 니샤: 혹시 학기 시작하기 전에[II.4] 도움이 필요하면 언제든지 연락주세요.
10 케빈: 네~ 감사합니다!

01 니샤: Hi! You are a new international student, right?
02 케빈: Yes. Hi! I'm Kevin. [Literally, I am called Kevin.][II.1] I am from America.
03 니샤: I'm Nisha from India.[II.1] [Literally, I am called Kevin.] Nice to meet you.
04 케빈: Nice to meet you, too.
05 니샤: How long has it been since you came to Korea, Kevin?[II.2]
06 케빈: It's only been two weeks.[II.3]
[Literally, It's not been outside of two weeks.]
07 니샤: Then, I bet you haven't adjusted to the time difference.
08 케빈: No, I've almost adjusted now.
09 니샤: Just in case, whenever you need help before the semester begins,[II.4] please contact me.
10 케빈: Yes, thank you!

Lesson 2 (p. 63)

Step 1 **Two classmates (미셸 Michelle, 매튜 Matthew) are talking to each other.**

01 미셸: 여름 방학 동안 어디 갔다 왔니?[II.1]
02 매튜: 보령머드축제에 갔었어.
03 미셸: 보령머드축제? 세계인의 축제라고 하던데 어땠어?
04 매튜: 사람도 엄청 많고 되게 재미있었어!
05 미셸: ㅎㅎ 뭐가 그렇게 재미있었어?
06 매튜: 낮에는 머드 슬라이드, 머드 런, … 그리고 밤에는 K-pop공연도 있었어.
07 미셸: 스트레스 다 풀렸겠네!
08 매튜: 응. 엄청 재미있었어! 근데 넌 뭐 했니?
09 미셸: 난 전주한옥마을에 갔다 왔어. 이거 거기서 찍은 사진이야.
(Showing a photo.)
10 매튜: 와~ 한복이 너한테 진짜 잘 어울리는구나![II.3]
11 미셸: 그리고 한옥에서 잤는데, 생각보다 편하더라고.[II.2]

01 미셸: Where did you visit during the summer break?[II.1]
02 매튜: I visited Boryeong Mud Festival.
03 미셸: Boryeong Mud Festival? I heard that it is a worldwide festival. How was it?
04 매튜: There were lots of people and it was extremely fun!
05 미셸: hh What was so fun?
06 매튜: (There were) mudslide, mud run, ... during the daytime. And there were also K-pop performances at night.
07 미셸: I bet you must have been completely relieved! [Literally, I bet your stress must have been completely relieved!]
08 매튜: Yep. I had lots of fun! Anyway, what did you do?
09 미셸: I visited Jeonju Hanok Village. This is a photo I took there.
(Showing a photo.)
10 매튜: Wow ~ This hanbok looks really good on you![II.3]
11 미셸: And I stayed at Hanok. I found out[II.2] that it was more comfortable than I thought.

Lesson 3 (p. 99)

Step 1 **Two close friends (정우, 지우) are talking about their plan for 추석.**

01 지우: 이번 추석에는 표 사기가 쉽지 않다고 들었어.[II.1] 너는 언제 고향에 가니?
02 정우: 난 올해 기차표를 일찍 사서, 이번 주 목요일 저녁에 갈 거야.
03 지우: 고향 친구들도 만나고, 맛있는 음식도 많이 먹고 좋겠다.
04 정우: 너는 언제 가?
05 지우: 난 이번 추석에는 고향에 가지 않고,[II.3] 친구들이랑 여행 가기로 했어.
06 정우: 난 너도 당연히 집에 가는 줄 알았는데….[II.4]
07 지우: 우리 부모님께서 괜찮다고 하셨어.[II.1]
08 정우: 넌 좋겠다~ 우리 부모님께서는 집에 꼭 오라고 하셨어.[II.2]

01 지우: I heard it's not easy to buy public transport tickets this 추석.[II.1]
When do you leave for your hometown?
02 정우: I bought a train ticket early this year, so I'll head (to my hometown) right after this Thursday's class.
03 지우: You can meet hometown friends, eat delicious homemade food, and more. It will be great!
04 정우: When will you go?
05 지우: I won't go to my hometown this 추석.[II.3]
Instead, I decided to go on a trip with friends.
06 정우: I thought you'd also definitely go home … .[II.4]
07 지우: My parents told me it's okay.[II.1]
08 정우: I envy you ~ My parents told me I must come home.[II.2]

Lesson 4 (p. 131)

Step 1 Two students (니샤 Nisha, 케빈 Kevin) at a college in Seoul are talking about their weekend trip.

01 케빈: 시험도 끝났는데, 주말에 무슨 계획 있어요?
02 니샤: 이번 주말에 부산에 한 번 가 볼까 하는데,[II.1] 교통편은 뭐가 좋을까요?
03 케빈: 고속버스를 타면, 요금도 싸고 휴게소에서 맛있는 음식도 먹어볼 수 있지만,
04 저는 KTX 타는 걸[II.2] 선호하는 편이에요.
05 니샤: KTX는 비싸지 않나요?
06 케빈: 그렇긴 하지만, 빨라서 서울에서 부산까지 2시간 30분이면 가거든요.
07 니샤: 아~ 그럼, 빠르니까[II.3] KTX를 타야겠네요.
08 케빈 씨는 계획 없어요?
09 케빈: 저는 친구들하고 DMZ에 가 볼까 해요.
10 니샤: DMZ까지 어떻게 갈 거예요?
11 케빈: 제가 운전할 줄 아니까[II.3,4] 차를 렌트해서 가려고요.

01 케빈: The exams are over now. What plans do you have this weekend?
02 니샤: I'm thinking of visiting Busan this weekend. What would be the best mode of transportation?
03 케빈: If you take an express bus, fares are cheap and you can also eat delicious foods at rest stops.
04 However, I prefer taking KTX.[II.2]
05 니샤: Isn't KTX expensive?
06 케빈: That's true, but because it is fast, it takes only 2 hours and thirty minutes from Seoul to Busan.
07 니샤: Oh~ I see. Then, it's fast,[II.3] so I'd better take KTX.
08 Do you have any plans, Kevin?
09 케빈: I am thinking of going to DMZ with friends.
10 니샤: How will you go to DMZ?
11 케빈: Because I know how to drive,[II.3,4] I intend to rent a car.

Lesson 5 (p. 161)

Step 1 Two close friends (지훈, 서연) are talking about yesterday's sports game.

01 서연: 어제 한국시리즈 경기, 누가 이겼어?
02 지훈: 두산이 이겼어. 완전 끝까지 마음 졸이면서 봤어.
03 서연: 왜? 어땠는데?
04 지훈: 처음에 롯데가 8대 5로 이기고 있었거든.[II.1]
05 근데, 마지막에 두산이 만루 홈런을 치면서 역전을 했어.
06 서연: 아~ 아쉽다! 이번에는 롯데가 이길 줄 알았는데….
07 지훈: 넌 롯데 팬이냐?
08 서연: 응. 너는 두산 팬이지?
09 지훈: 당연하지! 내 고향이 서울이잖아!
10 서연: 다음 경기는 경기장에서 같이 볼까?
11 지훈: 어. 안 그래도 내가 민지한테 같이 경기장에 가자고 했거든.[II.3]
12 서연: 아~ 그래? 그럼 내가 마크한테도 갈 수 있냐고 물어볼게.[II.2]
13 지훈: 그래, 좋아! 이번에는 우리 내기할까?
14 서연: 좋지! 자기가 응원하는 팀이 지면, 저녁 사기로 하자!

01 서연: who won in the Korean series game yesterday?
02 지훈: Doosan did. I was so anxious the whole time until the very end.
03 서연: Why? How was it?
04 지훈: Lotte was winning 8 to 5 in the beginning.[II.1]
05 However, a grand slam from Doosan turned the game around.
[Literally, Doosan hit a grand slam home run and turned the game around.]
06 서연: Too bad! I thought Lotte would win this time.
07 지훈: Are you a fan of Lotte?
08 서연: Yes. You are a fan of Doosan, right?
09 지훈: Of course! You know, my hometown is Seoul.
10 서연: Shall we watch the next match at the stadium together?
11 지훈: Yep. Actually, I told Minji that we should go to the stadium together.[II.3]
12 서연: Oh did you? Then, I will ask Mark if he can also go.[II.2]

13 지훈: That's great! Shall we bet (on the outcome) this time?
14 서연: Sure that's great! Whoever's team loses, let's have them buy dinner!

Lesson 6 (p. 189)

Step 1 Two people (서연, 캐런 Karen) are talking about their favorite dramas.

01 서연: 너 오늘 좀 피곤해 보인다?
02 캐런: 어제 드라마 보느라고[II.1] 밤을 새워서요.
03 서연: 뭐라구? 드라마 때문에 밤을 새웠다고?
04 캐런: 네. 보고 싶은 드라마가 있었는데, 시험공부하느라고 계속 못 봤거든요.
05 어제 시험이 끝나서, 한꺼번에 다 봐 버렸어요.[II.2]
06 서연: 어떤 드라만데?
07 캐런: 서울에 있는 병원이 배경인 의학 드라마예요.
08 서연: 아~ 요즘 화목에 하는 그 드라마 말이야?
09 캐런: 네.
10 서연: 밤 새워서 볼 만큼[II.3] 그렇게 재미있어?
11 캐런: 네. 주인공으로 나오는 남자 배우가 잘생기고 연기도 잘하거든요.
12 서연: ㅎㅎ 너 그 배우한테 아주 푹 빠져 있구나!

01 서연: You look a little tired today.
02 캐런: Because I stayed up all night yesterday, watching a drama.
03 서연: What? [Literally, What did you say?] You stayed up all night because of a drama? [Literally, you said that you stayed up …]
04 캐런: Yes. There was a drama I wanted to watch, but because I needed to study for an exam, I couldn't keep watching.
05 Because the exam was over, I finished watching all the episodes at once.[II.2]
06 서연: Which drama is it?
07 캐런: It's a medical drama with a hospital as its setting.
08 서연: Oh~ you're talking about the drama that airs on Tuesdays and Thursdays these days?
09 캐런: Yes.
10 서연: Is it interesting enough that you want to stay up all night watching it?[II.3]
11 캐런: Yes. The actor who plays the main character is handsome and gives great performances as well.
12 서연: haha you're really hooked on him!

Lesson 7 (p. 215)

Step 1 Sitting on a bench alone, 캐런 Karen is searching for something on his phone. 케빈 Kevin, passing by, strikes up a conversation.

01 케빈: 너 여기서 뭐 하고 있니?
02 캐런: 집 알아보려고 인터넷 보고 있어.
03 케빈: 왜? 학교 기숙사에서 나오려고?
04 캐런: 응, 방을 같이 쓰는 게 불편해서,
05 근처 원룸으로 옮기려고 해.
06 니가 사는 원룸은 어때?
07 케빈: 학교까지 걸어서 10분밖에 안 걸리고, 동네도 조용한 편이라서 좋아.
08 캐런: 방값은 얼마나 해?
09 케빈: 학교 기숙사보다는 좀 비싼 편인데,[II.1,2]
10 보증금 1,000만 원에 월세는 50만 원이야.
11 캐런: 그렇구나. 근데, 넌 그 집 어떻게 구했어?
12 케빈: 인터넷에서 구했어.
13 캐런: 나도 지금 인터넷에서 알아보고 있는데, 어떻게 찾아야 할지 모르겠어.[II.3]
14 케빈: 걱정마. 내가 도와 줄게. 오늘 수업 끝나고 같이 알아보자.

01 케빈: What are you doing here, Karen?
02 캐런: I'm searching for a house on the Internet.
03 케빈: Why? Do you intend to move out of the dorm?
04 캐런: Yes, because it's inconvenient to share a room (with my roommate),
05 I plan to move to a studio near (our school).
06 How do you like your studio?
07 케빈: It's good because it takes only ten minutes to walk to school and my neighborhood tends to be safe.
08 캐런: How much is the room price?
09 케빈: It tends to be a little more expensive than that of our school dorm.
10 It's ₩500,000 a month plus ₩10,000,000 for a security deposit.
11 캐런: Oh I see. How did you find that studio anyway?
12 케빈: I found it on the Internet.
13 캐런: I am also searching on the Internet, but I don't know how to find it.
14 케빈: Don't worry. I will help you. Let's search (for a house) together after class today.

English translation (of VIII. Reading)

Lesson 1

신입생 환영회 (Freshman welcome party)

We sincerely welcome you all who are accepted into Hankuk University.
We hope that many of you can participate in the welcoming party for the freshmen.

- Date and time: 9:00~11:00am, Feb. 20th, 2020
- Location: Auditorium
- Participants: Freshmen
- Program

9:00-9:30	Welcome, Faculty Introduction
9:30-10:00	Freshman Introduction
10:00-11:00	Introduction to College Life, Guide to Using the Library

한국어를 배우는 이유 (My reason for learning Korean)

Before I came to Korea, I studied Korean as a hobby. At that time, it was my dream to meet with famous Korean singers and actors/actresses. It has been three years since I came to Korea. I have been interested in learning about Korean history and culture. After graduating, I want to work in Korea. ___________ My current plan is to attend grad school and continue my studying.

Lesson 2

남산골한옥마을 (Namsangol Hanok Village)

■ Entrance fee Free
■ Hours April ~ October (09:00-21:00)
November ~ March (09:00-20:00)
■ Directions
Subway: Chungmuro station, Exit 4
Bus: Line 140, 604, Hanok village station, Toegyero 3-ga
■ Amenities
There is a Korean restaurant "Namsangak," and a traditional tea house "Kukhayngbang."
You can eat boxed lunch on the lawn at the park. You cannot cook at the park.
■ Cultural Experiences
Wearing *hanbok*, Writing Korean characters, Korean tea drinking

For more information, refer to the website.
https://www.hanokmaeul.or.kr/

서울의 박물관 (Museums in Seoul)

There are many museums in Seoul. Among them, the National Museum of Korea and War Memorial of Korea are especially popular among foreigners. The National Museum of Korea is the biggest museum in Korea. You can see famous cultural assets and learn about the Korean history. At the War Memorial of Korea, you can learn about the history of the wars that happened in Korea. You can also see various weapons that were used in the wars in person. These museums are located in the center of Seoul and are close to subway stations, so it's easy to visit them. Also, admission is free. It is good to visit them early because they are always crowded with visitors. Also, it is good to plan to look around for a long time since they have large collections.

Lesson 3

한가위 (Hangawi)

There is a saying that "No more or no less, may it always be like hangawi." Hangawi is a synonym for Chuseok, and the time around Chuseok is the best season of the year. First of all, the weather is good because the hot summer has passed and the weather gets cooler. Also, fruits and grains are abundant around Chuseok season so even poor people don't have to worry about food. (   ) People in the old days offered these words to each other with the hope that every day could be as good as the Chuseok season, year round.

세배 (Sebae)

The action of giving deep bows to the senior members of a family on Chuseok morning is called sebae. (1) Sebae is a greeting to one's elders in the family as they start the new year. (2) When you performing sebae, you offer greetings of the new year "I hope you will be healthier in the New Year!," "Have lots of good luck and stay healthy for a long time." (3) While giving seabae money, people offer well-wishes with remarks such as "Get a good job in the New Year," and "Meet and marry a good person in the New Year," which are called deokdam.(4)

Lesson 4

이천도자기축제 (Icheon Ceramics Festival)

Dear students,
You must be busy studying.
I would like to let you know about the porcelain making event, next Saturday.
In this event, you can learn about Korean porcelain and make it yourself at Yicheon, which is famous for porcelain. We are planning to depart at 9:00 am and return at 5:00 pm next Saturday. You can register this week and the participation fee is 30,000 won. Hope many of you can participate.
Korean Language Center, Hanguk University

천안 호두과자 (Cheonan Walnut Cookies)

One of the most popular snacks in rest areas on expressways or train stations are walnut cakes. Walnut cake is a kind of small cake that looks like a walnut, and it is filled with sweet red-bean paste and walnut. Walnut cake is popular for snacking or giving as a present. Walnut cake was first made at Cheonan, Chungcheongnam-do, so Cheonan walnut cake is the most popular. Cheonan has had walnut trees for a long time and walnut cakes first made by a bakery was sold at Cheonan station and then spread to the rest of Korea. Cheonan station has been a hub of transportation since a long time ago, and the people who passed Cheonan station enjoyed the walnut cake, which became a famous product representing Cheonan.

Lesson 5

한국 시리즈 결승전 중 교통 안내 (Traffic Announcement During the Korean Series, Final Match)

The Korean Series, Final Match
November 20 (Sun), 6:30 pm
Traffic Information Near Jamsil Baseball Stadium
Parking is not allowed near Jamsil Baseball Stadium starting from 4:30, 2 hours prior to when the final match begins. It would be appreciated if you use the subway or bus to come and see the game. If you want to park, please understand that you should use the parking lot at Jamsil Han river, even if it is inconvenient.

한국에서 인기있는 스포츠 (Popular sports in Korea)

It has been discovered that the most popular sports in Korea are baseball and soccer. According to the survey result, 35% of the respondents answered that they like to watch baseball the most. Soccer (33.6%), golf (15.9%), and basketball (10.2%) followed. The sports they most like to play were found to be soccer (21.3%), followed by hiking, swimming, tennis and yoga. According to the investigation, there have been more women who have been playing soccer or basketball, as compared to 5 years ago, and the number of people playing tennis and yoga is increasing.

Lesson 6

사극 드라마 축제 (Historical drama festival)

The historical drama festival will be held at the Youngin Folk Village from November 3 to December 1. During the festival, visitors can watch the filming of scenes at the folk village. They also have a chance to try on special makeup and historical costumes from dramas. On November 10, there will be an award ceremony for movie stars of Korean historical dramas, and visitors can participate in events such as the "star hand printing ceremony" and "signing events for fans" and spend time with the movie stars. In addition, splendid performances such as Nanta and traditional dance, a Taekwondo demonstration and B-boy are prepared. You can check the details and schedules of the event on the website (www.koreanfolk.co.kr).

외국인들이 한국어를 배우는 이유 (Reasons for foreigners to learn Korean)

Recently, foreigners who are learning Korean in Korea are increasing. (㉠) in order to find out why foreigners learn Korean, one newspaper company conducted a survey of 1,000 foreign college students who are studying in Korea. (㉡) and getting a job in their home countries (27%), going to graduate school in Korea (23%), enjoying Korean cultural contents such as K-pop, K-dramas (18%), making Korean friends (11%), etc., followed it. (㉢) as effective methods of studying Korean, there were various answers such as talking with Korean people, watching dramas or entertaining shows, listening to songs, writing a journal every day. (㉣)

Lesson 7

방 구하기 (Looking for a room)

Studio available near the Sinchon station of line # 2

■ 5-minute walk from "Sinchon Station Exit #1"

- Close to OO shopping center, XX mart
- Two rooms, one bathroom, a spacious living room
- A/C available
- Shared laundry room
- Deposit: 1,200만 원/ Rent: 50만 원 (including internet)

서울 고시원

- 5 minutes to Hongdae station, 1 minute to bus stop
- Private bathroom and shower
- TV in each room
- Internet & A/C included
- Separate floors for females and males
- Shared kitchen, lounge, laundry room
- Private room: 30만 원 per month, two person-shared room: 50만 원 per month

대학생들의 주거 형태 (Housing options for college students)

According to the survey results of the newspaper of Hankook University, about half of Korean college students live at home while attending school and 24.7% live in a dorm. While the survey conducted two years ago showed that 21% of the students lived off-campus and cooked for themselves and 7.5% lived at a boarding house, the survey this time showed that the figure dropped to 16.2% and 3.5% respectively. One student said that many students want to live alone but there are not that many students who can actually do that because the deposit and monthly rent of studios and officetels are continuously rising. It turns out that college students don't prefer boarding houses, as they consider their private lives important.

Appendix Ⅰ : Vocabulary index (Korean - English)

ㄱ

ㄴ

ㄷ

ㄹ

ㅁ

ㅂ

ㅇ

ㅈ

ㅊ

ㅋ

Vocabulary index (English - Korean)

A

B

C

D

E

F

G

H

I

J

K

U

V

W

Y

Appendix II : Words and expressions (organized by lesson)

Lesson 1 Are you the new international student?

1. New words & expressions in Conversation

NOUN

도움	help; assistance, support
반 년	half a year (= six months 육 개월)
사회학과	sociology department
선배	a classmate in a higher grade *선배님 (님 is honorific address term)
유학생	international student
후배	a classmate in a lower grade

PRONOUN

이쪽 this [Literally, this side; the person on this side]

VERB

도와주다	to give someone a hand; help
유학오다	to come to study abroad
인사하다	to greet; introduce

ADVERB

새로	newly
서로	each other; one another
언제든지	anytime

EXPRESSION

■도움이 필요하면	when (you) need help [Literally, when help is necessary]
■연락(을) 주다	to give someone a call; contact someone *(someone)한테/에게 연락(을) 주다

2. Additional words & expressions (Section II ~VI in the textbook)

NOUN

학점	credit; grade
학교 정문	main gate or entrance of a school
대강당	auditorium
학생회관	student union building
신입생 환영회	freshman welcome party; freshmen orientation
학생회	student union/association
신입생	incoming students; freshmen

VERB

도착하다	to arrive

EXPRESSION

■준비운동을 하다	to do warm-up exercise
■취직을 하다	to get a job
■양치질을 하다	to brush teeth
■~고 있다	be ~ ing (action in progress)
■도와주고 있다	to be helping [Lit., to be giving help for someone]
■필요한 것들	things that are needed
■시차 적응도 못 했겠네요	You must still be jet-lagged

Lesson 2 Where did you all visit for the field trip?

1. New words & expressions in Conversation

NOUN

견학	field trip
공연	performance
망원경	telescope; binocular
보령	Boryeong (a city in South Korea)
보령 머드 축제	Boryeong Mud Festival
북한	North Korea
온돌방	*ondolbang*, a room with the Korean floor heating system
전주	Jeonju (a city in South Korea)
전주 한옥 마을	Jeonju Hanok Village
축제	festival
한옥	*hanok* (a traditional Korean house)
DMZ	demilitarized zone

VERB

걸어 다니다	to walk around
묵다	to stay (at a hotel) *(a hotel)에 묵다, (a hotel)에서 자다
보이다	(for a person/thing) to be seen
어울리다	to look good on (a person) *(a person)한테/에게 어울리다

찍다 to take (photos)

ADJECTIVE

편하다 to be comfortable; convenient

ADVERB

가깝게 near; not far away

EXPRESSION

■당연하지! Of course!

■(망원경으로 보)니까 (I looked at it with a telescope), so …

■생각보다 more than (I) thought; unlike what (I) thought

■(한국 사람) 같아! (You) look like (a Korean)!

2. Additional words & expressions (Section II ~VI in the textbook)

NOUN

머드 런 mud run

머드 레슬링 mud wrestling

머드 슬라이드 mudslide

맛집 a restaurant that is famous for serving delicious food

쇼핑몰 shopping mall

동아리 club (on college campus)

대중교통 public transportation

남산한옥마을 Namsangol Hanok Village

도시락 lunch box

입장료 admission fees

VERB

풀리다 to disappear; go away
*스트레스가 풀리다 to be stressed out [Lit. for stress to disappear]; 스트레스가 쌓이다 to get stressed [Lit., for stress to be accumulated]

기다려지다 to look forward to ~

ADJECTIVE

끝내주다 to be wonderful; fantastic

편하다 to be comfortable; convenient

ADVERB

엄청 very much

EXPRESSION

■스트레스가 다 풀렸겠네! You must have been completely stressed out!

■세계인의 축제 worldwide festival

■세계인의 축제라고 하던데 (I) heard that (it) is a worldwide festival

■끝내주게 wonderful; fantastically

■기다렸다는 것을 알았다 (I) know that (he) waited ~

■나중에서야 only later

■돈을 내다 to pay for ~ [Lit., to put out money]

■싸가지고 가다 to pack (thing) and go

Lesson 3 Traditional holiday customs also gradually change.

1. New words & expressions in Conversation

NOUN

기차표 train ticket

명절 traditional holidays

송편 half-moon-shaped rice cake

연휴 holidays (in a row); consecutive holidays

추석 Chuseok, the Korean (version of) Thanksgiving Day (celebrated on August 15 on the lunar calendar)

추석연휴 Chuseok holiday

친척 relatives

풍습 customs

표 ticket

VERB

달라지다 to change

보내다 to spend one's time

초대하다 to invite

EXPRESSION

■**(표 사)기가 쉽지 않다.** It is not easy to (buy a ticket).

*verb base + 기가 쉽다/어렵다: it is easy/difficult to ~

2. Additional words & expressions (Section II ~VI in the textbook)

NOUN

한강 Han River in Seoul
알레르기 allergy
*알레르기가 있다 to have allergy
치마 skirt
참가비 fees to pay for participation
술 alcohol
반팔 short-sleeved shirt, half-sleeved shirt
자리 one's seat
일기예보 weather forecast
전공수업 major class/course
버스표 bus ticket
놀이기구 the rides at an amusement park
호수 lake
바위(들) rock(s)
볼거리 things to see; attractions
할거리 things to do
경치 scenery

VERB

배달시키다 to have things delivered
(차를) 렌트하다 to rent (a car)
내다 to submit (thing)
*(thing)을/를 내다
넘다 to exceed; go beyond
모이다 to gather; to meet
나가다 to go out
고장나다 to be broken
빌려주다 to lend (thing) to (person)
*(thing)을/를 (person)한테/에게 빌려주다
빌리다 to borrow (thing) from (person)
*(thing)을/를 (person)한테서 빌리다

ADJECTIVE

무섭다 to be scary

EXPRESSION

■그래도 돼요? Can you do that? [Lit., Is it okay although you do so?]
*그래도 is reduced from 그리하여도 "although (person) does so"
■하나도 (+ negative verb/adjective) anything at all [Lit., even one]
■식당이 생긴 줄 모르다 not to know if a restaurant opened
■(a place)에 들어가다 to enter (a place)
■메시지를 남기다 to leave a message
■너희들 you guys
(세계인의 축제라)고 하던데 I heard that (it is a worldwide festival)
스트레스가 다 풀렸겠네! You must have been completely stressed out!

Lesson 4 What would be the best transportation?

1. New words & expressions in Conversation

NOUN

고속버스 express bus
교통편 means of transportation
관광 안내 sightseeing guidance
사흘 three days *사흘 후에: in four days
일정 daily schedule
제주도 Jeju-do (island of South Korea)
지역 area
컨퍼런스 conference
택시기사 taxi driver
휴게소 rest area
KTX Korea Train Express

VERB

렌트하다 to rent (a car)
운전하다 to drive
추천하다 to recommend

ADVERB

오래 for a long time
즐겁게 pleasantly; joyfully

EXPRESSION

■(먹어 볼) 수 있다 to be able to (eat)
*~을/~ㄹ 수 있다
:to be able to~
■관광 안내를 잘 해주다 to give a good tour guides
■즐겁게 여행하세요! Have a nice trip!

2. Additional words & expressions (Section II ~VI in the textbook)

NOUN

연말 the end of a year
이어폰 earphone
무선인터넷 wireless internet

VERB

머무르다 to stay
산책하다 to take a walk
선호하다 to prefer

EXPRESSION

■(뭐가 좋은)지 모르다 not to know (what is good)
■(무슨 옷을 입)을 지 모르다 not to know (what clothes I will wear)
■세일 때 on sale
■운행시간이 정확하다 operation schdeule/hour is accurate
■그렇긴 하지만 it is so but …
■바깥 경치 scenery outside;
■좌석 마다 per seat;
■개인 모니터 individual monitor;
■뒤로 눕다 to lie back

Lesson 5 Did you watch the Korean series game?

1. New words & expressions in Conversation

NOUN

9회 the 9th inning
결승전 final match
경기 game; match
대구 Daegu (the name of a city)
두산 Dusan (the name of a baseball team)
마지막 the last; end
만루홈런 grand slam
삼성 Samsung (the name of a baseball team)
역전 turn around
팬 fan
한국시리즈 Korean Series (baseball league championship)

VERB

역전(을) 하다 to turn something around
이기다 to win (a person/team)
*(a person; team) 을/를 이기다

ADJECTIVE

안타깝다 to be sad, regrettable, pitiful or pathetic

EXPRESSION

■(마음을 졸이)면서 while (I) am being anxious
* ~(으)면서 while ~ ing
■끝까지 to the very end
■당연하지! Of course.
■안 그래도 actually; as a matter of fact

2. Additional words & expressions (Section II ~VI in the textbook)

NOUN

치맥 *chimak* (acronym of 치킨 chicken and 맥주 beer)
시합 (or 경기) game
병원 hospital
심리학 시험 psychology exam

VERB

응원(을) 하다 to support (someone); cheer (someone) up
지다 to lose; to be defeated
*(person/team)한테 지다

내기(를) 하다 to make a bet *(perso)와/과 내기를 하다
밤새우다 to stay up all night; keep awake all night
참여하다 to participate in
다치다 to get injured
생기다 (for something) to come up
*(-이/-가) 생기다

Lesson 6 Did you say you stay up all night watching a drama?

1. New words & expressions in Conversation

NOUN

내용 content(s); story
배경 background
배우 actor/actress
사극 historical drama
역사 드라마 historical drama
연기 acting; performance
왕 king
자막 caption; subtitle
조선 시대 the Joseon Dynasty
주인공 protagonist; main character

VERB

나오다 to star (as~)
*(a character)으로/로 나오다
밤새우다 to stay up all night (= 밤을 새우다)

ADVERB

사실 in fact
한꺼번에 at once

EXPRESSION

■(피곤해) 보인다 You look (tired)
*~아/~어 보이다 (for a person/ thing) to look/appear ~
■(그 사극) 말이야? Are you talking about (that historical drama)?

2. Additional words & expressions (Section II ~VI in the textbook)

NOUN

인턴쉽 internship
목소리 voice
용돈 allowance
섬 island

VERB

예약하다 to make an appointment
아껴쓰다 to use something sparingly
갚다 to pay back

ADJECTIVE

후회가 되다 to be regretful

EXPRESSION

■골프(를) 치다 to play golf
■길이 막히다 (for a road) to be jammed
■정신이 없다 to be out of mind
■머리(를) 자르다 to get a hair cut

Lesson 7 I was searching for a house on the internet.

1. New words & expressions in Conversation

NOUN

가구 furniture
방값 room rent
보증금 security deposit
부동산 (사무소) real estate office
화장실 bathroom; restroom

PRONOUN

니 you (as in 니가 used in the subject position of a sentence)
*니 is a variant of the standard counterpart 너. Note that when 너 is used in the subject position in a sentence, 네가 (not 너가) is correct.

VERB

구하다 — to find (something)
나오다 — to come out (from a place); move out (from a place)
*(a place)에서 나오다
알아보다 — to search (a thing)
옮기다 — to move (to a place)
*(a place)으로/로 옮기다

ADJECTIVE

안전하다 — to be safe

EXPRESSION

■그렇겠네요! — That must be so!

2. Additional words & expressions (Section II ~VI in the textbook)

NOUN

집밥 — homemade meal
동영상 — video clip
공용 화장실 — shared bathroom
결승전 — final match

VERB

이사가다 — to move out

EXPRESSION

■(부동산 사무소)를 통해서
■요리하기가 싫다 — to hate cooking
■식사를 제공해 주다 — to provide meals

Appendix Ⅲ: Grammar (organized by lesson)

BEGINNING 1

Lesson 1 Hi.; How are you?

(1) NOUN이에요/예요. "am/are/is NOUN"
(2) NOUN이요/요. "(It is) NOUN"
(3) 성함이 어떻게 되세요? "May I have your name?"

Lesson 2 I am an American.

(1) A은/는 B이에요/예요 "A is B"
(2) Name + 씨 "Mr. ... ; Mrs. ... ; Miss ..."
(3) NOUN은요?/는요? "What about ~ ?; How about ~?"
(4) Questions in Korean

Lesson 3 Are you a college student?

(1) A은/는 NOUN이/가 아니에요. "am/are/is not NOUN"
(2) 몇 학년이에요?" "What year are you in school?"
(3) 저도 NOIN이에요/예요. "I am also ~."

Lesson 4 What are you doing?

(1) Verbs and adjectives
(2) Conjugating verbs and adjectives
(3) Verb/Adjective + 아요/어요. sentence ending
(4) 안 + verb/adjective "not~"
(5) "Subject-Object-Verb" (SOV) word order

Lesson 5 What do you do?

(1) Verb/Adjective + 으세요/세요. sentence ending
(2) 무슨 + NOUN "What ~; What kind of ~"
(3) Make a request or suggestion using ~으세요/~세요.
(4) ··· 잘 하시겠어요. "You must be good at ..."

Lesson 6 How is your dorm?

(1) place name + -에 "in/on/at/to + place name"
(2) NOUN은/는/이/가 있어요 & 없어요.
(3) 근데 "but"
(4) NOUN은/는/이/가 + 어때요? "How is NOUN?"

Lesson 7 May I have your phone number?

(1) The subject-focus marker -이/-가
(2) The topic/contrast marker -은/-는
(3) Reading phone numbers
(4) Verb base + 을게요/ㄹ게요. "I will ~"
(5) NOUN은/는/이/가 어떻게 되세요? "What is~?"
(6) Expressing possession

Lesson 8 I'll buy it today.

(1) Verb base + 을래요?/래요? "Would you like to ~?; Do you want to~?"
(2) Korean numerals for the numbers: 1~10
(3) 그럼, ~ "if so~ ; Well, then ~"
(4) NOUN + 하고 "~ and ; with ~"

Lesson 9 Do you have any siblings?

(1) Verb/Adjective + 잖아요. "You know"
(2) 여기; 거기; 저기 "here; there; over there"
(3) 있으세요 and 계세요.
(4) 혹시 "I wonder ~; Do you happen to ~?"
(5) 좀 verb base + 으세요/세요. "Please do ~."
(6) 잠시만요. "Just a second, please."

Lesson 10 How many people are coming?

(1) Native-Korean and Sino-Korean numerals beyond 10
(2) Using native Korean numerals
(3) Using Sino-Korean numerals
(4) Verb/Adjective + 을까요?/ㄹ까요? "Shall I/we~?; Do you think~?
(5) 그렇게 ~? "that (much) ~?"

BEGINNING 2

Lesson 11 What time is it now?

(1) Telling time in Korean (Korean numerals)
(2) Verb/Adjective base + 아서요/어서요. "It is because ..."
(3) NOUN에 vs. NOUN에서 "at/on/in/from/to ~"

Lesson 12 Please have some *gimbap.*

(1) Past tense: Verb/Adjective base + 았어요/었어요.
(2) Object marker -을/-를
(3) Who ... What ... Verb/Adjective.
(4) ~네요 Expressing the speaker's spontaneous reaction or realization

Lesson 13 I am now becoming 25 years old.

(1) Talking about one's age (Korean numerals)
(2) Expressing a date
(3) Noun + 으로 보여요/로 보여요. "to look like ~"
(4) Adjective + 아/어 보여요. "to look ~"

Lesson 14 It is really cold today.

(1) ~이면/~면, ~으면/~면 "if ~ ; when ~"
(2) Weather expressions
(3) ~아 지다/~어 지다. "to become ~"
(4) ~아 죽다/~어 죽다. "~ to death"

Lesson 15 Let's go to eat lunch

(1) Responding to a negative question 안 ~; ~ 지 않
(2) Verb base + 으러 가다/러 가다. "to go for the purpose of ~"
(3) Verb base + 아 봤다/어 봤다. "to have done ~"
(4) Verb/Adjective + 은데/는데/인데 "Giving background information"

Lesson 16 Happy birthday!

(1) NOUN한테/한테서 "to [person]; from [person]"
(2) Verb/Adjective + 지만 " ... but; although ..."
(3) Verb base + 아/어 보세요. "Please try to ~."
(4) Verb base + 아/어 봐도 돼요? "Is it okay to try to~ ?; May I try ~ ?"
(5) Non-honorific speech level "The ~아 speech style"

Lesson 17 You speak Korean very well!

(1) Verb/Adjective +을/ㄹ 거예요. "will ~ [prediction; volition]"
(2) Verb/Adjective + 지요?/죠? Seeking the listener's agreement
(3) NOUN+으로/로 "by~; in ~; with ~" [Instrument/means]
(4) 잘 해요; 못 해요; 잘 못해요. Expressing one's ability
(5) Verb base + 으려고/려고 하다 "intend to ~"
Verb base + 으려고/려고 "intending to ~"
(6) Verb/Adjective base + 는데도/은데도 "even though~ ; even if ~"

Lesson 18 Would you like to go on a blind date?

(1) NOUN + 동안; Verb + 는 동안 "during ~; while ~ing"
(2) Noun-modifying forms of verbs ~는/은/ㄴ
(3) Noun-modifying forms of adjectives ~은/ㄴ
(4) Describing people's appearances
(5) 이; 그; 저 "this; that; that over there"
(6) ~거든요. "It is because …; … , you see."

Lesson 19 What do you usually do when you have time?

(1) Verb/Adjective + 다가 Depicting transition from one event to another
(2) 어떤 + NOUN "which ~/what kind of ~; some/any ~"
(3) The honorific speech level "The ~습니다 speech style"
(4) Verb/Adjective + 겠 ~ "must ~"
(5) Frequency expressions
(6) [NOUN 1]도 Verb/Adjective고 [NOUN 2]도 Verb/Adjective고 "to do NOUN 1 and to do NOUN 2 as well"

Lesson20 How was the blind date last time?

(1) 주다, 주시다, 드리다. to give [verbs of giving]
(2) ~아 주다/~어 주다. to do (something) for (someone)
~아 주시다/~어 주시다.
~아 드리다/~어 드리다.
(3) ~기로 하다. to decide to ~
(4) -을/-를 하다. (for someone) to do (something)
-이/-가 되다. for something) to be done
(5) 지난/이번/다음 + NOUN last/this/next ~

INTERMEDIATE 1

Lesson 1 Are you the new international student?

(1) NOUN (이)라고 하다 "to be called ~"
(2) Verb base 은/ㄴ지 [time span]이/가 되다 "It's been [time span] since ~"
(3) NOUN밖에 "nothing/nobody/no ~ but; only ~"
(4) Verb base + 기 전에 "before ~ing"

Lesson 2 Where did you all visit for the field trip?

(1) The ~는다 speech style
(2) Verb/Adjective + 더라고 "I found out/realized that ~"
(3) Verb/Adjective +는구나/구나 "Expressing your realization of a new fact"

Lesson 3 Traditional holiday customs also gradually change.

(1) ~다고/~라고 하다 Reported statement
(2) ~(으)라고 하다 Reported command
(3) Verb/Adjective base +지 않 "not ~"
(4) Noun-modifying form + 줄 알았다/몰랐다 "I mistakenly thought/ I did not know that ~"

Lesson 4 What would be the best transportation?

(1) Verb base + 을까/ㄹ까 하다 "to be thinking of ~ing"
(2) Noun-modifying form + 것 "the fact/thing that ~"
(3) Verb/Adjective + (으)니까 "since ~ ; because ~; ~, so … "
(4) Verb/Adjective base + 을/ㄹ 줄 알다/모르다 "to know how to do ~"
Verb/Adjective base + 을/ㄹ 줄 모르다 "to not know how to do ~"

Lesson 5 Did you watch the Korean series game?

(1) Verb/Adjective + 거든 Indicating that you plan to continue talking
(2) ~냐고 하다 Reported question
(3) ~자고 하다 Reported proposal

Lesson 6 Did you say you stay up all night watching a drama?

(1) Verb base + 느라(고) "because of ~ ing"
(2) Verb base + 아/어 버리다 Declaring that an action has been completed
(3) Verb/Adjective + 을/ㄹ 만큼 "to the extent that ~"

Lesson 7 I was searching for a house on the internet.

(1) Noun-modifying form + 편이다 "to tend to ~; It is more the case of ~ than the other"
(2) NOUN보다 (더/덜) "(more/less) … than ~"
(3) Verb base + 아야/어야 할지 모르다 "to not know whether … have to ~"

Appendix Ⅳ: Speech levels, styles, and types

The table shows two speech levels (Honorific vs. Non-honorific), four speech styles, and four speech types under each style. For rules, refer to Lesson 4 (Beginning Korean 1), Lesson 16 & 19 (Beginning Korean 2) and Lesson 1 (Intermediate Korean 1).

Sentence types	Speech levels			
	Honorific		Non-honorific	
	More Formal ⟪	⟫ More Informal	More Formal ⟪	⟫ More Informal
	"~습니다" style [Lesson 19]	"~아요" style [Lesson 4]	"~는다" style [Intermediate, L1]	"~아" style [Lesson 16]
Statement (with falling intonation)	~습니다/~ㅂ니다.	~아요/~어요.	~는다/~ㄴ다/~다.	~아/~어.
	1. 책을 읽습니다 2. 친구를 만납니다. I read a book. I meet a friend.	1. 친구를 만나요. 2. 책을 읽어요. I meet a friend. I read a book.	1. 친구를 만난다. 2. 책을 읽는다. 3. 한국어가 좋다. I meet a friend. I read a book. Korean is good.	1. 친구를 만나. 2. 책을 읽어. I meet a friend. I read a book.
Question (with rising intonation)	~습니까?/~ㅂ니까?	~아요/~어요?	~니? or ~냐?	~아/~어?
	1. 책을 읽습니까? 2. 친구를 만납니까? Do you read a book? Do you meet a friend?	1. 친구를 만나요? 2. 책을 읽어요? Do you meet a friend? Do you read a book?	1. 친구를 만나니? 2. 책을 읽니? Do you meet a friend? Do you read a book?	1. 친구를 만나? 2. 책을 읽어? Do you meet a friend? Do you read a book?
Proposal	-읍시다/~ㅂ시다.	~아요/~어요.	~자.	~아/~어.
	1. 책을 읽읍시다. 2. 친구를 만납시다. Let us read a book. Let us meet a friend.	1. 친구를 만나요. 2. 책을 읽어요. Let us meet a friend. Let us read a book.	1. 친구를 만나자. 2. 책을 읽자. Let us meet a friend. Let us read a book.	1. 친구를 만나. 2. 책을 읽어. Let us meet a friend. Let us read a book.
Command	~으시요/~십시오. * ~으시오/~시오.	~아요/~어요.	~아라/~어라.	~아/~어.
	1. 책을 읽으십시오. 2. 친구를 만나십시오. Read a book. Meet a friend.	1. 친구를 만나요. 2. 책을 읽어요. Meet a friend. Read a book.	1. 친구를 만나라. 2. 책을 읽어라. Meet a friend. Read a book.	1. 친구를 만나. 2. 책을 읽어. Meet a friend. Read a book.

* ~으시오/~시오 in commands is rarely used in daily conversation. It is usually used on sign boards for the public or in written (formal) documents.

Appendix Ⅴ: Irregular verbs and adjectives

1. "ㄷ" irregular verbs: ㄷ changes to ㄹ when followed by a vowel.

걷다 (to walk) : 걷 → 걸 + 어요 → 걸어요
걷 → 걸 + 으세요 → 걸으세요
걷 → 걸 + 었어요 → 걸었어요
걷 → 걸 + 을 거예요 → 걸을 거예요
걷 → 걸 + 으니까 → 걸으니까
걷 → 걸 + 으면 → 걸으면

Exceptions: *받다 (to receive) → 받아요
*쏟다 (to pour) → 쏟아요
*닫다 (to close) → 닫아요

Verb/Adj	습니다	아요/어요	으세요	았어요/었어요	을 거예요	으니까	으면
걷다 (to walk)	걷습니다	걸어요	걸으세요	걸었어요	걸을 거예요	걸으니까	걸으면
듣다 (to listen)	듣습니다	들어요	들으세요	들었어요	들을 거예요	들으니까	들으면
묻다 (to ask)	묻습니다	물어요	물으세요	물었어요	물을 거예요	물으니까	물으면
깨닫다 (to realize)	깨닫습니다	깨달아요	깨달으세요	깨달았어요	깨달을 거예요	깨달으니까	깨달으면

2. "ㄹ" irregular verbs/adjectives: ㄹ in the base drops when followed by ㄴ, ㅂ, and ㅅ.

놀다: (to hang out) 놀 → 놀 + 는군요 → 노는군요
놀 → 놀 + ㅂ니다 → 놉니다
놀 → 놀 + 세요 → 노세요

Verb/Adj	ㅂ니다	아요/어요	았어요/었어요	(으)ㄹ 거예요	니까	(으)면	는군요	세요
놀다 (to hang out)	놉니다	놀아요	놀았어요	놀 거예요	노니까	놀면	노는군요	노세요
들다 (to carry)	듭니다	들어요	들었어요	들 거예요	드니까	들면	드는군요	드세요
만들다 (to make)	만듭니다	만들어요	만들었어요	만들 거예요	만드니까	만들면	만드는군요	만드세요
멀다 (to be far)	멉니다	멀어요	멀었어요	멀 거예요	머니까	멀면	*멀군요	
살다 (to live)	삽니다	살아요	살았어요	살 거예요	사니까	살면	사는군요	사세요
알다 (to know)	압니다	알아요	알았어요	알 거예요	아니까	알면	아는군요	아세요
열다 (to open, unlock)	엽니다	열어요	열었어요	열 거예요	여니까	열면	여는군요	여세요
팔다 (to sell)	팝니다	팔아요	팔았어요	팔 거예요	파니까	팔면	파는군요	파세요
힘들다 (to be difficult, tiring)	힘듭니다	힘들어요	힘들었어요	힘들 거예요	힘드니까	힘들면	*힘들군요	

* The rules does not apply to adjectives.

3. "ㅂ" irregular verbs/adjectives: ㅂ in the base changes to 우 (or *오 for a few words) when followed by a vowel.

Vowel contraction

쉽다 (to be easy) : 쉽 → 쉽 + 어요 → 쉬 + 우 + 어요 → 쉬워요

쉽 → 쉽 + 었어요 → 쉬 + 우 + 었어요 → 쉬웠어요

쉽 → 쉽 + 어서 → 쉬 + 우 + 어서 → 쉬워서

쉽 → 쉽 + 을 거예요 → 쉬 + 우 + ~~을~~ 거예요 → 쉬울 거예요

쉽 → 쉽 + 으세요 → 쉬 + 우 + ~~으~~세요 → 쉬우세요

쉽 → 쉽 + 으니까 → 쉬 + 우 + ~~으~~니까 → 쉬우니까

쉽 → 쉽 + 으면 → 쉬 + 우 + ~~으~~면 → 쉬우면

*Exceptions: 집다 (to hold) → 집어요

씹다 (to chew) → 씹어요

Verb/Adj	습니다	아요/어요	았어요/었어요	아서/어서	을 거예요	으세요	으니까	으면
가볍다 (to be light)	가볍습니다	가벼워요	가벼웠어요	가벼워서	가벼울 거예요	가벼우세요	가벼우니까	가벼우면
고맙다 (to be thankful)	고맙습니다	고마워요	고마웠어요	고마워서	고마울 거예요	고마우세요	고마우니까	고마우면
귀엽다 (to be cute)	귀엽습니다	귀여워요	귀여웠어요	귀여워서	귀여울 거예요	귀여우세요	귀여우니까	귀여우면
눕다 (to lie down)	눕습니다	누워요	누웠어요	누워서	누울 거예요	누우세요	누우니까	누우면
더럽다 (to be dirty)	더럽습니다	더러워요	더러웠어요	더러워서	더러울 거예요	더러우세요	더러우니까	더러우면
덥다 (to be hot) (weather)	덥습니다	더워요	더웠어요	더워서	더울 거예요	--	더우니까	더우면
뜨겁다 (to be hot) (temperature)	뜨겁습니다	뜨거워요	뜨거웠어요	뜨거워서	뜨거울 거예요	--	뜨거우니까	뜨거우면
무겁다 (to be heavy)	무겁습니다	무거워요	무거웠어요	무거워서	무거울 거예요	--	무거우니까	무거우면
맵다 (to be spicy)	맵습니다	매워요	매웠어요	매워서	매울 거예요	--	매우니까	매우면
밉다 (to be hateful)	밉습니다	미워요	미웠어요	미워서	미울 거예요	미우세요	미우니까	미우면
쉽다 (to be easy)	쉽습니다	쉬워요	쉬웠어요	쉬워서	쉬울 거예요	쉬우세요	쉬우니까	쉬우면
어렵다 (to be difficult)	어렵습니다	어려워요	어려웠어요	어려워서	어려울 거예요	어려우세요	어려우니까	어려우면
차갑다 (to be cold) (temperature)	차갑습니다	차가워요	차가웠어요	차가워서	차가울 거예요	차가우세요	차가우니까	차가우면
춥다 (to be cold) (weather)	춥습니다	추워요	추웠어요	추워서	추울 거예요	--	추우니까	추우면
*곱다 (to be pretty)	곱습니다	고와요	고왔어요	고와서	고울 거예요	고우세요	고우니까	고우면
*돕다 (to help)	돕습니다	도와요	도왔어요	도와서	도울 거예요	도우세요	도우니까	도우면

4. "ㅅ" irregular verbs/adjectives: ㅅ in the base drops when followed by a vowel.

낫다 (to get better) : 낫 → 낫 + 아요 → 나아요
낫 → 낫 + 았어요 → 나았어요
낫 → 낫 + 을 거예요 → 나을 거예요
낫 → 낫 + 으면 → 나으면

Verb/Adj	습니다	아요/어요	았어요/었어요	을 거예요	으면	고	지만
낫다 (to get better)	낫습니다	나아요	나았어요	나을 거예요	나으면	낫고	낫지만
잇다 (to connect)	잇습니다	이어요	이었어요	이을 거예요	이으면	잇고	잇지만
짓다 (to build)	짓습니다	지어요	지었어요	지을 거예요	지으면	짓고	짓지만
붓다 (to pour; to swell)	붓습니다	부어요	부었어요	부을 거예요	부으면	붓고	붓지만

5. "ㅎ" irregular adjectives: ㅎ in the base drops when followed by a vowel.

Vowel contraction

노랗다 (to be yellow): 노랗 → 노랗 + 아요 → 노래요
노랗 → 노랗 + 았어요 → 노랬어요
노랗 → 노랗 + 아서 → 노래서

Verb/Adj	습니다	아요/어요	았어요/었어요	아서/어서	고	지만
까맣다 (be black)	까맣습니다	까매요	까맸어요	까매서	까맣고	까맣지만
하얗다 (be white)	하얗습니다	하얘요	하얬어요	하얘서	하얗고	하얗지만
그렇다 (be so; be that way)	그렇습니다	그래요	그랬어요	그래서	그렇고	그렇지만
이렇다 (be this way)	이렇습니다	이래요	이랬어요	이래서	이렇고	이렇지만
어떻다 (be how)	어떻습니까?	어때요?	어땠어요?	어때서?	어떻고?	--

6. "르" irregular verbs/adjectives: — in 르 in the base drops and additional ㄹ is added, when followed by a vowel.

contraction

모르다 (to not know) : 모르 → 모르 + 아요 → 몰ㄹ + 아요 → 몰라요

모르 → 모르 + 았어요 → 몰ㄹ + 았어요 → 몰랐어요

모르 → 모르 + 아서 → 몰ㄹ + 아서 → 몰라서

Verb/Adj	ㅂ니다	아요/어요	았어요/었어요	ㄹ 거예요	니까	아서/어서	면	지만
고르다 (to choose)	고릅니다	골라요	골라요	고를 거예요	고르니까	골라서	고르면	고르지만
누르다 (to press)	누릅니다	눌러요	눌렀어요	누를 거예요	누르니까	눌러서	누르면	누르지만
다르다 (be different)	다릅니다	달라요	달랐어요	다를 거예요	다르니까	달라서	다르면	다르지만
모르다 (to not know)	모릅니다	몰라요	몰랐어요	모를 거예요	모르니까	몰라서	모르면	모르지만
배(가) 부르다 (to be full)	배부릅니다	배불러요	배불렀어요	배부를 거예요	배부르니까	배불러서	배부르면	배부르지만
부르다 (to call; to sing)	부릅니다	불러요	불렀어요	부를 거예요	부르니까	불러서	부르면	부르지만
빠르다 (be fast)	빠릅니다	빨라요	빨랐어요	빠를 거예요	빠르니까	빨라서	빠르면	빠르지만

7. "ㅡ" irregular verbs/adjectives: ㅡ in the base drops when followed by a vowel.

contraction

바쁘다 (to be busy) : 바쁘다 → 바쁘 + 아요 → 바ㅃ + 아요 → 바빠요 (Use 아요 when the last vowel in the base is 아/오.)
[ㅏ: last vowel]

예쁘다 (to be pretty) : 예쁘다 → 예쁘 + 어요 → 예ㅃ + 어요 → 예뻐요 (Use 어요 when the last vowel in the base is not 아/오.)
[ㅖ: last vowel]

크다 (to be big) : 크다 → 크 + 어요 → ㅋ + 어요 → 커요 (Use 어요 when there is no vowel in the base.)
[no vowel]

Verb/Adj	ㅂ니다	아요/어요	았어요/었어요	을 거예요	면	아서/어서	지만
나쁘다 (to be bad)	나쁩니다	나빠요	나빴어요	나쁠 거예요	나쁘면	나빠서	나쁘지만
배(가) 고프다 (to be hungry)	배고픕니다	배고파요	배고팠어요	배고플 거예요	배고프면	배고파서	배고프지만
바쁘다 (to be busy)	바쁩니다	바빠요	바빴어요	바쁠 거예요	바쁘면	바빠서	바쁘지만
크다 (to be big)	큽니다	커요	컸어요	클 거예요	크면	커서	크지만
슬프다 (to be sad)	슬픕니다	슬퍼요	슬펐어요	슬플 거예요	슬프면	슬퍼서	슬프지만
쓰다 (to write; to use)	씁니다	써요	썼어요	쓸 거예요	쓰면	써서	쓰지만
아프다 (to be sick)	아픕니다	아파요	아팠어요	아플 거예요	아프면	아파서	아프지만
예쁘다 (to be pretty)	예쁩니다	예뻐요	예뻤어요	예쁠 거예요	예쁘면	예뻐서	예쁘지만

Appendix Ⅵ: Noun-modifying forms

The following show the noun-modifying forms of verbs and adjectives. For more details, refer to Lesson 18 in Beginning 2.

1. NOUN-MODIFYING FORMS OF VERBS

Dictionary form	Past tense form	Present tense form	Future tense form
Verb base + 다	Verb base + 은/ㄴ + NOUN	Verb base + 는 + NOUN	Verb base +을/ㄹ+ NOUN
Verb base (ending in a consonant): 먹다	먹은 음식	먹는 음식	먹을 음식
Verb base (ending in a vowel): 가다	간 식당	가는 식당	갈 식당

▶**Note 1:** The following table shows noun-modifying verb forms according to tenses.

Dictionary form	Past tense form	Present tense form	Future tense form
Verb base + 다	Verb base + 은/ㄴ	Verb base + 는	Verb base + 을/ㄹ
읽다 (to reda)	읽은	읽는	읽을
보다 (to see)	본	보는	볼
가다 (to go)	간	가는	갈
사다 (to buy)	산	사는	살
주문하다 (to order)	주문한	주문하는	주문할
먹다 (to eat)	먹은	먹는	먹을
드시다 (to eat)	드신	드시는	드실
가르치다 (to teach)	가르친	가르치는	가르칠
만나다 (to meet)	만	만나는	만날
시작하다 (to begin)	시작한	시작하는	시작할
일어나다 (to get up)	일어난	일어나는	일어날
끝나다 (to end)	끝난	끝나는	끝날
공부하다 (to study)	공부한	공부하는	공부할

▶**Note 2:** For the noun-modifying form of a "ㄹ" irregular verb, follow the rules, as shown in the table below.

Dictionary form	Past tense form	Present tense form	Future tense form
Verb base + 다	Verb base + ㄴ	Verb base + 는	Verb base + ㄹ
살다 (to live)	(살 → 살 + ㄴ) 산	(살 → 살 + 는) 사는	(살 → 살 + ㄹ) 살
만들다 (to make)	(만들 → 만들 + ㄴ) 만든	(만들 → 만들 + 는) 만드는	(만들 → 만들 + ㄹ) 만들
팔다 (to sell)	(팔 → 팔 + ㄴ) 판	(팔 → 팔 + 는) 파는	(팔 → 팔 + ㄹ) 팔

▶**Note 3:** The noun-modifying forms of ㄷ irregular verbs are:

Dictionary form	Past tense form	Present tense form	Future tense form
Verb base + 다	Verb base + 은	Verb base + 는	Verb base + 을
듣다 (to hear)	(듣 → 들 + 은) 들은	듣는	(듣 → 들 + 을) 들을
걷다 (to walk)	(걷 → 걸 + 은) 걸은	걷는	(걷 → 걸 + 을) 걸을
묻다 (to ask)	(묻 → 물 + 은) 물은	묻는	(묻 → 물 + 을) 물을
	Rule: 1) ㄷ changes to ㄹ 2) 은 is attached		Rule: 1) ㄷ changes to ㄹ 2) 을 is attached

▶**Note 3:** The following table shows the noun-modifying forms of the 이다 verbs.

Dictionary form	Past tense form	Present tense form	Future tense form
Noun이다 **Noun다**	**Noun이 + 던 /Noun이었+던** **Noun + 던 /Noun였+던**	**Noun이 + ㄴ** **Noun이 + ㄴ**	**Noun이 + ㄹ** **Noun이 + ㄹ**
학생이다 (to be) 가수다 (to be)	학생이던/학생이었던 가수던/가수였던	학생인 가수인	학생일 가수일

2. NOUN-MODIFYING FORMS OF ADJECTIVES

Dictionary form	Past tense form	Present tense form	Future tense form
Adjective base + 다	**Adjective base + 던**	**Adjective base + 은/ㄴ**	**Adjective base + 을/ㄹ**
Adjective base (ending in a consonant): 좋다	좋던 음식	좋은 음식	좋을 것
Adjective base (ending in a vowel):비싸다	비싸던 식당	비싼 식당	비쌀 것

▶**Note 1:** The following table shows noun-modifying adjective forms according to tenses.

Dictionary form	Past tense form	Present tense form	Future tense form
Adjective base + 다	**Adjective base + 던**	**Adjective base + 은/ㄴ**	**Adjective base + 을/ㄹ**
좋다 (to be good;nice)	좋던	좋은	좋을
괜찮다 (to be okay)	괜찮던	괜찮은	괜찮을
많다 (to be many)	많던	많은	많을
예쁘다 (to be pretty)	예쁘던	예쁜	예쁠
싸다 (to be cheap)	싸던	싼	쌀
비싸다 (to be expensive)	비싸던	비싼	비쌀
바쁘다 (to be busy)	바쁘던	바쁜	바쁠
크다 (to be big)	크던	큰	클
유명하다 (to be famous)	유명하던	유명한	유명할
편하다 (to be convenient)	편하던	편한	편할
대단하다 (to be incredible)	대단하던	대단한	대단할

▶**Note 2:** The table below shows the noun-modifying forms of "ㅂ" irregular adjectives.

Dictionary form	Past tense form	Present tense form	Future tense form
Adjective base + 다	Adjective base + 던	Adjective base + ㄴ	Adjective base + ㄹ
쉽다 (to be easy) 어렵다 (to be difficult) 춥다 (to be cold) 덥다 (to be hot) 반갑다 (to be glad) 맵다 (to be spicy)	쉽던 어렵던 춥던 덥던 반갑던 맵던	(쉽 → 쉬우 + ㄴ) 쉬운 어려운 추운 더운 반가운 매운 Rule: 1) ㅂ changes 우 2) ㄴ is attached	(쉽 → 쉬우 + ㄹ) 쉬울 어려울 추울 더울 반가울 매울 Rule: 1) ㅂ changes 우 2) ㄹ is attached

▶**Note 3:** For the noun-modifying forms of ㄹ irregular adjectives, follow the rules, as shown in the table below.

Dictionary form	Past tense form	Present tense form	Future tense form
Adjective base + 다	Adjective base + 던	Adjective base + ㄴ	Adjective base + ㄹ
멀다 (to be far) 길다 (to be long)	멀던 길던	(멀 → 머̶ㄹ̶ + ㄴ) 먼 (길 → 기̶ㄹ̶ + ㄴ) 긴 Rule: 1) Drop ㄹ 2) ㄴ is attached	(멀 → 머̶ㄹ̶ + ㄹ) 멀 (길 → 기̶ㄹ̶ + ㄹ) 길 Rule: 1) Drop ㄹ 2) ㄹ is attached

▶**Note 4:** The noun-modifying forms of adjectives ending ~있다/~없다 are shown below:

Dictionary form	Past tense form	Present tense form	Future tense form
Adjective base + 다	Adjective base + 던	Adjective base + 는	Adjective base + 을
재미있다 재미없다 맛있다 맛없다	재미있던 재미없던 맛있던 맛없던	재미있는 재미없는 맛있는 맛없는	재미있을 재미없을 맛있을 맛없을

Appendix Ⅶ: Reported speech constructions

1. Reported statement: ~다고/~라고 하다

Use ~**다고/~라고 하다**, when you report a person's statement (e.g., what was stated in the past).

▶You (Reporter): person -이/가 [what was stated + 다/라]고 하다.
WHO (subject) WHAT (object) SAY(verb)

"A person **says/said that** ~."

* The expression in [ ] is called "reported statement."
  Let's use [ ] to mark the boundary of reported statement.
* The verb/adjective used in "reported statement" is called "reported verb/adjective."
* 하다 in ~고 하다 is called "reporting verb" or "saying verb."

Use the ~는다 speech style for the reported verb/adjective in a reported statement, as shown below.
The ~는다 speech style is ~는다, ~ㄴ다, or ~다. (For more, see Appendix. VI.)

Present tense

▶ [... Verb base + 는다/ㄴ다]고 하다 (e.g., .. 읽는다고 해요, 어울린다고 해요)
▶ [... Adjective base + 다]고 하다 (e.g., .. 예쁘다고 해요)
▶ [... Noun (이)라]고 하다 (e.g., .. 학생이라고 해요, 가수라고 해요)

Past tense

▶ [... Verb/Adjective base + 았다/었다]고 하다 (e.g., .. 맑았다고 해요, 읽었다고 해요)
▶ [... Noun + 이었다/였다]고 하다 (e.g., .. 학생이었다고 해요, 가수였다고 해요)

Dictionary form	Present / Past	Reported statement	
		Full form	Reduced form
(Verb) 읽다 가다	읽는다 읽었다 간다 갔다	읽는다고 해요 읽었다고 해요 간다고 해요 갔다고 해요	읽는대요 읽었대요 간대요 갔대요
(Adjective) 예쁘다	예쁘다 예뻤다	예쁘다고 해요 예뻤다고 해요	예쁘대요 예뻤대요
(Consonant-ending Noun + 이다) 학생이다	학생이다 학생이었다	학생이라고 해요 학생이었다고 해요	학생이래요 학생이었대요
(Vowel-ending Noun + 다) 가수다	가수다 가수였다	가수라고 해요 가수였다고 해요	가수래요 가수였대요

2. Reported command: ~(으)라고 하다

Use ~(으)라고 하다 when you report a person's command (e.g., what was commanded in the past).

▶You (Reporter): Person-이/가 [what was commanded ~(으)라]고 하다.
WHO (subject) WHAT (object) SAY(verb)

"A person **tells/told** another to do ~."

* The expression in [ ] is called "reported command." " Let's use [ ] to mark the boundary of reported statement.

Use the ~(으)라 form of the verb in the reported command, as shown below.

▶ [... Verb base (ending in a consonant) + 으라]고 하다 (e.g., .. 읽으라고 해요)
▶ [... Verb base (ending in a vowel) + 라]고 하다 (e.g., .. 가라고 해요)

You can use the reduced form ~으래요/~래요 instead of the full form ~으라고 해요/~라고 해요 in more casual conversations, as shown in the table below.

Dictionary form (word base + 다)	Command	Reported command	
	Present	Full form	Reduced form
Consonant-ending verb base + 다 (읽다)	읽어라	읽으라고 해요	읽으래요
Vowel-ending verb base + 다 (오다)	와라 (오+아라)	오라고 해요	오래요

3. Reported question: ~냐고 하다

Use **~냐고 하다** when you report a person's question (e.g., what was asked in the past).

You (Reporter): Person-이/가 [what was asked ~냐]고 하다.
WHO (subject) WHAT (object) SAY (verb)

"**A person** asks/asked if/whether/who ~."

*The expression in [ ] is called "reported question." "Let's use [ ] to mark the boundary of reported statement.

Use the ~냐 form of the verb/adjective in the reported question, as shown below.

<Present tense>

▶ [··· Verb/Adjective base + 냐]고 하다: 가냐고 하다/ 예쁘냐고 하다
▶ [··· Noun (이)냐]고 하다 : 학생이냐고 하다, 가수냐고 하다

<Past tense>

▶ [··· Verb/Adjective base + 았냐/었냐]고 하다: 갔냐고 하다/ 예뻤냐고 하다
▶ [··· Noun 이었냐/였냐]고 하다 : 학생이었냐고 하다, 가수였냐고 하다

Dictionary form	Present/ Past	Reported statement	
		Full form	Reduced form
Verb (가다)	가다 갔다	가냐고 해요 갔냐고 해요	가내요 갔내요
Adjective (예쁘다)	예쁘다 예뻤다	예쁘냐고 해요 예뻤냐고 해요	예쁘내요 예뻤내요
Consonant-ending Noun (학생이다)	학생이다 학생이었다	학생이냐고 해요 학생이었냐고 해요	학생이내요 학생이었내요
Vowel-ending Noun (가수다)	가수다 가수였다	가수냐고 해요 가수였냐고 해요	가수내요 가수였내요

4. Reported proposal: ~자고 하다

Use **~자고 하다** when you report a person's proposal (e.g., what a person proposed in the past).

You (Reporter): Person-이/가 [what was proposed **~자**]고 **하다**.
WHO (subject) WHAT (object) SAY (verb)

"A person **proposes/proposed ~ing.**"

"A person **suggests/suggested ~ing.**"

*The expression in [ ] is called "reported proposal." Let's use [ ] to mark the boundary of reported proposal.

Use the ~자 form of the verb in the reported proposal, as shown below.

▶ [… Verb base + 자]**고 하다** : 가자**고 하다**, 먹자**고 하다**

* The reduced form of 가자고 해요 is 가재요.

Look at the following examples.

- 테드: 우리 KTX 타고 갈까요?

  미영: 마크 씨는 [고속버스 타자]**고 하던데**요. or 마크 씨는 고속 버스를 타 **재는데**요?

  Ted suggested taking an express bus.

- 아버지: 민지야, 우리 주말에 등산 갈까?

  민지 : 친구가 [같이 영화 보자]**고 했는데** or (친구가 같이 영화 보**잤는데**) 다음 주말에 가면 안 돼요?

  My friend suggested watching a movie. Can't we go next weekend?

- 민수: 마크가 오늘 저녁에 자기 집에서 게임하**재**.

  윤기: 다음 주가 시험이잖아. 정신 좀 차리라고 해! ㅎㅎ

  Mark suggested playing the game at his house tonight.